# THE VOICE
## AND
## VOICE
## THERAPY

# THE VOICE
# AND
# VOICE
# THERAPY

*Daniel R. Boone*
University of Denver

Prentice-Hall, Inc., Englewood Cliffs, New Jersey

© 1971 by Prentice-Hall, Inc., Englewood Cliffs, New Jersey

13-943084-9

Library of Congress Catalog Card Number 74-146738

Printed in the United States of America

Current printing (last digit):
12   11   10   9

*Prentice-Hall International, Inc., London*
*Prentice-Hall of Australia, Pty. Ltd., Sydney*
*Prentice-Hall of Canada, Ltd., Toronto*
*Prentice-Hall of India Private Limited, New Delhi*
*Prentice-Hall of Japan, Inc., Tokyo*

*to C.B.*

# Contents

*chapter one*

SYMPTOMATIC VOICE THERAPY           1

Hyperfunctional Voice Problems, 2. The Sites of Vocal Hyperfunction, 3. The Reduction of Vocal Hyperfunction as a Therapeutic Goal, 9. Summary, 13.

*chapter two*

THE VOCAL MECHANISMS AND HYPERFUNCTION      14

Respiration, 14. Phonation, 24. Resonance, 39. Summary, 44.

*chapter three*

DISORDERS OF VOCAL FOLD MASS AND
APPROXIMATION                   46

Dysphonias Related to Mass-Size Alterations of Vocal Folds,
49. Dysphonias Related to Problems of Vocal Fold Approximation, 60. Summary, 70.

*chapter four*

THE VOICE EVALUATION                                    71

The Voice Evaluation and Medical Information, 72. The Voice
Evaluation and the Case History, 76. The Voice Evaluation
and Observation of the Patient, 80. The Voice Evaluation and
Testing of the Patient, 83. Summary, 101.

*chapter five*

VOICE THERAPY FOR PROBLEMS OF
VOCAL HYPERFUNCTION                                     102

Voice Therapy for Young Children, 105. Voice Therapy for
Adolescents and Adults, 107. Voice Therapy Facilitating Techniques, 109. Summary, 155.

*chapter six*

VOICE THERAPY FOR SPECIAL PROBLEMS          156

Voice Therapy for the Deaf, 156. Voice Therapy for Functional Aphonia, 160. Voice Therapy for Ventricular Phonation, 164. Voice Therapy for Spastic Dysphonias, 166. Voice
Therapy for Vocal Cord Paralysis, 167. Voice Therapy for
Special Voice Symptoms, 171. Summary, 174.

*chapter seven*

THERAPY FOR RESONANCE DISORDERS             175

Therapy for Oral-Pharyngeal Resonance Problems, 176.
Therapy for Nasal Resonance Problems, 181. Summary, 195.

*chapter eight*

VOICE THERAPY FOR THE LARYNGECTOMY PATIENT     197

The Preoperative Visit, 198. Postoperative Medical Care of
the Laryngectomee, 201. The Postoperative Visit, 203. Physical Problems of the Laryngectomee, 208. Voice Training of
the Laryngectomee, 210. Psychosocial Adjustment, 221. Summary, 223.

BIBLIOGRAPHY                                            224
INDEX                                                   235

# Preface

Voice therapy is often a neglected part of the curriculum and clinical training of laryngologists and speech pathologists. Yet the majority of children and adults with hyperfunctional voice problems are highly responsive to voice therapy. This volume attempts to present, through an understanding of the vocal mechanism and its pathologies, a therapeutic philosophy for the successful treatment of people with varying kinds of aphonias and dysphonias.

*The Voice and Voice Therapy* represents the thinking and clinical approaches of many people. Any listing of those who have contributed to the clinical philosophies emerging from these pages will surely omit some names that should not be forgotten, but such a list I must attempt to make. Any clinician, particularly a voice clinician, is surely a composite of all the people with whom he has studied and worked. For me, this book would not have been possible without the thinking of J. L. Aten, Ph.D.; L. G. Best, Ph.D.; F. S. Brodnitz, M.D.; W. M. Diedrich, Ph.D.; R. M. Flower, Ph.D.; W. H. Gardner, Ph.D.; B. B. Gray, Ph.D.; V. Jordan, M.D.; F. M. Kirchner, M.D.; A. W. Knox, Ph.D.; W. Latas, M.A.; N. M. Levin, M.D.; K. Lyndes, M.A.; W. Maloney, M.D.; K. Merten, M.A.; J. F. Michel,

Ph.D.; J. B. Miller, Ed.D.; Col. R. C. Newell, M.D.; P. H. Ptacek, Ph.D.; G. O. Proud, M.D.; E. K. Sander, Ph.D.; R. L. Shelton, Jr., Ph.D.; D. L. Teter, Ph.D.; and W. H. Wilson, M.D. Since the clinical practice of voice therapy provides one with a continuous learning experience, I am most grateful for all that I have learned from the many patients with clinical voice disorders who have received voice therapy from me and my colleagues.

As a university professor, I hope that *The Voice and Voice Therapy* will give the serious student of voice disorders and their therapies a useful glimpse of current knowledge and its clinical application. In my attempt to integrate current research findings into some kind of clinical interpretation and direction, I have tried to avoid oversimplification and overstatement. Realizing that the state of our art has some way to go, I must point out that *The Voice and Voice Therapy* perhaps reflects where I am as much as where our theoretical-clinical knowledge is. To the student clinician I offer the encouraging advice to go ahead and work with people with voice disorders, for there is no clinical group in speech pathology more responsive symptomatically to what we do. These people need our help as voice therapists.

The book received valuable assistance from two colleagues in Denver, Colorado—D. L. Teter, Ph.D., and K. Lyndes, M.A.—both of whom provided many of the photographic illustrations. Clinical pathology pictures were provided by Teter from his work with the clinic population at Fitzsimons General Hospital, U.S. Army, Denver, under the direction of Col. R. C. Newall, M.D., chief of Otolaryngology. The photographs of laryngeal and thoracic structures were ingeniously prepared and photographed by Lyndes, with the full cooperation of the Department of Pathology and its chief, J. Minckler, M.D., at General Rose Hospital, Denver. Both Teter and Lyndes are speech pathologists and know the kinds of illustration relevant to the voice clinician.

The amazing transition from my rough draft (typed on a pre-World War II portable) to final copy was accomplished through the editing and typing of Mrs. B. B. Brueggemann. Only a devoted sister could give so much of her time and talent to the final development of a manuscript.

Hopefully, for my wife and four children the completion of the book will mean more time to spend in the Colorado mountains.

*The Voice and Voice Therapy* is an attempt to take some of the magic out of voice therapy. I hope there is something here not only for the student of voice therapy, but also for the clinical speech pathologist and the practicing laryngologist. I think there is.

DANIEL R. BOONE, PH.D.
*Professor of Speech Pathology,*
*University of Denver,*
*Denver, Colorado*

# THE VOICE
## AND
## VOICE
## THERAPY

*chapter one*

# Symptomatic
# Voice Therapy

*Most voice disorders are related to the misuse and abuse of the voice. Symptomatic voice therapy attempts to identify these vocal abuses and then eliminate or reduce them by direct symptom modification. This book concerns voice disorders—functional and organic, imagined or real—and what the voice clinician can do about them.*

The act of speaking is a very specialized way of using the vocal mechanism. The act of singing is even more so. Speaking and singing demand a combination and interaction of the mechanisms of respiration, phonation, resonance, and speech articulation. The best speakers and singers are often those persons who, by natural gift or training, or by a studied blend of both, have mastered the art of optimally using these vocal mechanisms. The patient with a voice disorder often uses his vocal mechanisms in a faulty manner. It is this vocal misuse which becomes the focus of our clinical attempt to help him use his voice more optimally. The goal of voice therapy, from our point of view, is to identify and eliminate the possible misuses of respiration, phonation, or resonance which contribute to the patient's vocal impairment. This symptom-oriented approach is what we mean by symptomatic voice therapy.

## HYPERFUNCTIONAL VOICE PROBLEMS

Although there are many types of vocal disorders related to various functional or organic pathologies at particular sites of the vocal mechanism, there does not appear to be a differential type of voice therapy for each kind of disorder. Rather, the concept of *hyperfunction* as introduced by Froeschels (*60*) provides a therapeutic philosophy for the clinician that is not bound to particular etiologies or pathologies, but provides a working method for reducing the vocal symptomatology of the average voice patient who misuses or abuses his vocal mechanism. Froeschels characterizes a hyperfunctional voice disorder as having too much muscular force in the wrong places. The accomplished speaker or singer uses the vocal mechanism in an optimum manner, getting "mileage" out of his voice by avoiding undue tensions in vocal production (respiration, phonation, and resonance). The patient will, of course, experience various bodily tensions, but if he is to master control of the phonatory mechanisms, these structures must be relatively free of tension. It would appear that the average person generates many of his own tensions, and that his "reality" is a composite of the external world and how he sees and responds to it. His tensions, whether externally imposed or self-generating or a combination of both, can contribute to a breakdown in his overall effectiveness, sometimes reflecting themselves in the development and continuation of a voice disorder. As Brodnitz has written, "Tenseness of muscle groups is a common occurrence in modern civilization. We live in a tense age, and the tenseness of a competitive atmosphere affects the vocal organs too. In this sense, vocal hyperfunction belongs to the large number of psychosomatic disorders that translate inner tension into tense organic behavior." (*24*, p. 47.)

It is the thesis of this text that most problems of vocal hyperfunction are highly remediable by symptomatic voice therapy. That is, once vocal abuses have been identified and eliminated, the patient experiences a better voice. Evidence continues to accumulate that the elimination of excessive force in respiration, phonation, and resonance will eliminate much of the patient's vocal problem (Arnold, *4*; Brodnitz, *24*; Murphy, *119*; Van Riper and Irwin, *162*; and Wilson, *168*). There are occasional cases where the voice disorder serves the patient and is only a symptom of a strong underlying psychological problem requiring the clinical services of a psychologist or psychiatrist. Often, however, the reduction of hyperfunctional vocal behavior will be accompanied by a reduction of vocal symptoms, regardless of the psychological needs of the patient. For years, voice therapy has frequently been avoided by the laryngologist or speech pathologist because of the mistaken belief that most voice problems are merely symptomatic of un-resolved psychological problems. However, the clinical evidence seems to say, "We can take the problem out of your voice. You'll still have your tensions and personality problems, *but your voice will sound like the rest of ours.*" A normal speaking voice does not have to be the product of an optimally functioning, healthy personality. The voice need not be the mirror of a maladapted personality, or, for that matter, a healthy personality, as any good actor will testify. A trial period of voice therapy aimed at reducing vocal symptoms appears to be in order for most patients with hyperfunctional voice problems.

## THE SITES OF VOCAL HYPERFUNCTION

Excessive muscular contraction and force of movement in respiration, phonation, or resonance can be labeled as vocal hyperfunction. An identification and description of the specific anatomical sites and physiological functions associated with vocal hyperfunction will provide the reader with an overview of the problem.

### RESPIRATION

The larynx is primarily a valvelike "guardian" watching over the airway and preventing the entrance of foreign bodies into the respiratory system. Yet, beyond this primitive capacity, man has developed the further ability to prolong his exhalation while the true vocal folds are gently approximated to produce phonation. Phonation as part of speaking or singing requires a continuous closing and opening of the vocal folds, with shortenings and elongations of the folds as needed for continuous variations in pitch. Variations in intensity require continuous and subtle fluctuations of air flow. The regulation of this outflow of air is basically involuntary and highly automatic in ordinary speech, but the public speaker or singer learns to rely heavily on a partial control of his breathing mechanism. Singers, for example, require an additional supply of air in excess of that obtained in normal inhalation, and are able to replenish their air supply quickly and efficiently. Most important, perhaps, singers must be able to sustain a prolonged exhalation. The trained speaking voice (a voice that does not tire easily) and the accomplished singing voice (a voice that is aesthetically pleasant and musically competent) require the greatest extent of respiratory movement in the lower chest and upper abdominal regions, for it is in the abdominal-lower thoracic area where the speaker or singer has the most voluntary control of respiration. Although it is possible to develop some control over respiration, particularly over the expirational phase of breathing, this control must be within the limits of the oxygen needs of the individual.

The average speaker tends to employ respiration somewhat inadequately for phonation. With the substantiation and validation of the myoelastic theory of phonation, it is surprising that so many laryngologists and speech pathologists put so little emphasis on the importance of adequate respiration for the development of good phonation. Our relative deemphasis of respiration in voice therapy may be related in part to our need to invalidate the techniques of our singing-teacher predecessors and put voice therapy on a "scientific basis." The fact remains that the larynx and its phonatory productions are dependent on an adequate outgoing air stream of sufficient subglottal pressure to set the approximated vocal folds into vibration. Therefore, it would appear certain that the everyday demand of phonation—let alone the artificial phonatory requirements of the actor, lecturer, or singer—require that we take in and control a sufficient quantity of air to permit a sustained subglottal air pressure great enough to produce vocal fold vibration.

Unusual force or muscle tension (hyperfunction) can be observed in various phases of respiration among normal persons and clinical voice patients. While the normal speaker without vocal pathology can tolerate vocal stresses related to inadequate and inefficient respiration, the patient with vocal pathology usually cannot tolerate such respiratory inefficiency. Perhaps the most common problem of respiration observed among voice patients is the attempt to speak on an inadequate expiration. The inspiratory phase may be inadequate for the phonatory task. The untrained singer may be observed to elevate his shoulders, using the neck accessory muscles for inhalation. Or the lecturer or the singer, in his need to get in a "big" breath, may, in taking a maximum inhalation, display an obviously distended abdomen, a fixed thorax, elevated shoulders with the associated neck accessory muscles in a hypertonic state, and possibly a head thrust forward in extension. Although such a "deep breather" may have increased his vital capacity, he is in no position to parcel out his exhalation for a controlled, sustained phonation. More commonly, perhaps, we see the patient who suffers not from too little or too much of an inhalation, but from improper utilization of his expiration. Sometimes this patient attempts to impose too stringent a conscious control over his breathing, relying little or not at all on the autonomic aspects of breathing related to the delicate balance between carbon dioxide and oxygen; such a patient was once described as a "cortical breather," one who could not turn over his breathing functions to the automatic phases of inspiration-expiration during his waking hours, but only during sleep was able to demonstrate anything approaching normal respiration. Usually, however, "cortical breathing" is less obvious, being characterized instead by the patient who exerts too much muscular force (perhaps by holding the abdominal muscles in a fixed, contracted state) while attempting to speak. Another hyperfunctional type of respiration is seen in the patient who attempts to speak on residual air: the inspiratory phase of breathing may be adequate; the patient exhales a normal tidal expiration; then he speaks on a portion of his residual air. Since there is little air pressure remaining at the end of the tidal breath, the patient experiences insufficient subglottal air pressure, with the result that his phonation is weak and often inaudible. Such an inefficient method of breathing can have negative effects on the laryngeal mechanism.

## PHONATION

From a physiological point of view, the larynx is not primarily an organ of voice, but serves as the upper, valvelike entry way to the respiratory tract. While most mammals are physically capable of using the laryngeal valving folds for phonation, a few species, such as rabbits and deer, are usually silent. At the other extreme is man, whose control over phonation has resulted in the fantastic achievement of human speech, with its requirements of sustained phonation, abrupt cessation of phonation, pitch variation, and changes in intensity. The vegetative, life-sustaining role of the laryngeal mechanism stands in sharp contrast to the role the laryngeal apparatus is called upon to play for purposes of human speech. Optimal phonation for speaking and singing requires continuous abduction-adduction of the vocal folds, with subtle changes in fold length and mass. The subglottal air pressure forces the gently approximated vocal folds apart, setting them into vibration. It is at the anatomical site of the glottal opening where the vast majority of hyperfunctional voice problems begin, because of inappropriate (inadequate or excessive) vocal fold approximation.

While the symptoms of vocal hyperfunction are often produced by the excessive force and contraction of muscles concerned with respiration and supraglottal resonance, there are specific types of hyperfunctional behavior at the site of the larynx. One of the most damaging is the hard glottal attack, described by Jackson and Jackson (86) and Peacher and Holinger (129) as the slamming approximation of the vocal processes of the arytenoid cartilages, often causing the formation of contact ulcers. The formation of other laryngeal pathologies, such as cord thickening, nodules, and polyps, is often the result of excessive force in vocal fold approximation, well described by Arnold (4). Probably for every patient the speech pathologist sees who has some degree of *dysphonia* (voice problem) with accompanying organic laryngeal pathology, there is a patient with a similar-sounding dysphonia but no structural change of the laryngeal mechanism. The hyperfunctional overadduction of the vocal folds will result typically in limiting free vibration of the folds, producing the tight dysphonia of the harsh voice or perhaps the laryngeal "stutter" of spastic dysphonia. Another extreme of improper adduction is the lax approximation of the vocal folds as heard in such conditions as the breathy voice or in the presence of the extreme problem of absent cord adduction, as dramatically observed in functional aphonia. Most clinical voice problems, with or without structural deviations, are characterized by faulty vocal fold approximation, with the patient usually exhibiting something in between the extremes of spastic dysphonia and functional aphonia.

There is much disagreement among voice authorities about the influence of inappropriate pitch level or fundamental frequency on the development of various vocal pathologies. While for some patients it might appear that an inappropriately low or high pitch level is a primary etiological factor in a vocal disorder, there are other patients whose faulty pitch levels have developed secondarily from the increase of vocal fold mass due to early polypoid or nodule growth. That is, sometimes the inappropriate pitch level produces the dysphonia, and sometimes the prolonged dysphonia produces vocal fold tissue changes with a resulting alteration in pitch. It appears that it is important for any speaker or singer to use the vocal mechanism optimally with regard to fundamental frequency. Speaking or singing at an inappropriate pitch level requires excessive force and contraction of the intrinsic muscles of the larynx, leading to vocal fatigue, or the hoarseness related to a tired vocal mechanism (Jackson and Jackson, *86*). Brodnitz has written:

> The most frequent causes of the formation of nodules in singers are: attempts to sing above the natural limits of the voice (baritones who try to become tenors, mezzosopranos who sing as sopranos), enforced production of the voice with hyperfunctional constriction and singing of highly dramatic parts by singers with lyric voices. Whether conservatively or surgically treated, a complete retraining of the techniques of singing and of the voice mechanism is necessary. [*24*, p. 116]

Another common pitch deviation is the inappropriately low pitch of the young professional person, such as the teacher or preacher, who speaks at the bottom of his pitch range in an attempt to convey some extra authority through his voice. Or there is the young professional woman who speaks at a fundamental frequency value well below the normative values of the average adult female. An inappropriate pitch level, whether it be too low or too high, requires unnecessary muscle energy to maintain the necessary vocal fold adjustments of length and mass to produce the "artificial" voice. Of the many variables we often identify as hyperfunctional voice behaviors, inappropriate pitch level is one of the easiest of the disorders to remedy. Sometimes just by raising or lowering the fundamental frequency slightly, the patient will experience a lessening of the energy he employs to speak, which will result in a noticeable decrease in his dysphonia. (voice disorder)

Among the greatest of all causes of vocal dysfunction are the various forms of vocal abuse. Continued talking, excessive laughing and crying, talking loudly over background noise, and screaming and yelling all take a toll, reducing the efficiency of the laryngeal mechanism. In presenting their well-developed compendium of abusive vocal events, Jackson and Jackson write:

> There is a great variation in the amount of abuse the larynx of different individuals will stand; but every larynx has its limit. To go beyond this limit means thickening of the cords, and a thickened cord means a hoarse voice. Not only is a thickened cord a poor vibrator but it throws great additional work upon the thyroarytenoidei. [*86*, p. 40]

The vocal fold edema, or vascular engorgement, which may result from excessive phonation, such as in screaming or yelling, produces by its additive nature an enlargement of the vocal folds which may produce an alteration in phonation; the patient may further add to his difficulty by attempting to compensate for this change in his voice by making new adjustments and contractions of the intrinsic and extrinsic laryngeal muscles. Coughing and excessive throat clearing frequently contribute to the problem of dysphonia and laryngeal pathology, perhaps adding edema and irritation to an already pathological condition. True infection of the larynx is often the primary etiological factor in dysphonia, with the patient experiencing acute or chronic laryngitis; instead of imposing upon himself a temporary period of voice rest during the infectious stage of the disease, the patient may continue to phonate, compounding his vocal fold irritation. Lecturing or serious singing "on top" of an existing laryngeal infection can have disastrous aftereffects and perhaps damage the vocal mechanism permanently. External irritants, particularly once laryngeal pathology has been established, may have an exacerbating effect on certain vocal pathologies; smoking, excessive alcohol consumption, smog, and dust have all been identified as culprits that help maintain various laryngeal disorders. It would appear that once any kind of vocal abuse has been identified, intelligent efforts by the patient to reduce future such abusive behavior might well result in a noticeable lessening of his vocal distress.

## THE VOCAL TRACT

The complexity of vocal resonance and speech articulation is, of course, a supraglottal phenomenon. Because both resonance and articulation are so complex from the point of view of voluntary and involuntary motor control, there is frequent hyperfunctional usage of particular supraglottal structures. The most immediate supraglottal area, the hypopharynx, is a common site of hyperfunction; this is where the patient may contract the pharyngeal constrictors and retract the tongue posteriorly, filling the hypopharyngeal opening. This posterior tongue retraction, coupled with pharyngeal constriction, produces an acoustical bottleneck which results in a restriction of oral resonance. The glossal filling of the hypopharynx may occur only during particular anxiety states of the patient or be conditioned to occur only during particular speaking events; at these times, however, the patient experiences extreme difficulty in "getting out" his voice. Posterior tongue retraction also occurs in the oral pharynx, producing a *cul de sac resonance* (this phenomenon is discussed in some detail in chapter 6 with regard to the voices of the deaf). Posterior tongue retraction is usually accompanied by high posterior arching of the tongue, often in direct contact with the soft palate; this glossal posterior arching is sometimes a predisposing factor to such resonance deviations as hypernasality or denasality. Although hyperfunctional carriage of the tongue may create many acoustical variations of voice, it is often not identified, erroneously, as a contributing cause of an existing dysphonia. Related to disorders of resonance is the hyperfunctional use of the soft palate, with the patient often keeping the velum in a fixed opened or closed position; this lack of palatal movement is sometimes directed volitionally by the patient as he attempts to create a *Godlike voice* or imitates nasalized speech patterns or attempts to sing like an *Irish tenor*. Prolonged attempts at artificial resonance may create unnecessary constriction and tension in those structures contributing to the resonance effects. Unfortunately, focal hyperfunction of the vocal tract does not usually remain that focal, so that hyperfunctional postures affect adjacent and related muscles.

One of the most commonly observed types of hyperfunctional behavior in the vocal tract is speaking with mandibular constriction, or talking "through one's teeth." The patient makes most of the muscle adjustments required for continuous speech almost wholly with his tongue, with the mandible locked in a passive role. This means that for the various adjustments required for producing vowels, the patient changes the dimensions of his oral cavity by flattening or elevating the tongue, with little or no size change contributed by the opening of the mandible. It is no wonder that the majority of these patients with mandibular restriction complain of symptoms of vocal fatigue, pain, or fullness in the hyoid area after prolonged speaking or singing. The entire burden of articulation is on the tongue. Mandibular restriction is a commonly observed diagnostic entity in many patients with hyperfunctional voice disorders. Recognizing this, Froeschels (59) developed the *chewing approach* in voice therapy. Voice clinicians using the chewing approach for selected voice patients generally report its efficacy, not only in promoting greater mobility of the mandible, but in reducing other oral hyperfunctional postures.

Hyperfunction is sometimes observed in the patient's overuse of the tongue tip and lips in speech articulation. Such a patient overarticulates, frequently accompanying his overarticulations with hard and abrupt glottal attacks. He maintains a posture of articulatory precision with excessive constriction and force, his speech and voice lacking ease and naturalness of production. At another extreme is the patient who speaks with a masked expression and dullness of articulation. His voice quality may be muffled and his overall speech-voice production restricted in sound.

Hyperfunctional behavior may be observed, then, in such supraglottal areas as: the hypopharynx and oropharynx, characterized by pharyngeal constriction with tongue retraction; the nasopharynx, characterized by fixed and inappropriate velar posturing; the mandible, characterized by mandibular restriction, or the patient speaking through clenched teeth; and the tongue and lips, characterized by inappropriately precise articulation with excessive tongue and lip posturing. Less specific and more difficult to identify is the overall hyperfunction of the vocal tract demonstrated by the patient who "projects" his voice by increasing the tonicity of the walls of the resonating cavities; he achieves this primarily through the contraction of the pharyngeal constrictors and the elevation-retraction of the tongue. Vocal "projection" appears often to be more a self-delusion of the performer than an acoustic reality to the listener. The performer is rewarded by his efforts at overcontraction by a feeling that he is *doing something.* And he is. In his attempt to make himself heard clearly, he is sharpening his articulation and increasing the volume of his voice. Projection, therefore, appears to be more a phenomenon of articulation and volume intensity than of resonance. Excessive muscle energy expended for the contraction of the pharyngeal constrictors produces hyperfunctional vocal behavior which adds little to the sound of the voice and produces an unnecessary amount of muscle fatigue.

### THE REDUCTION OF VOCAL HYPERFUNCTION AS A THERAPEUTIC GOAL

The patient with a presenting vocal complaint usually shows symptoms related to the improper functioning of phonatory or resonance mechanisms. These voice symptoms often appear to be related to specific abuse and/or misuse of the vocal mechanism, with or without the development of laryngeal pathologies. It is our thesis that once the possible abuses and misuses of the vocal mechanisms are identified, these symptoms can be eliminated or minimized by voice therapy. Such a symptomatic approach, however, must not ignore the question of *why* the patient has developed his vocal symptoms and *how* these voice problems continue to serve him.

Such a symptomatic therapy approach as the one developed in this text would have little validity if limited to the mechanical interactions of respiration, phonation, resonance, and articulation. Laboratory data often suggest such a mechanical approach: witness our values of vital and tidal capacities, our measures of subglottal air pressure, our measurements of fold length and mass with regard to fundamental frequency, our high-speed cinematography of vocal fold physiology, and our cinefluorographic-spectrographic analyses of various resonance parameters. While these data are vital to our understanding of phonatory and resonance physiology, which in turn is important if we are to provide our patients with effective voice therapy, they do not help us answer the questions of why the voice disorder arose and how its continuation serves the patient.

A voice disorder often begins as the natural sequela of a true organic disease. The patient may attempt his normal speech-voice pattern within an overall milieu of physical exhaustion accompanying or following a severe, debilitating illness; he is required to expend an unusual amount of effort to speak *normally*, and this produces strain and sometimes permanent damage to the laryngeal mechanism. Wyatt (*174*), in describing vocal problems originating in physical alterations of the vocal mechanism, listed certain endocrine imbalances related to systemic illnesses, puberty, pregnancy, menstruation, and menopause as conditions that might cause initial vocal symptoms. Some voice problems seem to have their origin in acute local diseases of the respiratory tract, including the larynx or pharynx; the acute problem may force the individual to produce his voice with unusual effort, resulting in a hyperfunctional voice behavior which may well persist after the acute infection is over. Or the vocal trauma of a particular event, such as yelling at a basketball game, may produce temporary laryngeal changes which cause compensatory vocal behaviors that persist and become the individual's particular *set* for subsequent vocal behavior. Acting, lecturing, or singing under exceptional conditions (inappropriate pitch range, too loud, too long) may produce temporary phonation changes, requiring the individual to attempt various vocal effects to overcome his temporary dysphonia; such vocal compensations may become a permanent part of the patient's vocal repertoire.

*Why* voice symptoms begin cannot always be answered in terms of an initial laryngeal structural change secondary to physical change from illness or trauma. Vocal behavior, as well as other forms of verbal behavior that meet the needs of the organism, tends to be repeated (Krasner, *94*). For example, consider the individual who, when attempting to answer the phone, experiences a phonation break in his voice; his listener then makes an appropriate comment, and the speaker subsequently modifies or continues his voice-break behavior in the present and future phone situations. Or there is the child who, during a particularly anxious moment, is unable to control his exhalation sufficiently to make the verbal responses he wants to make, and so becomes aphonic; the reaction of others as well as his own reaction to this event will have a profound influence on whether such an aphonic response recurs. His first inappropriate vocal response may well have been accidental. His reaction to it will play an important part in whether he seeks similar vocal events in the future or whether such vocal behavior is so repugnant to him that he discontinues it. As for the reaction of others, his initial use of the particular voice pattern, whether by accident or imitation, may produce such desirable responses from his listeners that he is encouraged to continue it.

While the *why*, or the precipitating causes, of voice pathologies are many and varied, *how* they maintain themselves or how the symptoms serve the speaker is even more complex. Undoubtedly, for many voice patients the initial event is long past, and the patient speaks the way he does today because this is the way he spoke yesterday. If the mode of phonation satisfies the total adaptive needs of the individual, he continues to use it. On the other hand, if he finds the penalty for continuing the atypical voice pattern too great, he may decide to discontinue it. By trial and error, or from the advice of friends, or by reading such a book as this, the patient makes an attempt to modify his way of speaking. Often he will be successful, and his phonatory problems will disappear. Frequently, however, his compensatory endeavors to change will only compound his hyperfunctional phonatory behavior, and his problem will continue. As Jackson and Jackson (*86*) explained in their description of *myasthenia laryngitis,* prolonged hyperfunctional use of the voice, and the various vocal compensations the patient may use to overcome his voice problem, may lead to a hypofunctional voice weakness characterized by a weakened laryngeal mechanism (such as bowing of the folds).

An improper voice production quickly becomes automatic and involuntary, and as such is resistant to voluntary modification. The individual has very little volitional control over respiration, phonation, and resonance, and his best motor control of these mechanisms is evidenced when he attempts to match an acoustical model of a voice, his own model, or an external one provided for him. With the acoustical voice model clearly before him, his tidal breath is usually sufficient, his glottal adjustments are made with little volitional control, and his vocal tract (pharyngeal constriction, velopharyngeal closure, tongue positioning) automatically adjusts so that the outgoing phonation approximates the voice model. Phonation and resonance are the result of highly automatic motor behavior. The fact that maladaptive vocal behavior, like any other phonation, becomes a highly automatic motor response appears to be the primary reason why poor vocal habits maintain themselves. Successful voice therapy, therefore, requires that after identifying possible abuses or misuses in vocal behavior, the trained observer, speech pathologist, or laryngologist initiate corrective voice therapy procedures which will replace incorrect motor responses with more optimal ones.

Symptomatic voice therapy cannot always be successful with patients whose aberrant voice patterns serve them well, consciously or subconsciously. How often we hear that the abnormal voice is only a maladaptive symptom of a neurotic personality, a view articulately espoused by Moses in his classic work, *The Voice of Neurosis* (*118*). Moses argues that to eradicate the symptom focally is only to encourage the patient to develop another symptom, perhaps more maladaptive than the voice disorder. The voice clinician will see patients whose psychological needs are so served by their vocal symptoms that all attempts at symptom modification meet with failure. Or he will see the dysphonic patient who has received intensive psychotherapy directed toward a general problem of psychological adjustment, but who, despite his relatively good psychological health, continues to demonstrate dysphonia. Occasionally it is reported, although this writer has never seen such a case, that the elimination of a patient's vocal symptom results in the development of a new symptom.

Symptomatic therapy for all kinds of maladaptive verbal behavior has received vigorous support in the growing literature of behavioral psychology (Sloane and MacAulay, *148*). The basic premise of the behavioral approach is that by isolating a maladaptive response, determining a baseline of frequency of the response, and developing an operant shaping-training program specific to the problem, the original response will diminish by incremental shaping until it reaches an acceptable goal or target value. One widely used method of behavioral therapy, developed by Wolpe (*171*), is systematic desensitization (gradual deconditioning of anxiety responses), which closely parallels the symptomatic modification of voice problems without necessarily taking neurotic implications of such problems into account. For those voice problems without organic structural changes of the laryngeal mechanism, this statement by Rachman in 1967 about the efficacy of behavioral therapy deserves serious consideration by the voice clinician:

In the experimental investigations and in the clinical reports there is overwhelming evidence that substantial improvements in neurotic behavior can be obtained by systematic desensitization (and other methods of behavior therapy) even when little or no attention is paid to the possible or presumed underlying causes of the illness. [*136*, p. 103]

Some voice problems approach the psychiatric dimensions of a conversion hysteria, where the patient fixates on his somatic disorder, often in the absence of true organic disease. A direct attack in removing the patient's symptoms is again warranted. The problem of symptom transfer—finding a new symptom at a new somatic site after the original symptom has been removed—does not appear to be the clinical reality it was once feared to be. Rachman, in the study referred to above, provides an impressive reference list of behavioral studies which eliminated focal symptoms of neurotic and psychotic patients, with no transfer of symptoms. Stevens, in describing 300 patients with conversion hysteria, wrote in 1968 (*155*) that during amytal sodium interviews he did not once encounter a symptom transfer or psychotic reaction after an interview which reduced the patient's conversion symptom.

While reduction of vocal hyperfunction as a therapeutic goal is feasible for the overwhelming majority of voice patients, the clinician will occasionally encounter patients whose functional voice symptoms are not remedied by symptomatic voice therapy. Some of these patients will quickly be recognizable as persons whose difficulties are related primarily to serious problems of psychological adjustment; such patients should be referred, whenever possible, to a clinical psychologist or psychiatrist. For others, perhaps an initial exposure to symptomatic voice therapy proves to be an inadequate treatment with the patient showing no reduction of symptoms; while symptomatic voice therapy may be ineffective for some patients, a trial period is not harmful and should be attempted.

### SUMMARY

The processes of respiration, phonation, and resonance demand an optimum blending by the successful user of voice. Most vocal pathologies are related to hyperfunctional usage of some or all of these mechanisms, producing various alterations of phonation or resonance, with or without the subsequent development of laryngeal pathology. While the differentiation of functional from organic voice disorders is essential for the laryngologist in his need to identify true larygeal disease, vocal therapy approaches differentiate very little between functional and organically caused dysphonias. Our recommended therapy approach requires that the patient's vocal abuses or misuses be identified whenever possible, and that the voice therapy then be directed at reducing the identified hyperfunctional behavior. The thesis of this text is that direct symptom modification will in most cases reduce the patient's voice symptoms. While symptomatic voice therapy will not be successful for all voice disorders, particularly those which effectively serve the maladapted individual's needs, it will produce considerable improvement in the majority of patients with hyperfunctional voice problems. Such a symptom-oriented approach requires that the voice clinician have a thorough understanding of the mechanisms specific to voice production, and that he be flexible enough to adjust his therapeutic approach to the needs of the particular patient. *The Voice and Voice Therapy* is devoted to providing the voice clinician with an understanding of the mechanisms of normal and pathological voice; its emphasis will be on developing a philosophy of voice therapy, the implementation of which can be seen in the clinician's application of specific therapeutic procedures.

*chapter two*

# The Vocal Mechanisms and Hyperfunction

*Knowledge of the basic anatomy and physiology of the vocal mechanisms permits the clinician to understand what the patient is doing in respiration, phonation, and resonance. The problem of vocal hyperfunction is usually related to use of too much force at various sites of the vocal mechanism. We shall consider separately each of the primary vocal mechanisms—respiration, phonation, and resonance—listing briefly the anatomical structures involved, describing the physiology of the mechanisms, and discussing how the mechanism is related to observed clinical hyperfunction.*

## RESPIRATION

Man has learned to use respiration for speech, sustaining his exhalations for purposes of phonation. Both speaking and singing require an outgoing air stream capable of activating vocal fold vibration. When the speaker or singer "trains" his voice, he frequently focuses on developing conscious control of the breathing mechanism. This conscious control, however, must always be consistent with the physiological air requirements of the individual. It is often the conflict between the physiological needs and the speaking-singing demands for air that causes faulty usage of the vocal mechanism. Our dependence upon the constant renewal of our oxygen supply imposes upon us certain restrictions and limitations as to how many words we can say, or how many phrases we can sing, on one expiration.

Some familiarity with the anatomy and function of the respiratory structures should be helpful in developing a working understanding of the mechanics of respiration as it applies to phonation:

STRUCTURES OF RESPIRATION

Respiratory Tract
    Nasal Cavity
    Pharynx
    Oral Cavity
    Larynx
    Trachea
    Bronchi and Bronchioles
    Alveoli Sacs
    Lungs
    Pleurae
Thoracic Bone Structure
    Spinal Column
    12 Paired Ribs
Muscles of Inspiration
    Diaphragm (the primary muscle of inspiration)
    External Intercostals
    Pectoralis Major and Pectoralis Minor
    Costal Elevators
    Serratus Anterior and Serratus Posterior
    Neck Accessory Muscles (primarily the Sternocliedomastoid)
Muscles of Expiration
    Abdominals (no abdominal contraction except during conditions of forced
        expiration, such as laughing, yelling)
        Internal Oblique Abdominal
        External Oblique Abdominal
        Transverse Abdominal
        Rectus Abdominal
    Internal Intercostals
    Posterior Inferior Serratus

Some of the structures of the respiratory tract can be identified in the line drawing and unusual photograph in figure 1. Because of the elasticity of lung tissue and its tendency to shrivel upon removal from the thorax, these cadaver lungs have been stretched out for the photograph and grossly resemble their normal shape and relative size as they would have appeared

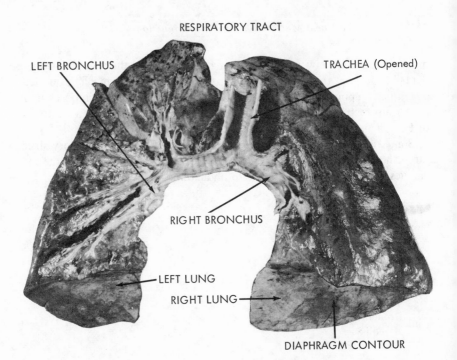

LEFT BRONCHUS

TRACHEA (Opened)

RIGHT BRONCHUS

LEFT LUNG

RIGHT LUNG

DIAPHRAGM CONTOUR

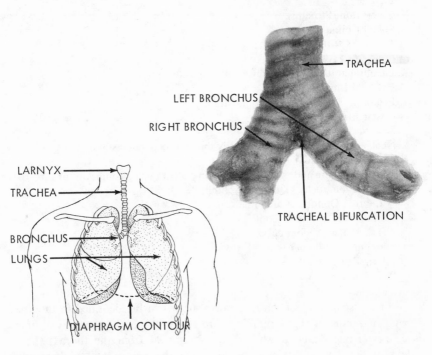

TRACHEA

LEFT BRONCHUS

RIGHT BRONCHUS

TRACHEAL BIFURCATION

LARNYX

TRACHEA

BRONCHUS

LUNGS

DIAPHRAGM CONTOUR

Fig. 1. Respiratory tract.

16

toward the end of an expiratory cycle. They were undoubtedly larger when inflated toward the end of an inspiratory cycle.

## MECHANISM OF RESPIRATION

In order to understand the physiology of respiration, it is necessary to remember the high degree of elasticity of the lungs. This elasticity is seen dramatically in the collapse and shriveling of the tissue of lungs which are removed from the body at surgery or in postmortem examination (see fig. 1). The tendency to collapse also exists in the living organism, and is directly related to lung elasticity and to internal and external air pressures. On  inspiration, as the thoracic cage increases in size, the elastic lung tissue follows the thoracic expansion, increasing the size of the lungs. As the lungs increase in size, the air already captured within them from previous inhalation is reduced in total pressure, since the same amount of air has more space. This decrease in air pressure within the lungs (intrapulmonary pressure) represents a minus value differential between intrapulmonary pressure and the outside air pressure—atmospheric pressure being around 760 mm. Hg. (millimeters of mercury)—and the outside air rushes in to fill the vacuum. When the intrapulmonary and atmospheric pressures are equalized, the expiration process begins. It is characterized by a decrease in the size of the thorax and an elastic recoil of the lungs, resulting in an increase of intrapulmonary pressure. When the intrapulmonary pressure exceeds that of the atmosphere, there is an immediate outflow of air until the two pressures are equalized, at which time the inhalation process begins again. Zemlin has described this differential effect of air pressure very well:

The moment inspiration begins, intrapulmonic pressure begins to fall below atmospheric, and at the height of inspiration the intrapulmonic pressure is lowest, amounting to $-1$ to $-2$ mm. Hg. . . . As the inspiration phase comes to an end, the intrapulmonic pressure begins to rise, and at the very end of inspiration (with the laryngeal valve open) it is the same as atmospheric. As expiration movement begins, the lungs contract elastically as rapidly as the diminishing chest cavity permits, and the air within the lungs is compressed. Intrapulmonic pressure exceeds atmospheric by about 2–3 mm. Hg, and the air rushes out of the lungs until once again the intrapulmonic pressure reaches atmospheric. [177, pp. 96–97]

For the average adult, the constant exchange of carbon dioxide for renewed oxygen requires from 13 to 18 breaths per minute, depending on muscular exertion, body temperature, and other physiological demands. For many years, Zoethout and Tuttle included in their *Textbook of Physiology* (*178*) the following respiratory values, which are as valid today as they were when first set down in the 1920s:

The rate (respiratory) varies with age:
At birth ...................................from 40 to 70 per minute
5 years .......................................about 25 per minute
15 years ......................................about 20 per minute
30 years ......................................about 16 per minute
It is also influenced by the position of the body:
Reclining ...........................................13 per minute
Sitting .............................................18 per minute
Standing ............................................22 per minute
Sleep decreases the rate by as much as 25 percent.

Descriptions of lung volume or lung capacity tend to be confusing because of an overabundance of conflicting terms. Therefore, any discussion of normal respiratory values as they apply to various forms of human breath function should define terms. We shall develop some working definitions for the terms used with the normative respiratory values shown in figure 2.

*Tidal capacity.* Tidal air is the total volume of air inspired or expired during each normal respiratory cycle.

*Complemental air.* Complemental air is the maximum volume of air that can be inspired beyond the normal tidal inhalation. The term "inspiratory reserve volume" is often used now instead of complemental air (Comroe, *37*).

*Supplemental air.* Supplemental air is the maximum volume of air that can be expired beyond the end of a normal tidal expiration. The supplemental air volume is sometimes called the "expiratory reserve volume."

*Residual air.* Residual air is the volume of air in the lungs at the end of a maximal expiration. It is the volume of air remaining in the lungs that can not be exhaled.

*Vital capacity.* Vital capacity is the total volume of air measurable within the lungs. Vital capacity would represent the sum of tidal capacity, complemental air, and residual air.

Typical air volumes using these terms can be found in figure 2, which presents a collation of different authors' air-volume values for the adult male. Typical adult female values would be slightly lower, depending of course on the relative size of the individual's thoracic cage.

Of primary interest to the voice clinician is the individual's tidal capacity, as the average voice demand requires no more than an average tidal breath. Of some relevance, however, is both how well the individual can empty his lungs and how well he can sustain his exhalation. An important measure

FIGURE 2. TYPICAL AIR VOLUMES OF THE ADULT MALE

| Author | Vital Capacity | Tidal Capac- ity | Comple- mental Air | Supple- mental Air | Residual Air |
|---|---|---|---|---|---|
| Murray and Lewis (*121*) | 3500 cc | 500 cc | 1500 cc | 1500 cc | 1000 cc |
| Gray and Wise (*66*) | 3700 cc | 500 cc | | | 1640 cc |
| Wise, McBurney, and Mallory (*170*) | 3700 cc | 457 cc | 1600 cc | 1600 cc | |
| Tabor (*156*) | 3700 cc | 500 cc | 1600 cc | 1600 cc | 1500 cc |
| Zemlin (*177*) | 3500–5000 cc | 750 cc | 1500 cc | 1500 cc | 1000-1500 cc |
| Millard and King (*109*) | 4100 cc | 500 cc | 1800 cc | 1800 cc | 1200 cc |
| Greene (*67*) | | 500 cc | 1500-2000 cc | 1500-2000 cc | |
| Curry (*42*) | 3000 cc | 500 cc | 1500 cc | 1500 cc | |

indicating lung elasticity and the quickness of air evacuation is the *vitalor test*. Here the subject is asked to take a maximal inhalation and then force out his exhalation as quickly as possible. A measurement is made of the amount of air he is able to expire in one second (see the Vitalor Test Report in figure 3). In quiet breathing, the length of time of inspiration is very similar to that of expiration; the use of tidal breath and a portion of supplemental breath during speaking, however, is represented by a relatively short inspiration with a prolonged expiration, parceling the outflowing air stream to meet particular phonatory demands. The time ratio of inspiration-expiration for quiet breathing is, grossly, 1/1.5. Speaking and singing are characterized by prolonged exhalation. Otis and Clark (*124*), in reporting studies designed to measure time of inspiration relative to time of exhalation for speech activities, found that a subject will take about as long to say something (counting to 25, repeating the alphabet, reciting poetry) as is required, regardless of the degree of ventilation. Otherwise, the length of expiration is highly dependent on the length of the verbal response. The inspiration-expiration time ratio for speaking, therefore, would be anywhere from 1/2 to 1/20, depending on the length of the passage the speaker wishes to say. In singing, the inspiration-expiration time ratio may be even greater, with the singer taking in a quick breath and sustaining his phonation according to his ability and the demands of the singing passage.

It would appear from the studies of Campbell (*29*; *30*) that the diaphragm and external intercostals are active during normal at-rest inspiration; at-rest expiration is characterized primarily by diaphragm—external intercostal relaxation and the natural elasticity of lung and thoracic structures, with assistance from the compressed abdominal viscera below. Expiratory muscles, such as the abdominals and internal intercostals, do become active in expiration for such acts as coughing and prolonged sound production, "par-

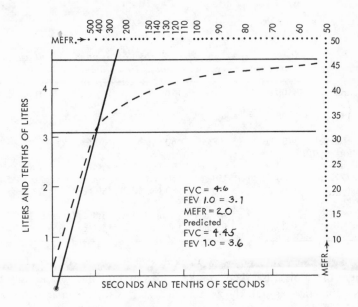

SECONDS AND TENTHS OF SECONDS

Predicted:

1. V.C. ___4. 45___ Liters

2. FEV₁ ___3. 6___ Liters

Found:

1. V.C. ___4.6___ Liters

2. FEV₁ ___3.1___ Liters

3. MEFR ___210___ L/min

Fig. 3. A vitalator test. The patient was asked to take in a big breath. According to his age and size, his predicted vital capacity (V.C.) and forced expiration volume (FEV) were respectively 4.45 and 3.6 liters. His tested V.C. was found to be 4.6 liters, and the amount of air he could exhale in one second (his FEV) was found to be 3.1 liters. This lower forced expiration reading is an indication of some reduction of the patient's lung expiratory function.

ticularly when the pressure developed is large or the lung volume at which the effort is made is low" (Campbell, *30*, p. 130). While the abdominal muscles are the primary muscles of expiration, they participate only minimally in normal speaking or breathing. During laughing, singing, or playing wind instruments, according to Bishop (*17*), it is the progressive, fine contraction of the abdominal muscles which helps control the rate of exhalation of lung volume far beyond normal tidal capacity. Bishop's data in studying respiratory values in man indicate that human abdominal muscles respond primarily during a "voluntary maximal breath." It would appear from the above findings, then, and from recent laboratory data such as those reported by Campbell (*29*) and Bishop (*17*), that the classic view of dia-phragmatic-abdominal breathing is wrong. While the diaphragm appears to be the primary muscle of inspiration, the abdominals do not function as natural antagonists, except under conditions of prolonged or forceful expira-tion. It may well be that at the peak of inspiration, the normal elasticity of the lungs is sufficient to produce enough subglottal pressure to set the approximated vocal folds into vibration. As air moves out of the lungs and these natural elastic forces become diminished, it is then necessary, if one is to continue a forceful expiration, to contract the abdominals in order to further extend the smooth, steady rate of air flow. The well-trained singer demonstrates his ability to combine the natural elasticity of his lungs with a gradual and incremental contraction of the abdominals and other accessory muscles of expiration. Proctor described the trained singer's mastery of expiration when he wrote:

Most singers are capable of sustaining single tones for more than 30 seconds, and phrases that extend over 15 seconds are not unusual in song. Even if the singer has a very large vital capacity (6 liters) he can sustain a tone requiring a flow of 0.15 l/sec for only 40 seconds. [*135*, p. 213]

A basic requirement for the trained speaker or singer is the ability to pro-long expiration, which is really the ability to maintain a smooth, steady air flow.

Under the average demands of speech, both *subglottal pressure* and the rate of air flow through the larynx must be relatively stable if one is to maintain a fairly steady fundamental frequency and intensity level. To pro-duce and maintain a loud, steady pitch level requires a steady subglottal pressure of approximately 27 cm of air flow. The normal elasticity of the lungs is sufficient to produce this kind of subglottal pressure for simple vocal demands, such as those we might experience in relaxed conversation. During a more prolonged expiration, however, we would have to employ special expiratory contraction of the abdominals and internal intercostals (Mead, et. al., *105*). In singing, with its natural changes of pitch and loud-ness, there are obvious and noticeable changes in subglottal pressure and air-flow rate. The flow of air from the alveoli sacs out and up to the level of the glottis, and particularly the force of that air, may be measured by several methods, as described by Kunze (*96*) and Ladefoged (*97*), yielding sub-glottal pressure values. At lower pitch frequencies there appears to be less glottal resistance to the air flow (reduced subglottal pressure), so that a greater amount of air flow occurs. With regard to fundamental frequencies of the voice, then, it would appear that lower pitches are characterized by relatively lower subglottal pressures and greater air-flow rates, while higher pitches phonated by the same individual result in increased subglottal air pressure and a corresponding decrease in air-flow rate.

Cavagna and Margaria (*31*) studied six male subjects with regard to subglottal pressure, mean rate of air-flow through the glottis, lung volume, and sound-pressure levels in dB (re $0.0002$ dyne/cm$^2$). Their results, similar to those of Isshiki (*85*), were that air-flow rates increased as the subjects produced louder phonations. When low phonation intensities were produced, minimal air-flow values through the glottis were, grossly, about two liters of air per minute (for adult male subjects). It appears to take very little air flow for the average speaker to phonate in his optimal pitch range at low intensities. Under demanding phonatory conditions, such as serious singing, the primary respiratory task is to prolong the expiration, maintaining an even, steady rate of air flow. Bouhuys and his colleagues (*22*) have reported that in studying experienced singers for subglottal pressure and air-flow rate, they have found that good singers increase both subglottal pressure and air-flow rate when producing the same pitch level at increasing loudness levels. The untrained singer, and the average speaker for that matter, governs loudness differences of the same pitch level by glottal resistance and increased subglottal pressure, rather than by also increasing his overall rate of air flow.

### RESPIRATION AND HYPERFUNCTION

It would appear that control of expiration is far more important for developing good phonation than is increasing the size of one's vital capacity. In no way does a large inspiration appear necessary for a prolonged controlled expiration. In fact, because of the natural elasticity of thoracic and lung structures, a "super" inhalation probably causes excessive elastic recoil, producing alterations of both subglottal pressure and air-flow volume. Most phonatory tasks require little more than a normal, tidal inspiration. The expiratory activity which follows such an easy inspiration is initiated by the normal elasticity of the lungs, which produces the emitted air flow; the closing glottis in turn inhibits this flow, producing the necessary subglottal pressure.

Relatively few voice problems appear to be the direct result of improper use of the respiratory mechanism. Nevertheless, some individuals do need a certain amount of respiration training, and the majority of voice patients will enjoy more optimum phonation if some attention is given to taking the strain (or hyperfunction) out of breathing. Let us consider separately some of the common faults in respiration which are sometimes observed in the voice patient:

*1. Speaking on residual air.* The patient exhales much of his tidal breath before initiating phonation. The resulting lack of sufficient air flow and subglottal pressure usually produces an increase in glottal tension as he attempts to maintain phonation. With such increased glottal tension, the patient sounds as if his voice focus is in his larynx, and his voice often lacks adequate intensity and resonance. Learning to initiate phonation earlier in the tidal expiration can often quickly reduce this type of problem and obviate the need to develop respiration capacities by teaching a special kind of breathing.

*2. Phonating with insufficient loudness.* The patient complains of inadequate voice loudness, particularly in certain situations. Intensity of the voice is directly related to the amount of air flow and degree of subglottal air pressure. Anything the patient can do to increase his overall inspiration may aid him in maintaining an adequate expiration. As he increases his air flow, his voice will be perceived as louder. For purposes of normal conversational loudness, the patient needs no more than the average tidal expiration. For forced expiration (singing, yelling, speaking at high intensity levels), he might well profit from some instruction in diaphragmatic-abdominal breathing, where he will be taught to perform some abdominal muscle contraction to help sustain the required air flow. In chapter 5 we shall consider some other ways of increasing the perceived loudness of the voice, such as by slightly elevating the voice pitch and opening the mouth wider.

*3. Speaking with shortness of breath.* Some patients attempt to phonate when they have literally "run out of breath." In cases where the patient is unable to sustain his expiration beyond that required to say three or four words, the problem is often related to anxiety and cannot be treated by breathing exercises per se; the required treatment would be to diminish the anxiety. Some patients with certain physical conditions (emphysema, tuberculosis, quadriplegia, to name a few) have serious problems in inspiration-expiration; in these cases some breathing exercises to promote more efficient use of respiration are often helpful. Breathing exercises for physically impaired patients are often provided by inhalation therapists, physical therapists, pulmonary physicians, and some speech pathologists.

*4. Speaking with unnecessary focus on breathing.* A great many voice patients, particularly adults, concentrate far too much on their breathing in an attempt to overcome their phonatory difficulties. The myth continues that if you have a voice problem you should work on respiration. Actually, few voice patients need to work on increasing their respiratory efficiency. Patients who deliberately attempt to "take in" a big breath do so by forced enlargement of the thorax; this is almost always followed by a rapid, uncontrolled expiration, produced in part by the natural recoil elasticity of lung and thoracic structures. The ideal respiration for conversational phonation is the easy tidal breath cycle, with a slightly extended expiration to match the length of verbalization. Teaching the patient easy conversational phonation, coupled with the natural breathing that goes with it, is probably our most productive respiration "training" for the typical voice patient.

5. *Struggling to take in a breath.* When breathing in, some voice patients are observed to elevate their shoulders, using their neck accessory muscles. Such a method is poor, in that it requires a comparatively strenuous action to produce only a minimal inspiration. Occasionally one sees a patient who elevates his upper chest and flattens his abdomen on inspiration, collapsing his upper chest and extending his abdomen on expiration; this is a reversal of classic diaphragmatic-abdominal breathing, where the abdomen extends on inspiration and flattens on expiration. Observable variations in mode of breathing should be identified and corrected if they appear to contribute to an overall milieu of working too hard to phonate.

PHONATION

The airway requires various kinds of protective structures to prevent the infiltration of liquids, the aspiration of food particles and fluids during deglutition (swallowing), and the inhalation of foreign bodies during respiration. In most higher mammals, particularly man, the larynx serves as the basic valvelike entryway to the respiratory tract. All incoming and outgoing pulmonary air must pass through the valving, glottal opening of the larynx. Negus (*122; 123*) writes that that primary biological role of the larynx is to prevent foreign bodies from moving into the airway, and also to fixate the thorax by stopping the air flow at the glottal level, which permits the arms to perform heavy lifting and extensive weight-supporting feats. This primitive, valvelike action appears to be the primary function of the larynx in man. Using the laryngeal valving mechanism for phonation is undoubtedly an evolved, secondary function, which has required the development of intricate neural controls that permit man to use the approximating valvelike vocal folds for the precise phonations required in speaking and singing. The valving action of the larynx functions because, first, we have a fixed framework (the laryngeal cartilages); second, we are able to open (abduct) and close (adduct) the valve, primarily by using the intrinsic muscles of the larynx; and third, the valving mechanism receives external support from the extrinsic muscles of the larynx.

No attempt will be made in this text on therapy to present a detailed description of laryngeal anatomy and physiology. The serious student of voice therapy should be familiar with the various structures listed and have some familiarity with their function.

STRUCTURES OF PHONATION (see figure 4)

Laryngeal Cartilages
  Cricoid Cartilage (see figure 5)
  Thyroid Cartilage (see figure 6)
  Arytenoid Cartilages (see figure 7)
  Epiglottis Cartilage (see figure 8)
  Corniculate Cartilages
  Cuneiform Cartilages
Laryngeal Ligaments
  Cricothyroid Ligament
  Cricoarytenoid Ligament
  Vocal Ligament
  Ventricular Ligament
  Thyroepiglottic Ligament
Hyoid Bone
Intrinsic Muscles of Larynx (see figure 9)
  Cricothyroid
  Thyroarytenoid
  Posterior Cricoarytenoid
  Lateral Cricoarytenoid
  Transverse Arytenoid
  Oblique Arytenoid
  Aryepiglottic
Extrinsic Muscles of Larynx
  Thyrohyoid
  Stylohyoid
  Digastric
  Mylohyoid
  Geniohyoid
  Stylopharyngeus
  Palatopharyngeus
  Omohyoid
  Sternothyroid
  Sternohyoid
  Cricopharyngeus
  Thyropharyngeus

*MECHANISM OF PHONATION*

Vocal fold vibration (phonation) first requires fold approximation. Figure 10 shows the pre-phonation phase of the vocal folds, with the folds in a typical abducted-exhalation position. It appears that during quiet breathing, the average subject maintains a rather fixed glottal aperture, perhaps not too unlike the fold positioning photographed in figure 10. With many subjects we see a slightly larger opening on inhalation than on exhalation. When the

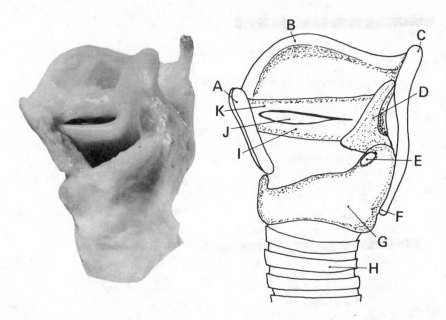

Fig. 4. A lateral left view of the larynx is shown with the left thyroid cartilage removed. The untouched photograph is remarkable in its view of the ventricle opening between the true folds and the false folds. Structures may be identified by viewing the line drawing letter identifications: (A) cut edge at lamina of thyroid cartilage; (B) arch of the thryoid cartilage; (C) superior horn of the thyroid cartilage; (D) arytenoid cartilage, right; (E) articular facet of the cricoid and arytenoid cartilage; (F) inferior horn of the thyroid cartilage; (G) cricoid cartilage; (H) tracheal ring; (I) vocal fold, right; (J) ventricle; (K) ventricular fold or false fold.

neural command is given for vocal fold adduction, approximation is extremely rapid. The two primary laryngeal adductors, the lateral cricoarytenoid and the thyroarytenoid, have contraction times as brief as about 15 msec, "exceedingly fast and . . . surpassed only by the extrinsic eye muscles" (Martensson, 102). We might assume, then, that vocal fold adduction can be achieved in 15 to 20 msecs. As the folds almost approximate, the expiratory air flow is obstructed at the level of the glottis, increasing the subglottal air pressure. Zemlin writes:

It is extremely important to note that complete obstruction of the air passageway is not necessary to initiate phonation. If the glottal chink is narrowed to about 3 mm, a minimal amount of air flow will set the folds into vibration. [177, p. 175]

The subglottal pressure which builds up when the folds above are approximated develops enough force to blow them apart. This air-flow force is

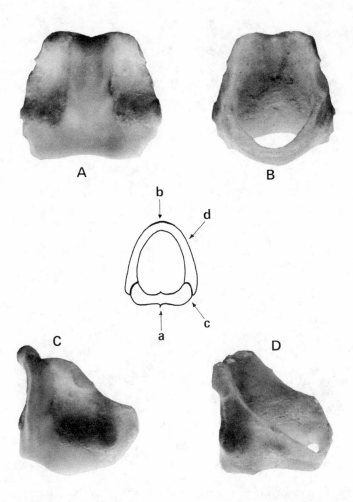

Fig. 5. Four views of the cricoid cartilage. In all photographs, ligament and muscle attachments and the membranous covering have been removed, showing the bare cartilage. The line drawing shows the overall superior contour of the cricoid and the anatomical site of the cricoid photograph [(a) indicated that photograph A was taken from that view]. Photograph A shows the posterior surface of the cricoid; the difference in texture (smooth and rough) is related to ossification; the smooth portions represent the ossification. (C) shows the right lateral view of the cricoid ring with the cartilage tipped upward, exposing the superior rim of the signet portion of the cartilage; upon this clearly defined rim rotate the two arytenoid cartilages. (D) shows a right lateral view of the cricoid; note the contrast in thickness between the thin anterior portion of the ring and the high signet posterior portion.

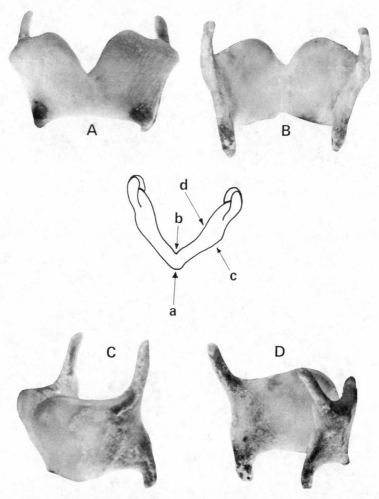

Fig. 6. Four views of the laryngeal thyroid cartilage. The line drawing of the superior view of the thyroid cartilage indicates the side of the cartilage photographed. A-a shows a direct frontal view of the thyroid. B-b shows a posterior view of the cartilage; note the clear extension of the inferior and superior horns on each side. C-c shows primarily the thyroid cartilage wall. D-d shows the thyroid posteriorly from a three-quarter view.

opposed both by the static force of the muscle and ligament mass itself and by the *Bernoulli effect*. The Bernoulli effect is the medial displacement of the vocal folds towards one another due to a vacuum produced in the glottal chink by the air stream. While air-flow rate has been constant until the flow reaches the constricting glottis, it then increases its velocity, rushing through what is left of the glottal opening. The resulting vacuum attracts the folds

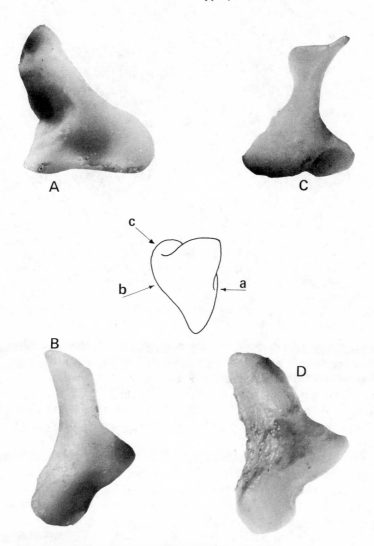

Fig. 7. Four views of an arytenoid cartilage after removal of ligament, muscle, and membrane attachments. Photograph A shows a lateral view of the indentation (fovea) toward the base which receives the attachment of the thyroarytenoid muscle (vocal fold) and the higher indentation on the left margin receives the fibers of the ventricular fold; the muscular process to which the posterior and lateral cricoarytenoids are attached may be seen at the right base. (B) shows a medial view of an arytenoid which has been tilted up slightly to the left; the right angular corner is the vocal process. (C) shows a posterior-lateral view of the muscular process at the base; note toward the right base the cricoarytenoid articular facet (point of joint articulation). In D, a view similar to B, the camera lens picks up the base of the cartilage as well as its medial wall; the curving base of the arytenoid allows it to rotate upon the cricoid rim below.

A                          B

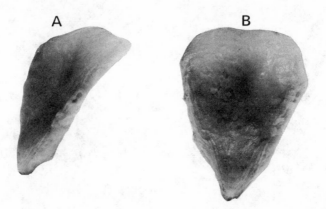

Fig. 8. In these two views of the epiglottis, the epiglottis has been removed from its attachment on the lower, internal surface of the thyroid cartilage. For the purposes of photography, the cartilage has been denuded, excising away its ligament and muscle attachments and its membranous covering. (A) shows the epiglottis from a frontal-lateral view; the rotation of the cartilage permits us to see the concave epiglottal contour. (B) shows the epiglottis in its whole anterior dimension which represents the lingual surface.

together, and is thus partially responsible for completing their vibratory cycle of being blown apart initially by the outgoing air stream and then returning to medial approximation. The other force besides the Bernoulli effect which aids the vocal folds in returning to their position of neutral approximation is probably the resistance of the vocal ligaments and the thyroarytenoid muscles and their membraneous covering, the conus elasticus.

The vibratory cycle of the vocal folds can be summarized as follows: The intrinsic adductors of the larynx approximate the folds in the neutral approximation position, where the natural size/mass and elasticity of the folds determine the rate of vibration; the emitted air flow passes through the approximation opening, blowing the folds apart; the static mass of the folds tends to bring them back to their neutral position; the Bernoulli vacuum effect draws the folds even closer together than when they are in their neutral approximation state; the vibratory cycle repeats itself.

In normal phonation, the expiratory phase of respiration is initiated at about the same time that the folds are approximated together. It would appear that the phenomenon of breathy phonation is achieved partially by the expiratory cycle beginning and getting well under way before the folds are fully approximated. The opposite problem, the hard glottal attack, is characterized by fold adduction occuring before expiration begins, resulting in a sudden burst of phonation. The force of the emitted air flow, its subglottal pressure, must be strong enough to overcome the inertia of the approximated vocal folds.

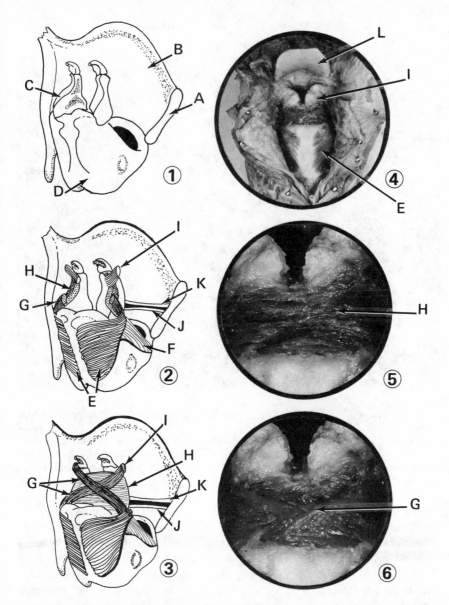

Fig. 9. Intrinsic muscles of the larynx. (1) Basic laryngeal cartilage structures: A, cut away of right thyroid ring; B, left thyroid cartilage wall; C, left arytenoid cartilage; D, posterior cricoid cartilage. The other sketches and photographs identify the following intrinsic muscles by letter: (E) posterior cricoarytenoid; (F) lateral cricoarytenoid; (G) oblique arytenoid; (H) transverse arytenoid; (I) aryepiglottic; (J) thyroarytenoid (vocal fold); (K) ventricular fold. (L) identifies the epiglottis.

During normal phonation, the vocal folds approximate one another in their total anterior-posterior dimension. In figure 11, line drawings show

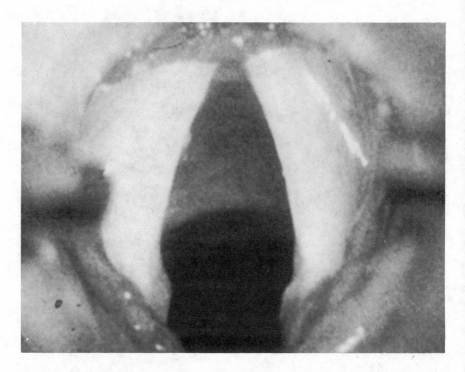

Fig. 10. The normal vocal folds photographed using indirect mirror laryngo-scopy, showing the open glottis during a normal expiration. The anterior portion of the two folds is at the top of the picture; the mirrored view of the right fold is to the left, the left fold to the right; the posterior, vocal process ends of the folds are at the bottom of the picture. The dark central inverted V area is the open glottis.

the relative approximation contours of the vocal folds during normal phona-tion, and also during normal inspiration, normal expiration, and whispering. The vocal folds appear slightly shorter during phonation and whispering in the line drawings, as they do in the normal larynx; that is, the vocal folds will always be longer in the open, abducted position than in the closed, adducted one (Hollien and Moore, *81*). The configuration of the glottis for whispering is characterized by an open, posterior chink, with the arytenoid cartilages and their vocal processes angled in an open, inverted V position. While the vocal folds are parallel to one another during whispering, they do not firmly approximate. This lack of adduction, particularly in the pos-terior chink, produces frictional sounds when the outgoing air stream passes through, producing what we perceive as whispering.

The vocal folds appear to be maximally long during at-rest breathing and shortened somewhat during phonation. In fact, at the lower end of one's pitch range, at the level where conversational phonation is generally found, the vocal folds are considerably shortened. Hollien and his colleagues

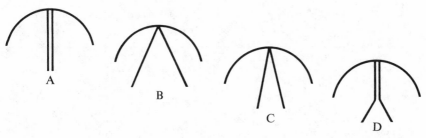

Fig. 11. Various glottal configurations. (A) The vocal folds are approximated for phonation. (B) The folds are widely abducted for forced inspiration. (C) The folds are in the typical expiratory (non-phonatory) position. (D) shows the typical inverted Y glottis for whisper with anterior ⅔ (vocal folds) laxly approximated and the posterior ⅓ (arytenoids) rotated in an abducted, open position. In drawings B and C, inspiration and expiration, the glottal surfaces were drawn deliberately longer to represent the increased length of the vocal folds during inspiration-expiration as contrasted with their shortened length during phonation and whisper.

(76; 77; 78; 79; 80; 81) and Sonninen (151) have found that the length of the vocal folds increases systematically, almost in a "stair-step" fashion, corresponding to increases in pitch level. By using X ray laminagraphy, which permits cross-sectional, coronal viewing of the vocal folds, Hollien found that the mean thickness or mass of the folds systematically decreased as voice pitch increased. It appears, then, from the multiple studies conducted on vocal fold length and thickness by the Hollien group, that fundamental frequency or voice pitch level is directly related to the length and thickness of the individual's vocal folds. The relative differences between men and women in vocal fold length (approximately 18mm for men and 10mm for women) and vocal fold thickness appear to be the primary determinants of differences in voice pitch between the adults of the two sexes (the typical fundamental frequency for men is around 125 cps; for women, around 200 cps). A table of normal pitch values, including pitch range and fundamental frequency, is given in figure 12. When an individual phonates at increasingly higher pitch levels, he must lengthen his vocal folds to decrease their relative mass. Increases of pitch, therefore, appear to be related to a lengthening of the vocal folds, with a corresponding decrease of tissue mass and an increase of fold tension. Lowering of the voice pitch is directly related to relaxation and shortening of the folds, which results in increased tissue mass and reduction of fold tension. An excellent discussion of the pitch-raising–pitch-lowering mechanism may be found in the chapter on the mechanics of phonation in Zemlin's *Speech and Hearing Science* (177), where the author arranges our current knowledge of pitch physiology into a readable narrative of "what happens" when varying pitches are produced.

FIGURE 12. NORMAL FUNDAMENTAL FREQUENCY ($F_0$) AND PITCH RANGES FOR FOUR VOICES (BASS, TENOR, ALTO, AND SOPRANO)

| Note on Piano | Physical (cps) | (bass) | Typical $F_0$ and Pitch Range (tenor) | (alto) | (soprano) |
|---|---|---|---|---|---|
| $C_6$ | 1,024 | | | | 1,040 |
| B | 960 | | | | |
| A | 853 | | | | |
| $G_5$ | 768 | | | | |
| F | 682 | | | 700 | |
| E | 640 | | | | |
| D | 576 | | | | |
| $C_5$ | 512 | | 550 | | |
| B | 480 | | | | |
| A | 426 | | | | |
| $G_4$ | 384 | | | | |
| F | 341 | 340 | | | |
| E | 320 | | | | |
| D | 288 | | | | |
| $C_4$ | 256 | | | | $F_0$ 256 |
| B | 240 | | | | |
| A | 213 | | | $F_0$ 200 | |
| $G_3$ | 192 | | | | |
| F | 170 | | | | 170 |
| E | 160 | | | | |
| D | 144 | | $F_0$ 135 | 140 | |
| $C_3$ | 128 | | | | |
| B | 120 | | | | |
| A | 106 | $F_0$ 100 | | | |
| $G_2$ | 96 | | 95 | | |
| F | 85 | 80 | | | |

Another determinant of voice pitch is subglottal air pressure, which, when increased, is usually accompanied by a corresponding increase in pitch level. It appears that at the upper end of the natural pitch range, increased tension of the vocal folds results in increased glottal resistance, requiring increased subglottal pressure to produce higher-frequency phonations. Increased tension of the vocal folds requires greater air pressure to set the folds into vibration. Van den Berg (*161*) has written that the average person must slightly increase subglottal pressure in order to increase voice pitch; however, because increasing subglottal pressure has an abducting effect on the vocal folds, the folds must continue to increase in tension to maintain their approximated position. While the primary determinant of pitch appears to be the mass and tension of the vocal folds, increases in pitch level are usually characterized by increasing subglottal pressures.

The vocal folds can elongate and stretch only so far. If the singer wants to extend his pitch range beyond what normal vocal fold stretching can do, he is forced to produce a *falsetto* voice. We might describe the production of the falsetto voice in this manner: the folds approximate with tight, posterior vocal-process adduction; the posterior cartilaginous portion is so tightly adducted that there is little or no posterior vibration; the lateral por- tions of the thyroarytenoid muscles are not contracted; the inner vocalis section is extremely tightened and contracted around the vocal ligament; the glottal edge is extremely thin and is the primary vibrating structure during falsetto. Judson and Weaver (*90*) have described the falsetto as an effect produced by strong contraction of the internal fibers of the thyroary- tenoid muscles, with the external fibers relatively relaxed. Using high speed photography, Rubin and Hirt (*140*) have shown that in posterior vocal- process adduction during falsetto, only the muscular section of the glottis vibrates.

Toward the bottom of their pitch range, some speakers will produce the *glottal fry,* a bubbling, cracking kind of low-pitched phonation. Perhaps the nearest-sounding noise to this glottal phenomenon would be the sputter of a low-powered outboard motor. Zemlin (*177*) reports that the folds are approximated tightly, with a flaccid appearance "along their free borders." Moore and von Leden (*114*) have found during fry a double vibration of the folds followed by a prolonged period of approximation, with this period of fold closure representing the greater time period of the vibratory cycle. Vocal fry may well be the normal vibratory cycle one uses near the bottom of one's normal pitch range. While fry may or may not be considered a vocal abnormality, some voice patients work to eliminate it by slightly raising their pitch levels.

Related to the production of voice pitch and the pitch range of any indi- vidual is *voice register.* It appears that a particular register characterizes a certain pattern of vocal fold vibration, with the vocal folds approximated in a similar way throughout a particular pitch range. Once this pitch range reaches its maximum limit, the folds adjust to a new approximation contour, which produces an abrupt change in vocal quality. Van den Berg (*161*) describes three primary forms of voice register: chest, mid-voice, and fal- setto. Hollien and his colleagues (*78*), in their laminagraphic X ray studies of vocal fold movement, describe two vocal registers: normal and falsetto. In the frontal, coronal view of the folds sketched in figure 13, one can easily see the thickened folds of the chest or normal register contrasted with the thin folds of the falsetto register. From the perceptual viewpoint, voice register is confined to the similar sound of the individual's voice at various pitches. While this similar quality is undoubtedly related to the similarity in vocal fold approximation and vibration characteristics, teachers of voice are desirous of blending the various registers together, so that the difference in quality of voice becomes almost imperceptible as the singer goes from one register to the next. Some singers seem to have only one register; no matter how they change their pitch, their voices always seem to have the same quality, with no discernible break towards the upper part of the pitch range. Such persons' frontal X rays would probably show a relatively stable contour in the approximations of the vocal folds. An excellent review of the

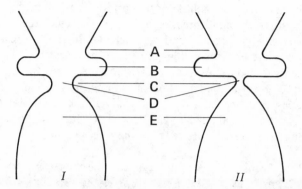

Fig. 13. A line tracing of a tomogram which presents an X ray frontal view of the vocal folds, showing vocal fold approximation contours for I, chest register, and II, falsetto register. (A) ventricular fold; (B) open ventricle; (C) vocal fold; (D) glottis, opening between folds; (E) trachea. Note the thicker fold approximation for the chest register as opposed to the thinner, superior approximation of the two folds during the production of the falsetto register.

literature and detailed description of voice register may be found in Luchsinger and Arnold's *Voice—Speech, and Language; Clinical Communicology: its Physiology and Pathology (101)*.

The normal singing and speaking voice is characterized by continuous fluctuations of both pitch and loudness. The mechanisms of pitch change, although not fully known at the present time, are better understood than the mechanisms of intensity. Intensity of the voice appears to be related to three factors: subglottal air pressure, amount of air flow, and glottal resistance.

Otis and Clark (*124*), in their studies on the effects of ventilation on phonation, found that intensity increases were caused primarily by elevated subglottal pressures, but in association with more rapid air-flow rates. The trained user of voice—the actor, the lecturer, the singer—probably produces intensity increases of voice by increasing both subglottal pressure and air-flow rate, rather than by increasing glottal tension. This point of view is supported by Bouhuys and his colleagues (*22*), who found, in their detailed study of pressure-flow events during singing, that experienced singers increased both subglottal pressure and air-flow rate when they sang the same pitched tones at increasing loudness levels. Inexperienced singers attempting to increase loudness have been observed to increase subglottal pressure and glottal tension, with a resulting decrease in air-flow rate.

As voice intensity is increased, the vocal folds tend to remain closed for a longer period of time during each vibratory cycle, and the greater intensity of voice is characterized by greater excursion of the vibrating folds. It would appear that as intensity increases, the increased glottal tension impedes the rate of air flow. At lower pitch levels this tension during intense phonations is minimal, causing the singer, for example, to "run out of air" sooner when producing varying intensities at low pitches than at high ones. It appears that the speaker or singer who continually requires a loud voice could use his vocal mechanism more optimally if he would develop his expiratory skills, relying more on increased subglottal air pressure and increased air-flow rates, and less on increased glottal tension, to achieve louder intensities.

*PHONATION AND HYPERFUNCTION*

Many voice problems are the result of faulty vocal fold approximation. Sometimes the folds are laxly approximated, so that the patient has a breathy voice; at the opposite extreme is the tight over-approximation observed in spastic dysphonia. More subtle hyperfunctional phonation problems would include speaking at inappropriate pitch levels, speaking with a sameness of pitch and intensity, speaking with the precision of hard glottal attacks, and abusing the vocal apparatus by excessive throat clearing, coughing, yelling, etc. We should consider the various phonatory hyperfunctions in the light of what we know about the normal phonation mechanism. In each type of hyperfunction listed, it can be observed that that particular vocal behavior requires extra effort in using the voice.

*1. Using the breathy voice.* A vocal nodule or a polyp along the glottal margin will produce, by its mass, faulty approximation between the two vocal folds, resulting in breathiness. This kind of breathiness can best be corrected by reducing or eliminating the space-occupying mass. More commonly, the breathy voice is achieved by incomplete, lax, fold approximation, coupled with the initiation of phonation well after the outgoing air flow has been started. This type of breathiness may well be functional in origin and be reduced or eliminated by voice therapy directed at increasing the firmness of glottal approximation.

*2. Using a tight, strained phonation.* The best example of the strained, overly tight voice is the phonation heard in spastic dysphonia. Here the patient overadducts his folds with so much glottal tension that normal, free vibration of the folds is not possible. Unfortunately, attempts to reduce this problem through voice therapy are frequently ineffective. There are many patients, however, whose problems are not intense enough to be classified as spastic dysphonia, but whose voices reflect severe glottal tension and excessive fold approximation; these individuals profit well from voice therapy aimed at producing an easier phonation.

*3. Using a dysphonic voice with a normal vocal mechanism.* Some of the hoarsest voices may be heard in patients who have normal larynges. The ease with which most of us can imitate various kinds of dysphonia is some validation of the observation that one "can just put his vocal folds together in a poor way" and produce a rather severely dysphonic voice. To produce dysphonia with a normal phonatory mechanism, one has to approximate the folds with some type of register variation, or with some kind of approximation inconsistency, or whatever. The voice therapy approach that is most successful here is to search with the patient—using the voice-facilitating approaches developed in chapter 5—for the best phonation he is able to produce. If normal phonation can be produced, then the therapy consists of practicing those approaches which maintain the relatively normal phonation.

4. *Using an inappropriate pitch level.* It would appear that speaking at the very bottom of one's pitch range or well above optimum pitch levels requires an unnecessary amount of effort. When the vocal folds are basically near their natural size, without excessive contraction or elongation, they seem to produce their best phonation. Excesses of pitch, if identified by the voice clinician, can usually be easily altered to more optimum levels.

5. *Speaking in a monotone.* It takes a considerable amount of effort to speak in a monotone. A monotonic voice is characterized by little or no variation of pitch or loudness. Such masking of phonatory effect can be reduced in voice therapy by encouraging the patient to practice pitch-loudness variation.

6. *Using the hard glottal attack.* The abruptly starting phonation of hard glottal attack requires much unnecessary effort. The speaker who "bites his words out" so crisply frequently pays the penalty of increased edema (swelling) and irritation of the folds, so that while his phonation at the beginning is normal, his voice eventually becomes dysphonic. For this sort of voice which is the opposite of the breathy one, our focus in therapy is on taking the work out of phonation; in the beginning we often deliberately introduce the lax approximation of folds and the resulting breathiness as an opposite way of phonating. Hard glottal attack, once identified, can usually be minimized with therapy, often with an immediate positive effect on the patient's voice.

7. *Abusing the voice.* Frequently it is not the singing or speaking phonation that harms the vocal mechanism, but the individual's nonverbal abuse of his voice. For example, excessive throat clearing, excessive coughing, extreme screaming and yelling, and making loud vocal noises can have adverse effects on the larynx. Most voice disorders of children appear to be related to this kind of vocal abuse and respond more effectively to the identification and reduction of such abuses than to any other kind of voice therapy.

8. *Increasing voice loudness by increasing glottal tension.* The best way to produce a louder voice is to increase the flow of air. The trained singer or actor, for example, produces the loudness he desires by increasing the strength of his expiration. Many of the rest of us produce a louder voice by

increasing glottal tension; here the focus of the voice seem to be at the level of the larynx, and the voice lacks adequate resonance. An occasional loud voice produced by any manner does not seem to hurt the mechanism much; improperly produced loudness by an actor night after night in a play, however, can inflict real damage on the laryngeal mechanism. The patient who often needs to produce a loud noise might well profit from some instruction in how to increase his expiratory control.

## RESONANCE

The phonation produced at the level of the glottis would be a very thin sound without adjacent resonating structures to amplify it. A patient was observed several years ago with a massive open wound immediately superior to his laryngeal thyroid cartilage. Before the would was sutured, there was a gaping opening above the larynx, so that the anterior surface of the epiglottis was exposed. When the patient was asked to phonate, his air stream would come out of the wound opening. His thin voice lacked all superior resonance. Without the supraglottal structures to amplify the fundamental frequency, his overall voice quality did not sound human. At present, we do not clearly understand the role of infraglottal resonators and their effects on the voice; we know far more about the supraglottal resonators. The serious student of voice should have some awareness of both the infraglottal and supraglottal structures and their possible functional effects on voice.

### STRUCTURES OF RESONANCE

Infraglottal Structures
    Trachea
    Bronchial Tubes
    Lungs
    Rib Cage
Supraglottal Structures
    Laryngeal Ventricle
    Epiglottis
    Thyroid Cartilage
    Aryepiglottal Folds
    Pharynx
    Tongue
    Oral Cavity
    Facial Muscles
    Cheek Muscles
    Mastication Muscles
    Velum
    Hard Palate
    Nasal Cavity
    Paranasal Sinuses

A vibrator, such as the string of a violin or the vocal folds, originates a fundamental vibration (or sound waves) which by itself produces weak, barely audible sounds. This vibrating energy is usually amplified by a resonating body of some type. For example, a violin string, when plucked, will set up a fundamental vibration; this vibration becomes resonated by the bridge to which the strings are attached, which then sets into vibration the sounding board below and in turn the main resonating body of the violin (the chest), which provides open cavity resonance. When all the violin parts are working together in harmony, the fundamental tone of the involved string becomes louder and fuller in quality. The same string stripped out of its mount on the violin and then plucked (even with the same amount of tension to the string) will sound less intense and thinner in quality. The violin provides a ready example of the two main types of resonance, the *sounding board effect* and the *open cavity effect.* When a particular string of the violin is bowed, the air waves which develop are low in amplitude and barely audible; however, since the vibrating string is stretched tightly over the bridge of the violin, it sets into vibration the bridge itself. The bridge functions as a sounding board. The sounding board then vibrates, setting into vibration the air over a much larger area, increasing the loudness of the tone. The sounding board vibration also introduces the sound waves into the violin cavity itself. This sounding board phenomenon is well described by Gray and Wise:

In the forced vibration of a surface of a sounding board, the vibration of the fork or the strings is communicated directly through some rigid but elastic body, such as the bridge, to the "sounding-board," so that the body vibrates with approximately the frequency of the impressed force. It is the sounding board itself which gives out the tone of great power. The phenomenon is considered by some to constitute amplification, but not resonance in the strict sense of the word. However, as commonly used, the word *resonance* may apply to amplification either by cavity resonance or the sounding board. [*66*, pp. 92–93]

The main body, or chest, of the violin provides cavity resonance to the vibrating string. The string vibrating alone, which is similar to laryngeal vibration without supraglottal resonance, will produce a barely audible tone. The cavity resonance provided by the body of the violin increases the volume of the vibrating string. The size and overall shape of the resonating cavity have an obvious relationship to the resonance of a vibration. It appears that for every frequency of vibration there is an ideal resonating cavity size and shape. The ideal is represented by that cavity which seems to give the loudest tone and the tone with the fullest amount of amplification to its overtones. This observation can be easily tested by placing a tuning fork over a large glass, varying the amounts of water in the glass. At a particular level of water, the glass will provide optimum resonance, heard as the increase in loudness of sound. The lower the frequency of the vibrating wave, the larger the size of the resonating cavity. The thinner string of the violin requires a much smaller resonating body than the larger string of the bass viola, which requires a resonating body as tall as the man who plays the instrument.

The relative size of the supraglottal resonators is always changing. The pharynx is probably the most important resonating cavity and sounding board for the voice. The lower end of the pharynx, the hypopharynx, begins immediately behind the rising aryepiglottic folds and above the cricopharyngeus opening over the esophagus, and, as such, plays a primary role in resonance. Both the hypopharynx and the middle pharynx, the oropharynx, are highly influenced by tongue positioning. A tongue placed far forward produces a large hypopharyngeal and oropharyngeal opening; posterior retraction of the tongue can grossly restrict this pharyngeal opening. Since the size of the pharynx has much to do with voice resonance, any filling of the pharynx with posterior tongue retraction will have noticeable effects on resonance. (*19; 57*). The tongue is not the only structure which contributes to the change of the size of the pharynx. The lower and middle pharyngeal constrictors, when contracted, can reduce the total dimensions of the pharynx; also, the supralaryngeal muscles which elevate the larynx will shorten the vertical dimension of the pharynx. The pharyngeal tube may shorten or lengthen, broaden or narrow, according to the vocal requirements of the speaker. When phonating a high pitch, for example, the rising larynx will carry up the attachment ends of the lower and middle pharyngeal constrictors, which will reduce the height of the pharynx; conversely, any downward excursion of the larynx, such as in singing at the lower frequencies of one's range, will lengthen the pharyngeal cavity. These pharyngeal size adjustments provide, in effect, the necessary adjustments in cavity size to maintain the appropriate resonance for the fundamental frequencies being emitted. The third pharyngeal area is the nasopharynx, which begins roughly at the level of the hanging soft palate (velum) and rises upward in a vertical course to about the level of the eustachian tubes, where the pharyngeal opening slants anteriorly into the nasal cavities. The lower end of the nasopharynx—where the velum makes contact with the superior pharyngeal constrictors—is a critical area for the absence or presence of nasal resonance. When the velar port is open, the opening between the velum and the pharyngeal wall will permit the nasal escape of air flow and sound waves, resulting in various degrees of nasal resonance. Alterations in the closure of this velopharyngeal port (too open or always closed) may produce unpleasant resonance effects.

While the pharynx may correctly be thought of primarily as a cavity resonator, we should not forget that the pharyngeal constrictors themselves, with their mucosal lining, produce sounding board effects. The degree of the pharyngeal sounding board effect is determined by the surface tonicity of the pharyngeal tissue. Increased contraction of pharyngeal constrictors will not only make the pharyngeal cavity smaller, but will provide a taut pharyngeal wall, increasing the elasticity of the surface tissues. Higher frequency vocalizations receive their best resonating effects under a fairly high degree of pharyngeal wall tension. Lower frequencies, on the other hand, are better amplified by a pharynx that is relaxed and somewhat inelastic.

The oral cavity, or mouth, is as essential for resonance as the pharynx. Of all our resonators, the mouth is capable of the most variation in size and shape. It is the constant size-shape adjustment of the mouth which permits us to speak. Our vowels and diphthongs, for example, are originated by a laryngeal vibration, but shaped and modified by size-shape adjustments of the oral cavity. The mouth has fixed structures (teeth, alveolar processes, dental arch, and hard palate) and moving structures; in our study of voice resonance, it is the moving structures, primarily the tongue and velum, with which we are most concerned.

The tongue is the most mobile of the articulators, possessing both extrinsic and intrinsic muscles to move it. Each of the extrinsic muscles can, upon contraction, elevate or lower the tongue at its anterior, middle, or posterior points and extend it forward or backward. The intrinsic muscles control the shape of the tongue by narrowing, flattening, lengthening, or shortening the overall tongue body. More detailed descriptions of tongue anatomy and speech physiology can be found in Van Riper and Irwin (*162*) and Gray and Wise (*66*). The various combinations of intrinsic and extrinsic muscle contractions can produce an unlimited number of tongue positions with resulting size-shape variations of the oral cavity. These tongue positions and their relationship to the formation of specific vowels and vowel formants have been clearly described (*131*). Less well understood is how the tongue functions with regard to sensory feedback (Bosma and others, *21*). That is, it is not clear how man knows where his tongue is and what it is doing. It would appear that his tongue is not richly endowed with proprioceptors and that, therefore, his knowledge of its position is relatively dependent on tactual sensation. In any case, our desire to alter tongue position in voice therapy is often hampered by the patient's inability to know where his tongue is and by his frequently observed inability to volitionally move his tongue to a more optimum intraoral position.

The structural adequacy and normal functioning of the velum are likewise important for the development of normal voice resonance. The elevation and tensing of the velum are vital for achieving velopharyngeal closure. A lack of adequate palatal movement, despite adequacy of velar length, can cause serious problems of nasality. While the velum probably serves as a sounding board structure in resonance, it plays an obviously important part in separating the oral cavity from the nasal cavity. The movement and positioning of the velum changes the size and shape of three important resonating cavities: the pharynx, the oral cavity, and the nasal cavity. Therefore, any alteration of the velum (such as a soft palate cleft) may have pronounced influence on resonance, whether the velum acts as a sounding board structure or as an important wall of a resonating cavity.

Once air flow and sound waves travel above the velopharyngeal opening and on into the nasal cavity, there is very little the patient can do to alter the resonance of his voice. There is some evidence that in the normal-sounding voice, some nasal-cavity resonance contributes to the total sound. Variations in nasality may be heard in such conditions as allergies and nasal infections, sometimes with an attendant lack of nasal resonance (denasality).

The sounding board and open cavity structure of the human vocal tract are sometimes misused in such a way as to create the following resonance problems.

*RESONANCE AND HYPERFUNCTION*

Unnecessary pharyngeal constriction and malpositioning of the tongue are the two most common hyperfunctional behaviors which affect resonance. Lack of mouth opening, as observed in the person who speaks through clenched teeth, will usually have a noticeably deleterious effect on resonance. Inappropriate posturing of the velum, such as keeping the velopharyngeal mechanism open when it should be closed, will also produce an undesirable resonance effect.

*1. Speaking with a taut pharynx.* There are certain people in some occupations, such as the carnival barker or dime-store demonstrator, who have a metallic, hard resonance to their voices. Such metallic resonance (the sound is almost impossible to describe) is produced by the tight contraction of the pharyngeal constrictors creating a relatively taut pharyngeal surface. No doubt this firmer surface not only decreases the horizontal dimensions of the pharynx, but changes its sounding board characteristics. Voice therapy directed toward changing such metallic resonance focuses on pharyngeal relaxation, utilizing such therapeutic approaches as the chewing method (see chapter 5).

*2. Speaking with faulty tongue position.* Proper placement of the tongue is critical for developing more optimum resonance. Baby-talk resonance, which is easily created by bringing the overall tongue carriage forward, is as easily corrected by developing a more posterior carriage of the tongue body while speaking. Posterior tongue carriage can result in "cul de sac" resonance, particularly when the tongue body is so far back that it makes contact with the pharyngeal wall. Excessively high tongue carriage may be a concomitant of nasality. Some complaints of resonance change are reported to occur only in certain situations; that is, it may be only during the patient's anxious moments that he places his tongue faultily and thus experiences a change of resonance. Improper tongue carriage as a factor in poor resonance can often be identified and then adjusted through voice therapy.

*3. Speaking with little mouth opening.* There is no speaking habit more retarding for the development of good voice than speaking with little or no mouth opening. Such patients are frequently observed to speak literally through clenched teeth. This places the entire burden of speech articulation on the lips and tongue, with no mandibular movements assisting in the oral cavity size adjustments required for normal speech. The outgoing air stream and sound waves do not receive full amplification in such a restricted oral cavity. The insistence of most singing teachers that their pupils open their mouths to produce the best-sounding voice is relevant for the voice clinician. Learning to open one's mouth is an excellent way of developing a better-sounding voice, because it seems to promote greater vocal-tract relaxation and provide a larger oral cavity for resonance amplification.

*4. Speaking with excessive mouth opening.* A few patients speak with excessive mouth opening, creating some resonance distortion. For example, patients with neuromuscular difficulties, such as the athetoid cerebral palsied child, will lower their mandibles excessively as they speak, with much distortion of voice quality. Any successful attempt in voice therapy to develop a more normal posturing of the mandible will usually result in some improvement in voice quality.

*5. Speaking with improper palatal movement.* Some deviations in nasality (hyper-, hypo-, and assimilative) are obviously related to improper palatal function. When such nasal-resonance deviation is related to functional misuse of the velopharyngeal mechanism (and not to structural inadequacy, such as cleft palate), it is often possible through voice therapy to develop a more oral-sounding resonance. Specific recommendations on voice therapy for resonance disorders may be found in chapter 7.

SUMMARY

The outgoing air stream is the primary activating force of the larynx. Therefore, the treatment of voice disorders requires the clinician to have some knowledge of basic anatomy and the physiology of respiration. Separate consideration was given to some of the common faults of respiration which may be observed in the voice patient. The laryngeal mechanism was described as a valve-like protector of the air way which, in man, also has the capability of phonation. A description of the physiology of phonation included review of the mechanisms of normal phonation, whisper, falsetto, pitch and intensity changes, and register. Commonly observed hyperfunctional phonatory behaviors were described. The possible contribution to normal voice of both infraglottal and supraglottal resonance was described. Examples of causes of inefficient resonance included unnecessary pharyngeal constriction, malpositioning of the tongue, and inadequate mouth opening.

*chapter three*

# Disorders of
# Vocal Fold Mass
# and Approximation

*Most disorders of phonation are related either to mass-size changes
of the vocal folds themselves, or to a lack of optimum approxima-
tion-adduction of the folds. Some of our changes in vocal fold mass
may be due to functional causes, such as speaking at too high a
voice pitch, or to organic tissue conditions, such as enlarging vocal
nodules. Similarly, some approximation difficulties are related to a
functional inability to bring the folds together well, while others
are related to organic problems of cord paralysis or structural
interferences which keep the folds apart, such as polyps occupying
the open glottis. We shall approach the problems of dysphonia from
a mass-approximation point of view, rather than from the more
traditional functional or organic one. Our reason for looking at the
phonation process (the mass and size of the vocal folds, and how
well the folds approximate one another) is that in voice therapy
there often is no differential approach to functional versus organic
problems.*

Under the broad label of *dysphonia* fall many deviations of phonation. The
listener may use various terms to describe the voice disorders he hears—

*hoarseness, breathiness, harshness, huskiness, stridency,* to name only a few—but, unfortunately, there is little common agreement as to what these terms mean. What is *hoarseness* to speaker A may be *huskiness* to speaker B. Our own private vocabularies for voice defects hinder us in developing an understanding of voice problems. This lack of a common vocabulary for the various parameters of voice production and voice pathology is perhaps related to the number of different kinds of specialists who are concerned with voice—the laryngologist, the singing teacher, the speech-voice scientist, the speech pathologist, and the voice-and-diction teacher. The laryngologist is interested primarily in identifying the etiological aspects for purposes of treatment; the singing teacher uses imagery in his attempt to get the desired acoustical effect from his student; the speech-voice scientist has the laboratory interest of the physicist; the speech pathologist often attempts to use the knowledge and vocabulary of all three of these disciplines; and the voice-and-diction teacher assesses the dynamics of voice production and uses whatever he must to "get" the best voice. It is no wonder that interdisciplinary communication among voice specialists breaks down.

Our difficulties in understanding the human voice and its disorders are further complicated by our lack of common perception of what is a normal voice and what is a voice problem. What is an abnormal voice to one listener may well be a normal voice to another. There is a wide range of voices accepted by the general public as normal. Some of our leading television and movie personalities have, as part of their image, a deviant kind of voice quality, and this perhaps contributes to public acceptance of a deviant voice as normal. Many dysphonic voices are heard in the people around us, and we accept this as "the way they talk." Milisen (*108*) listed the incidence of voice disorders in 1957 as "approximately 1 percent of the total population of this country." In a recent study of 32,500 school-age children, Senturia and Wilson (*143*) found that 1,962 (or about 6 percent) of them had voice deviations.

If more stringent criteria are used for the determination of whether or not a voice problem is present, the incidence figure will rise. We may be tolerant of a slight huskiness in the voice of an eleven-year-old boy, but not in the voice of a teacher or minister, and from the professional actor or singer we demand optimum vocal production. This sort of variation in our standards makes recognition of a voice problem difficult. Further complicating the problem is the fact than any one individual's voice will vary according to the time of day, to whom he is speaking, his degree of fatigue, the role he is assuming, etc.

The general public tolerance of and indifference to voice problems makes the early identification of voice pathologies difficult. Hoarseness which persists longer than several days is often identified by the laryngologist as a possible symptom of serious laryngeal disease. And it may be. Hoarseness is certainly the acoustic correlate of improper vocal fold functioning, with or without true laryngeal disease. The distinction between organic disease of the larynx and functional misuse has been a prominent dichotomy in the consideration of phonatory disorders. It is important for the laryngologist, in his need to rule out or identify true organic disease, to view the laryngeal mechanism by laryngoscopy in order to make a judgment with regard to organic-structural involvement. In the absence of structural deviation, he describes the voice disorder as functional. This functional-organic dichotomy persists in the literature of voice therapy, despite warnings that "such a dichotomy is completely inadequate in describing any but the most primitive of human behaviors. Etiologies of vocal disorders always exist along a continuum." (Murphy, *119*, p. 2). It is usually impossible to separate the organic voice problem from the functional one. For example, continuous faulty abuse and misuse of the vocal cords may lead to the development of vocal nodules. The structural or organic problem results from the functional misuse, and to separate the functional from the organic in such cases makes little sense. Or, the child may experience dysphonia with relatively normal vocal folds, perhaps with only a slight edema or swelling. With little or no structural change of the vocal folds, the functional-organic dichotomy would have us identify such a disorder as a functional one. From the point of view of voice therapy, however, there would be little difference between our therapeutic approaches, which in either case would be to reduce the vocal abuse-misuse.

Rather than struggle with the functional-organic dichotomy, which really does not tell us much, we would understand our voice patients and their dysphonias better if we focused on the process of phonation, the size and mass of the vocal cords, and the degree of cord approximation. Normal phonation requires that the vocal folds have appropriate tension and vibration, and any alteration of cord size is likely to produce phonation changes. Hollien and his colleagues (*76; 79; 80*) have demonstrated by their vocal fold measurements that there is a direct correlation between the size and mass of the vocal folds of an individual and his fundamental frequency. Lengthening of the folds causes an increase in their inherent tension, which increases their rate of vibration, elevating the voice pitch; decrease of fold length is essential for phonating at the bottom of one's pitch range. Another aspect of vocal fold size and mass is register. As we indicated in chapter 2, the approximating edges of the vocal folds differ for chest-register phonation as opposed to falsetto-register phonation; the inferior approximating surface of the vocal fold is the primary point of contact for lower chest-register frequencies (with a broader surface of contact), while the falsetto-register fold contact is a thinner, more superior point of contact. Inconsistencies in register may well have their origins in inappropriate mass-size adjustments of the vocal folds. Vocal fold increases in size and mass are brought about also by such obvious factors as puberty, with its increase in the size of the laryngeal structures; virilizing drugs, with their enlargement of the vocal folds (Damste, (43); laryngeal abuse-misuse, with its swelling of fold tissue; infection followed by edema; and many other causes which we shall consider separately.

Normal phonation requires that, in addition to proper mass-size adjustments, the two vocal folds approximate one another optimally along their entire length (from the anterior commissure up to, and including, the vocal process). The easy imitation of voices by some actors suggests that we are able to vary the strength of fold approximation. Consistent with this observation is the further one that most functionally caused dysphonias are related directly to under- or overadduction of the vocal folds. In underadduction, the folds are too laxly approximated, resulting in a breathy type of phonation. Sometimes after prolonged hyperfunctional use of the voice, the folds will bow posteriorly; actually, this posterior bowing is the incomplete adduction of the vocal processes, resulting in lack of posterior closure of the thyroarytenoids. Overadduction of the folds results in the tight valving of the glottal mechanism, so much so that the individual may be unable to phonate for speech. Spastic dysphonia is a clear example of a severe overadduction problem: the voice sounds strained, like the kind of phonation we hear from someone attempting to talk while lifting a heavy object; the valving action of the larynx (fixed, tight adduction) overrules the individual's desire to phonate, and phonation becomes almost impossible. Often such conditions that increase the mass-size of the vocal folds—e.g., cord thickening, nodules, or polyps—will, by their size, make the optimum adduction of the vocal folds impossible. Glottal growths, such as nodules and polyps, interfere with the approximating edges of the vocal folds, often producing open chinks between the approximating folds on each side of the growth. Any structural interference between the approximating edges of the vocal folds will usually result in some degree of dysphonia. Occasionally unilateral or bilateral paralysis of intrinsic muscles of the larynx will result in paralysis of one or both of the vocal folds, either in an open (abducted) or closed (adducted) position, producing serious problems of fold approximation. Before considering separately the various forms of approximation difficulties, let us review the disorders of mass-size and approximation which cause various degrees of dysphonia (figure 14).

### DYSPHONIAS RELATED TO MASS-SIZE ALTERATIONS OF VOCAL FOLDS

We shall discuss separately the various mass-size alterations of the vocal folds, deferring any detailed therapeutic considerations until chapters 5, 6, and 7.

FIGURE 14.  DISORDERS OF VOICE CAUSING CHANGES IN MASS-SIZE AND/OR
APPROXIMATION CHARACTERISTICS OF THE VOCAL FOLDS

| Voice Disorder | Mass-Size Change | Approximation Change |
|---|---|---|
| Laryngitis | X | |
| Cord thickening | X | X |
| Vocal nodules | X | X |
| Vocal polyps | X | X |
| Papilloma | X | X |
| Contact ulcers | X | |
| Leukoplakia | X | |
| Hyperkeratosis | X | |
| Hemangiomas | X | X |
| Granulomas | X | X |
| Carcinomas | X | X |
| Pubertal changes | X | |
| Endocrine changes | X | |
| Functional dysphonia | | X |
| Spastic dysphonia | | X |
| Functional aphonia | | X |
| Vocal cord paralyses | | X |
| Ventricular dysphonia | | X |
| Laryngofissure | | X |
| Cordectomy | | X |
| Laryngectomy | | X |

## LARYNGITIS

Functional or infectious laryngitis is described by the Ballengers (*13*) as an inflammation of the laryngeal mucosa and focal folds. In functional laryngitis, the patient experiences a moderate amount of hoarseness secondary to phonatory trauma. Typical functional laryngitis may be heard in the voice of an excited spectator after a football or basketball game. In the excitement of the game, with his own voice masked by the noise of the crowd, the rooter screams at pitch levels and intensities he normally does not use. The inner glottal edges of the vocal folds become swollen (edematous) and thickened, an expected consequence of excessive friction. This increased edema of the folds is accompanied by irritation and increased blood accumulation. The acute stage of functional laryngitis is at its peak during the actual yelling or traumatic vocal behavior, with the vocal folds much increased in size and mass. Brodnitz (*25*) writes that functionally irritated vocal folds appear on laryngoscopic examination to be much like the thickened, reddened folds of acute infectious laryngitis. There is an important difference in treatment, however. For functional or *nonspecific laryngitis*—which is usually the result of continued irritation by such things as allergy, excessive smoking and alcohol drinking, and vocal abuse—the obvious treatment is to eliminate the vocal irritant whenever possible. In the case of functional laryngitis secondary to yelling or a similar form of vocal abuse, elimination of the abuse will usually permit the vocal mechanism to return to its natural state. The temporary laryngitis experienced towards the end of the basketball game is usually relieved by a return to normal vocal activity, with most of the edema and irritation vanishing after a night's sleep. Chronic misuse of the voice, however, may lead to persistent vocal fold inflammation and the development of *polypoid* thickening, which may result in persistent laryngitis (Lowenthal, *100*). Chronic laryngitis may typically produce more serious vocal problems if the speaker attempts to "speak above" his laryngitis: The temporary edema of the vocal folds alters the quality and loudness of the phonation; the speaker increases his vocal efforts; the increase in effort only increases the irritation of the folds, thereby compounding the problem; and finally, if such hyperfunctional behavior continues over time, what was once a temporary edema may become a more permanent polypoid thickening, sometimes developing into vocal polyps or nodules. For this reason, functional laryngitis should be treated promptly by eliminating the causative abuse and, if possible, by enforcing a short period of complete voice rest.

For the laryngitis that is a frequent symptom of upper-respiratory infection, the best voice therapy is a general systemic and topical treatment of the infection. While the focus of treatment is the medical elimination of the illness, the thickening and irritation of the vocal folds secondary to their infection makes it important that the patient do little or no talking during the acute stage of the laryngeal disease. Luchsinger and Arnold write of infectious laryngitis:

If the patient tries to overcome the temporary hoarseness through increased vocal effort, such as in trying to sing with a cold, he may develop a localized hematoma, which may degenerate into an acute polyp. The wisdom of vocal silence when the throat hurts should be respected. [*101*, p. 178]

Acute, infectious laryngitis is not responsive to voice therapy. The patient should treat the infection and enforce upon himself temporary voice rest until his phonation feels and sounds normal.

*CORD THICKENING*

Prolonged abuse/misuse of the voice or chronic infection of the vocal folds may lead to actual tissue changes. Jackson and Jackson (*86*) list "chronic edema, hyperplasia, hypertrophy, fibroid tumors, and chronic polypoid corditis" as the common sequelea of continued abuse of the vocal folds. The free glottal edges of the folds become granular and somewhat rounded, with occasional blood vessels seen on their superior surfaces. The normal pearly-white surface of the fold becomes inflamed in its entire length, with increased redness often observed in the middle of the true vibrating fold.

Typically, cord thickening, nodules, and polyps develop at the junction of the anterior and middle third of the cord. Arnold (4) explains this "third" site of pathology as being the true midpoint of the vibrating membranous portion of the vocal fold. Therefore, as the midpoint of the two vibrating folds, it is their site of maximum contact during vocal fold approximation.

Many laryngologists believe that the tissue enlargement in cord thickening is due to irritative reactions to mechanical trauma. Because of some irritation (infectious or functional), the free glottal edges become edematous. Continued phonation during this edematous stage usually results in increased vascularity (blood flow) to the area, frequently inducing small hemorrhages of irritated blood vessels. This produces further swelling of the vocal fold structures, which leads to fibrotic, callous-like formations. These thickenings are often the predecessors of nodules and polyps, with the nodules similar to callous formations and the polyps usually more vascular and hollow in structure. Once cord thickening has developed, the patient will give evidence of a persistent change of voice quality. With the increase in mass of the vocal folds, there will usually be a dysphonia, characterized by a lowering of fundamental frequency and some breathy escape of air during phonation.

Voice therapy directed toward reducing aspects of abuse and misuse of voice production is often the best treatment for reducing cord thickening. The efficacy of voice therapy for cord thickening is well illustrated by the following case:

A six-year-old girl was referred for a voice evaluation because of chronic hoarseness. On indirect laryngoscopy it was found that the child had bilateral cord thickening with no demonstrable history of allergy or infection. The parents were counseled to do what they could do to help the child eliminate unnecessary crying and yelling, and the child was sent home. On a subsequent visit to the laryngologist, with no change in cords as observed by laryngoscopy, it was decided to "strip" the thickenings surgically. This was done with excellent results. Three weeks after surgery the child demonstrated clear cords bilaterally, free of thickening. After a postoperative period of approximately three months, the family returned to the laryngologist, complaining of the child's recurring hoarseness. Laryngoscopy found the child once again to have bilateral cord thickening, with the early formation of a vocal nodule on one fold. It was then decided to begin voice therapy. Special efforts were made to identify particular vocal abuses by the child, and a school playground situation was isolated as the cause of continuous vocal strain. Elimination of this and other adverse vocal behavior resulted in the gradual elimination of the vocal nodule and the near elimination of the bilateral thickening.

The above case illustrates that surgical treatment of cord thickening, without making attempts to remove the abusive causes of the problem, will not always lead to a permanent solution of the vocal problem. It would appear that reducing the source of the irritation (such as eliminating an allergy, reducing smoking, or curbing vocal abuse) is probably the best management of the problem.

*VOCAL NODULES*

Vocal nodules appear to be one of the most common disorders of the larynx, sometimes requiring removal by surgery, sometimes voice therapy, and frequently a combination of surgery followed by voice therapy. FitzHugh, Smith, and Chiong (*58*) report that of some 300 cases of benign lesions of the vocal folds, 134 involved vocal nodules. The primary cause of vocal nodules appears to be prolonged hyperfunctional use of the vocal mechanism. When the vibrating vocal folds approximate one another with excessive force, their approximating inner margins begin to show irritation at the midpoint (the anterior, middle one-third junction, as in vocal fold thickening). With this irritation repeated day after day, increased callous-like layers of epithelium begin to cover the irritated site. Eventually, a clearly recognized nodule develops on one cord, or, more commonly, on both. (A typical unilateral nodule is shown in figure 15.) As long as the patient continues his abusive vocal behavior, the nodules will remain and tend to enlarge.

No particular kind of voice typifies the patient with vocal nodules. In children there is usually some dysphonia, characterized by huskiness, low intensity, and frequent throat clearing. Van Riper and Irwin (*162*, p. 188) state that the "majority of writers who have dealt with the subject of vocal nodules emphasize the use of a voice pitched too high." One occasionally sees an excited child who comes to be treated for a voice that is "too high," but what has happened here usually is that the increased mass produced by the nodule on the vocal fold has resulted in a lower fundamental frequency, and the child, in a compensatory action to overcome the dysphonia, has commenced to speak in a louder voice, elevating his voice pitch as he does so. Both Arnold (*4*) and Brodnitz (*24*) make strong cases for treating vocal nodules in children by voice therapy, both stating that even large vocal nodules in children respond very well to the reduction of vocal hyperfunction. It is not unusual to see the soft, pliable nodules of children (sometimes called "screamer's nodules") disappear quickly with the elimination of shouting or yelling in the home or on the playground. Helpful approaches for reducing vocal abuse in children will be outlined in chapter 5.

In adults we more frequently see bilateral nodules, usually accompanied on each side by obvious open chinking of the glottis. The open glottal chink on each side—produced by the coming together of the bilateral nodules, which are in exact opposition to one another—results in a lack of firm

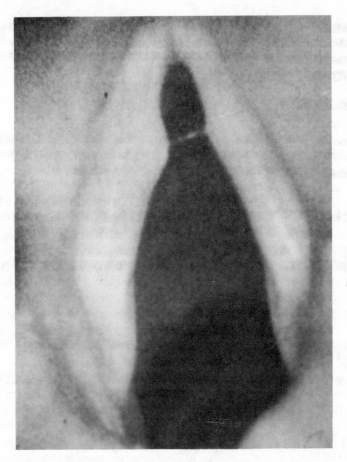

Fig. 15. By mirror laryngoscopy a well developed nodule may be seen on the patient's right vocal fold (at left of picture). Slight cord thickening may be observed on the corresponding site of the right fold. A typical mucous spittle thread is crossing the glottis between the right nodule and the left fold thickening.

approximation of the folds. This leads to a breathy, flat kind of voice (someday we will have a better and more exact terminology), lacking appropriate resonance. The patient complains of the need to clear his throat constantly, often feeling that there is excessive mucus or a foreign body on the vocal folds. The typical patient with a vocal nodule will say that his voice tires easily and that when he first starts to use it each day, it sounds much better. With prolonged singing or speaking, his phonation rapidly deteriorates. Small nodules and recently acquired ones can often be eliminated by voice therapy. Larger nodules in adults, and long-established ones, are often optimally treated by surgery, followed by a brief period of complete voice rest and then voice therapy. It is not unusual clinically to see the surgical removal of nodules in adults, only to have new nodules appear several weeks later. Unless the underlying hyperfunctional vocal behaviors are identified and reduced, vocal nodules have a stubborn way of reappearing.

*VOCAL POLYPS*

Vocal fold polyps usually occur at the same site as vocal nodules, the junction of the anterior, middle one-third of the fold as shown in figure 16. Polyps are more likely to be unilateral than bilateral. Brodnitz (*24*, p. 60) writes that "our present-day knowledge does not yet permit us to explain satisfactorily in all cases why one patient develops a nodule, another one a polyp, or a contact ulcer." A vocal polyp, like the vocal nodule or contact ulcer, usually develops secondarily to vocal fold abuse. Clearly defined polyps are usually the result of prolonged vocal abuse, their early genesis being similar to that of vocal nodules. The early thickenings of the fold become irritated, resulting in hemorrhages. These small hemorrhages are

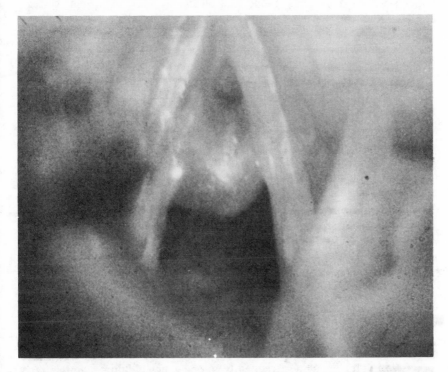

Fig. 16. By mirror view a large broad-based vocal polyp may be seen attached to the right vocal fold. This polyp hangs below the glottis, actually below and unattached to the normal left vocal fold.

frequently observed after the speaker has engaged in a prolonged but temporary period of vocal abuse, such as yelling at a basketball game. As the hemorrhage is absorbed, the tissue at the site may become swollen and somewhat distended, forming the polypoid body. While the nodule is similar to a callous formation, the polyp is more vascular in origin and is often the enlarged, engorged structure of a small blood vessel. The eventual polyp formation is usually broad-based at the site of irritation, lying at the free approximating edge of the vocal fold. There are some polyps that have narrow-neck attachments to the folds; that is, the main body of the polyp hangs within the glottis, its only attachment being a narrow neck adjoined to the free margin of the fold. This narrow-neck polyp may hang free within the glottis, producing no dysphonia unless its body gets between the two approximating edges of the folds. If it hangs below the level of cord approximation, or is blown above on exhalation, its additive mass may not contribute to a dysphonia.

The voice symptoms of patients with vocal polyps are many and varied. Luchsinger and Arnold (*101*) report that Motta, in his study of twenty patients with vocal polyps, found that all twenty had "high, light voices." It is frequently asserted by voice clinicians that polypoid problems of the vocal folds are often associated with high-pitched voices. However, patients with wide-based vocal polyps, because of the general additive mass to the folds, will usually sound hoarse and breathy—much like patients with vocal nodules. Narrow-neck polyps that do not interfere with fold approximation often produce no voice changes that can be "heard."

While early polypoid formations are responsive to voice therapy, well-established polyps of long standing are probably best treated initially by surgical removal. In their experience with 500 patients with vocal polyps, Holinger and Johnston (*74*) treated most of the patients surgically, with follow-up voice therapy. Surgery alone is not enough; it must be followed by attempts, through voice therapy, to eliminate the vocal abuses that might have caused the irritation in the first place. For advanced polyps, the best approach appears to be surgical removal, then brief voice rest, and then voice therapy. The kind of voice therapy initiated would be consistent with the evaluational findings (chapter 4) and would be designed to reduce any identified hyperfunctional vocal behaviors (chapter 5).

### PAPILLOMA

Papilloma is perhaps the most common of all benign tumors of the larynx in childhood. It occurs most frequently among young children, and relatively rarely among youngsters beyond puberty. The cause of these wartlike tumors is unknown, and they often vanish about as quickly as they appear. When the papillomatous growth appears on the vocal folds, its additive effects will produce varying degrees of dysphonia. Its real danger, however, is that it may grow rapidly enough to seriously interfere with the opening of the airway. For this reason, papilloma is considered a serious laryngeal disease, requiring close follow-up by a laryngologist. Surgical removal of a large papilloma is the preferred method of treatment, and *in no case* is the child with papilloma a candidate for voice therapy to reduce hyperfunction. The basic purpose of surgery for papilloma is to preserve the airway; moreover, because of this tumor's propensity for recurrence and rapid growth, the patient must be closely followed postoperatively to see that airway patency remains.

Papilloma usually disappears at puberty, regardless of treatment. If the lesions persist after puberty, they are often removed more easily than in early childhood, and with less chance of recurrence. It should be mentioned that in rare cases the papilloma must be closely watched for the possibility of its turning into a cancerous growth, a change which is extremely unlikely to occur in children (*164*).

The rapid growth of papilloma and its possible choking effect on the airway makes its early diagnosis important. For this reason, the voice clinician—particularly the public-school speech clinician—should be alert to any child who shows dysphonia. Any child who is hoarse for more than a few days should be given an indirect laryngoscopic examination by a physician to rule out the possible presence of papilloma. Again, the treatment of papilloma is medical/surgical, not voice therapy.

*CONTACT ULCERS*

Contact ulcer is usually located bilaterally on the free, approximating margins of the vocal processes. Peacher (*127*) writes that contact ulcer is found primarily in men, and that the incidence of the disorder is not too high. Both Moses (*118*) and Brodnitz (*25*) write that contact ulcers are frequently found in the hard-driving type of man who is under a great deal of daily tension. He frequently speaks in a voice pitch slightly too low for optimum phonation, and often with a hard glottal attack, literally slamming together the approximating surfaces of the vocal processes. Luchsinger and Arnold write:

Similar to migraine headache, laryngeal contact ulcer seems to occur frequently in individuals with a perfectionist personality who are compulsive hard workers, make demands on themselves, and tend to *build up inner tensions* without relaxation or exteriorized discharge. In psychoanalytic parlance, one might say that such persons "swallow" their tensions and problems until they "choke" from their unresolved conflicts. [*101*, p. 270]

The low-pitched voice with noticeable hard glottal attack appears to be characteristic of the patient with contact ulcers. These posterior ulcerations rarely produce any hoarseness. The patient's primary complaint is that his voice tires easily and that he has occasional pain in the laryngeal area, particularly after prolonged phonation. On laryngoscopy, some contact ulcers are found to have granulated tissue around the ulcer crater. The preferred treatment for all but the most severe contact ulcers appears to be vocal rehabilitation. Identification and reduction of vocal hyperfunctional behaviors will usually eliminate the contact ulcer in time (*127*; *128*; *129*). Large ulcerations with surrounding granulations may require surgical treatment followed by voice therapy. Voice rest alone, without voice therapy, can be considered only a temporary therapy for contact ulcers.

### OTHER GROWTHS ON THE VOCAL FOLDS

There are several kinds of benign growths which may be found on the vocal folds and contribute to dysphonia, but which are *not* the result of vocal abuse/misuse and are *not* responsive to vocal rehabilitation. Lesions of *leukoplakia,* which may appear in other places also, are caused primarily by chronic irritation, "particularly from the tars of tobacco smoke" (*141*). Leukoplakia is treated primarily by removing the cause of the irritation, e.g., by eliminating the smoking. Severe cases of laryngeal leukoplakia require surgery and a close watch by the laryngologist. Another medical problem is laryngeal *hyperkeratosis,* a mass of accumulated keratin (a scleroproteinous pigmented spot or covering) which may grow on the inner glottal margins, causing pronounced hoarseness. Hyperkeratosis requires the close supervision of a laryngologist, since it occasionally develops into a malignancy. It should not be treated by the non-medically-trained voice clinician. In a third type of condition, patients who require intralaryngeal intubation for breathing during surgical procedures will occasionally experience laryngeal trauma from the tubing, and, as a result, develop *hemangiomas* or *granulomas.* Both these types of additive tissue lesions are directly related to glottal trauma, and while they may produce moderate dysphonias, their effects are usually short-lived. Temporary voice rest, strictly enforced, will usually reduce the traumatically produced lesions. Usually, no formal voice therapy is required.

Occasionally, growths in the larynx are found to be *cancerous*. When a malignancy is identified, the preservation of life requires its prompt removal. In the case of laryngeal malignancy, the earlier the diagnosis the more effective the treatment will be. For those patients requiring the total removal of the larynx (*laryngectomy*), the need for developing a new pseudo-vibrator in place of the removed vocal folds requires extensive and highly specialized voice rehabilitation, which will be discussed in chapter 8.

## PUBERTAL GROWTH OF THE LARYNX

Although we have been focusing on the pathological aspects of mass-size changes of the vocal folds, we must not ignore the dramatic increase in the size of the human larynx at the time of puberty. During the peak years of puberty (which differ between boys and girls), the length and overall mass of the vocal folds increase dramatically. Hollien (*76*), Hollien and Malcik (*80*), and Hollien and Curtis (*79*) have related the mass-size of the vocal folds to fundamental frequency for the two sexes at various ages. For example, Hollien and Malcik report a fundamental frequency range of 210.2 to 269.7 cps among six 10-year-old boys, and of 115.9 to 137.1 cps among six 18-year-old boys. The lower pitches of the older group are the result of the increased mass-size of the vocal folds.

These rapid changes in the size of the vocal folds and other laryngeal structures produce varying vocal effects during the pubertal years. Boys experience a lowering of their fundamental frequencies of about one octave; girls, a lowering of about two or three notes. This change does not happen in a day or two. For several years, as this laryngeal growth is taking place, the boy will experience temporary hoarseness and occasional pitch breaks. The wise parent or voice clinician witnesses these vocal changes with little comment or concern. The mass-size increases of puberty tend to thwart any serious attempts at singing or other vocal arts. Luchsinger and Arnold (*101*) point out that much of the European literature on singing makes a valid plea that the formal study of singing be deferred until well after puberty. Until the child experiences some stability in laryngeal growth, the demands of singing might be inappropriate for his rapidly changing mechanism.

An excellent summary of the effects of puberty on phonation may be found in Weiss's "The Pubertal Change of the Human Voice" (*165*). The voice clinician who has many dealings with adolescents should become familiar with the dramatic voice changes experienced by youngsters at the time of puberty. These mutational voice changes and their temporary dysphonias usually do not require voice therapy.

## ENDOCRINE CHANGES OF THE VOCAL FOLDS

Most of the inappropriate voice pitches we hear are not related to the structural changes of the vocal folds that result from endocrine problems. Occasionally, however, we see a patient whose voice is too low or too high for his or her sex and age, indicating endocrine imbalance. An extreme example of endocrine causation would be castration before puberty, which, by preventing vocal mutation, maintains the boyish voice throughout life, as demonstrated by the castrato singer in early opera (Moses, *117*). We occasionally see men who do not experience voice mutation, directly as a result of poor gonadal, sexual development; such cases are rare and sometimes respond well to the glandular treatment of the endocrinologist. More commonly, the inappropriately high voice in the postpubertal male is functional in origin, related to the continuous overuse of the cricothyroid muscle, as documented by Arnold (*101*) in his myographic studies of falsetto. Sometimes the high pitch is the result of habit and personality-identity problems; this kind of voice problem is highly amenable to voice therapy, particularly in the absence of any endocrine causation. Specific therapy procedures for these functional mutational voice problems will be presented in chapter 6.

Seen relatively rarely are voice problems resulting from cord mass-size alterations related to thyroid abnormalities, pituitary disease, and adrenal diseases (Luchsinger and Arnold, *101*). Any endocrine imbalance which interferes with laryngeal growth may result in aberrant, higher voice pitches. Abnormal growth of the vocal folds, such as seen in some forms of pituitary gland malfunction, may result in inappropriately low-pitched voices. The effects of virilizing agents on the voices of women have been discussed by Damste (*43*), who reports that of 400 adult women who visited the E. N. T. Clinic at Utrecht, Netherlands, with various voice complaints, 40 had voice problems related to their having used virilizing drugs. Certain hormone-like drugs may cause considerable alteration (increase in mass and size) of the vocal folds in women, leaving them with a permanent lower fundamental frequency which is almost wholly resistant to voice remediation.

Any change in the overall size and mass of the vocal cords will probably produce some change in the vibrating characteristics of the voice. We have considered the various mass-size changes of the vocal folds which may contribute to varying kinds of dysphonia, some responsive to voice therapy and some for which voice therapy is inappropriate.

### DYSPHONIAS RELATED TO PROBLEMS OF VOCAL FOLD APPROXIMATION

The quality and strength of phonation is highly related to the degree of vocal fold approximation. Any of the mass-size increases (such as nodules, polyps, or papilloma) may, if on the inner glottal surfaces, prevent the free glottal edges from optimally approximating. In this section we will consider other approximating problems related to functional underadduction (folds too loosely together) or functional overadduction (folds too tightly together); various paralyses of one or both vocal folds; and the use of the ventricular bands or false cords as a phonation source, with the true folds abducted apart.

CORD THICKENING, NODULES, POLYPS, AND PAPILLOMAS AS OBSTRUCTIONS
TO APPROXIMATION

Besides the additive effects of cord thickening, nodules, polyps, and papillomas, with their obvious consequences for vocal fold vibration, these mass structures sometimes extend into the glottis, preventing the folds from making their normal approximation. The larger the mass on the free margin of one or both cords, the greater its obstructive effects and the greater the dysphonia. In the illustrations of nodules and polyps in figures 15 and 16, one can see that the mass of these vocal lesions could preclude optimal approximation of the folds. In cases of severe bilateral nodules, one will often observe open chinking of the folds on each side of the nodule. The outgoing air stream escapes through these openings quite audibly, so that what we hear is a breathy voice. The effects of obstructive masses which prevent cord approximation must be recognized by the voice clinician, since they may prevent the patient from achieving a "good-sounding" voice, no matter what he does.

FUNCTIONAL DYSPHONIA

Much of what is classified as functional dysphonia is the inability of the patient to approximate his vocal folds in an optimum manner, his approximation being either too lax or too tight. In addition, the patient complains of many vague disorders—throat "fullness," pain in the laryngeal area, dryness of mouth while talking, neck tightness, etc.—which are usually related to vocal fatigue. Those voice problems which are not the result of an organic pathology may be called functional dysphonia—a term which conveys very little to the voice clinician other than the important implication that there is no structural pathology present. (It would appear that a voice improperly used over time may well produce some structural change of the laryngeal mechanism, such as cord thickening or vocal nodules.) A functionally caused dysphonia does not necessarily sound different from an organically caused one. The same subjective terms (harsh, hoarse, breathy, strident, weak, etc.) are commonly used to describe both. Some of the hoarsest voices heard are made by people whose larynges demonstrate no organic pathology whatsoever; on the other hand, serious organic problems, such as beginning cancer, may produce no acoustic alteration of the voice at all. In general, voice-therapy approaches do not distinguish between functional and organic voice problems. The functional aspects of the majority of organic voice problems appear to have been well validated by Brodnitz (24), Luchsinger and Arnold (101), Perkins (130), Greene (67), and Murphy (119), to name but a few, all of whom indicate that separate voice-therapy approaches for functional and organic problems would be unrealistic.

It would seem best to approach functional dysphonia by first identifying the particular aberrant vocal behaviors. One form of dysphonia comprises disorders of *loudness*, the most common of which seen clinically appears to be an excessively weak voice. Most overly weak voices exist in the absence of organic pathology (the *phonasthenia* of Parkinson's disease would be an example of the occasional organic problem seen) and are often reflective of a general problem of poor interpersonal relationships. The patient may be so shy and insecure when he attempts to speak to people that he is unable to produce a strong enough air stream to trip his vocal folds into vibration. For such a patient, working on respiration and loudness per se would be less effective than attempting to improve his self-concept and interpersonal relationships. There are some individuals who, for whatever reason, speak in a soft voice, but who are quite responsive to symptomatic therapy to increase vocal intensity.

The most common words applied to functional dysphonia are "hoarse," "breathy," and "harsh." At the level of the larynx, the patients who produce these voices usually approximate their folds too loosely or too tightly. Laxity of approximation generally produces an escape of air, perceived as *breathiness*. Sometimes, as Brodnitz(24) suggests, the breathy, tired voice appears only after prolonged hyperfunctional voice use. It may emerge late in the day, after the patient has done a lot of phonating, particularly if such phonation has required a good deal of effort and force. *Harshness* is usually perceived in a phonatory milieu of hard vocal attack (sudden approximation of the vocal cords), pitch and intensity problems, and overadduction of the folds; however, harshness may well be more of a resonance phenomenon characterized by tongue retraction and constriction of the pharyngeal constrictors, and sometimes accompanied by nasality. Harshness to most people means a voice which indicates that a lot of effort and force has gone into its production.

Functional dysphonia often becomes "the" voice of the person. This is the way he talks. This is him. For such persons, voice therapy is not often successful and in many cases should not be initiated, particularly if the patient wants his voice "that way." But for patients who are motivated to change the quality of their voices, and who are diagnosed as having functional dysphonia, voice therapy is remarkably successful.

*SPASTIC DYSPHONIA*

The most extreme overadduction problem of the vocal folds is spastic dysphonia. Here the overadduction of the folds interferes so much with the outward escape of the air stream that phonatory vibration is almost impossible. The voice is characterized by "a strained, creaking, choked vocal attack and a tense, squeezed voice, accompanied by extreme tension of the entire phonatory system" (Luchsinger and Arnold, *101*, p. 328). The vocal symptoms are most severe when the patient attempts to speak to other people; he may have no problem in talking aloud to himself, in singing, in laughing, or in any other vocal action that does not involve interaction with people. The patient soon learns to expect phonation difficulties whenever he attempts to talk to someone, and in this sense the disorder is similar to the problem of stuttering. The patient overadducts his cords and attempts to force the airstream through the tight glottal closure, producing the "laryngeal stutter" (*101*). While some authorities, e.g., Heaver (*72*) and Moses (*118*)· view spastic dysphonia as a functionally caused problem symptomatic of difficulties in interpersonal adjustment, Robe, Brumlick, and Moore (*137*) conclude that its origin is in the central nervous system. Most voice clinicians appear to view spastic dysphonia as a symptom of personality maladjustment and not as a disorder originating in the central nervous system.

The onset of spastic dysphonia is relatively abrupt and frequently follows an unpleasant, traumatic event. Often the patient will recount in detail the events surrounding the onset of the voice disorder, and in so doing will usually describe the relative consistency of the disorder. It has been my observation with several spastic dysphonic patients that such individuals give their vocal and personal histories with a rather fixed smile, and with a penchant for historical detail not ordinarily seen in the average patient. A typical history was given by a 42-year-old housewife whose voice problems appeared to be directly related to the death of her teenaged son:

The patient described what happened when her son was hospitalized with severe pneumonia: she and her husband went down to the hospital canteen for a cup of coffee. When they returned to the boy's room they found that he had died during their absence. In the woman's shock, she was unable to speak for several days. Gradually, over a period of several weeks, her voice returned. Several years later a second child was hospitalized, also with pneumonia. While driving the boy to the hospital, the woman experienced severe difficulties in talking, similar to the sort she had suffered after the first boy's death. These voice difficulties persisted with no remission for several years. The patient would speak with a rather placid, smiling face, and at the same time would continuously push, or force out, her breath. She exhibited no normal phonation except when she laughed, which she would do frequently, using this relatively easy phonation as a "starter" for her verbal responses. Subsequent attempts at voice therapy, later combined with psychiatric therapy, were not successful in changing her spastic dysphonia.

The general prognosis for improving the voice of the patient with spastic dysphonia is not good. The patient's persistent use of the primitive valving action of the larynx when attempting to speak to someone is highly resistant to voice-therapy modification, as we shall discuss further in chapter 6. Continued research on the psychiatric implications of the disorder and on its possible etiology in the central nervous system is badly needed. It would appear that a behavioral modification approach at the present time is perhaps the best choice of treatment; that is, the voice therapist should establish a baseline of "good" phonation, such as the laugh, and attempt to extend this incrementally until easy voice patterns are maintained in everyday conversation. However, it must be pointed out that in our few attempts to use this behavioral approach with spastic dysphonia, we have been discouraged by the high rate of recurrence of the symptoms after a good voice has been established.

## FUNCTIONAL APHONIA

In contrast to the overadducted vocal fold approximation of spastic dysphonia, the patient suffering from functional aphonia underadducts, keeping the folds apart. Only rarely is aphonia not functional in origin. The patient has no speaking voice at all, managing a whisper for most social situations. On laryngoscopic examination the vocal folds appear to be normal; however, when the patient is asked to phonate, the folds generally abduct to a position further apart than they were in before the command was given. Functional aphonia is frequently described as a *hysterical* or *conversion* symptom, according to Aronson, Peterson, and Litin (*8; 9*), who found these two terms used by various laryngologists for 20 functional dysphonic and aphonic patients they had observed. While functional aphonia may well be a form of conversion hysteria, Brodnitz (*24*, p. 65) recommends that we avoid using the term in the "presence of the patient because of the social stigma attached to it." Usually the patient has had several temporary losses of voice before the disorder becomes permanent. One might speculate that the temporarily aphonic patient may derive some reinforcing gains from his loss of voice, such as not having to give a speech or not being able to preside over a meeting. Aphonia may become permanent after moments of acute stress, maintaining itself for various reasons. Aronson, Peterson, and Litin (*8*) report that the onset of functional dysphonia or aphonia in 10 out of 27 patients they studied was associated with an event of acute stress; in 13 of the 27 patients it was associated with stress over a longer period of time. The onset of functional aphonia is sometimes related to the patient's having experienced some laryngeal pathology or other disease. For example, Boone (*20*) describes the physical origin of functional aphonia in two patients, one who became aphonic after a meningitis attack, and the other after a laryngeal operation, when he could not end the voice rest imposed upon him by the laryngologist. Both these aphonic patients were highly responsive to voice therapy.

The patient with functional aphonia, who has no voice at all, generally presents to the voice clinician a more favorable prognosis than the patient with functional dysphonia. Most aphonic patients are probably similar to the 27 patients described by Aronson and his colleagues (*8*), who reported that "no serious psychopathology warranting immediate psychiatric help was found in any patient." While the aphonic patient may in the beginning derive primary gain from his lack of voice, in that it allows him to avoid certain situational stresses, his problem soon becomes a habitual response, and he talks today with no voice "because that is the way he talked yesterday." As long as the aphonia serves the patient well, whatever the gains may be, voice therapy will not be too effective. However, most aphonic patients desperately want to regain the use of their voices, waiting only for the clinician to show them how. The clinician should never confront the aphonic patient with "you could use your voice if you wanted to." Rather, some baseline phonations are achieved—usually the patient can cough (*20*)—and these primitive phonations are gradually shaped into a usable voice for purposes of speech. Details of therapeutic procedures to be used with aphonic patients are presented in chapter 6.

For years I would refer aphonic patients almost immediately for psychiatric consultation and therapy. If any voice therapy was given, it was done so concurrently with psychotherapy provided by the psychiatrist or psychologist. Finally, one day, a psychiatrist confronted me with the observation that most patients with functional aphonia were "psychologically not much different from the rest of us," and why didn't the speech pathologists "just treat them." Since that time, by employing the kind of behavioral approaches outlined by Sloane and MacAulay (*148*), my colleagues and I have made good therapeutic progress with patients with functional aphonia. It would appear that functional aphonia, like other types of conversion symptoms, may be treated successfully by the direct symptom-modification approach proposed by such behaviorists as Wolpe (*171*), Rachman (*136*), and Stevens (*155*). The voice clinician interested in symptomatic therapy for such problems as functional aphonia will find relevant reading in these cited sources, for they hint that a trial period of therapy will usually be most helpful and rarely harmful. They indicate that the clinician should focus on a symptom and gradually "condition it away"—good advice for the voice clinician working with functional aphonia.

*VOCAL CORD PARALYSIS*

Most voice problems related to vocal fold paralysis result in dysphonias that are somewhere between normal functioning and no voice at all. By vocal cord paralysis we mean the inability of one or both cords to move because of lack of innervation to particular intrinsic muscles of the larynx. The interruption of the innervation of the larynx can be central or peripheral;

it would appear that most cord paralyses are due to interruptions of the peripheral nerve fibers to the larynx, either the superior laryngeal nerve or the recurrent laryngeal nerve. Brodnitz (24) writes that the most frequent cause of vocal cord paralysis is "damage to the nerve during a thyroid operation." Among the other causes he lists are damage during removal of a parathyroid tumor, traumatic damage, and compression of a nerve by tumors or enlarged glands (such as goiter) in the neck and chest.

Paralysis of the superior laryngeal nerve is rare, and if this nerve were damaged bilaterally, the patient would experience paralysis of the crico-thyroid muscles and be unable to elevate his voice pitch. Unilateral damage to the superior laryngeal nerve would result in one fold elongating for pitch elevation and the other fold remaining relatively unchanged; the voice would be hoarse, lacking pitch variation and adequate loudness.

Paralysis of the recurrent laryngeal nerve may also be unilateral or bilateral. Of relevance here is Semon's Law—cited in Luchsinger and Arnold (101) as having been formulated in 1881—which explains a sequence of paralysis found in the larynx after paralysis of the recurrent laryngeal nerve as follows: first the abductor muscles are involved, with the midline positioning of the paralyzed cord(s) developing eventually into an adductor paralysis. This sequential change does not appear to be valid today. Rather, the laryngologist sees static, fixed paralyses of one type or the other: adductor paralysis (the involved cord(s) cannot move to the adducted, central position) or abductor paralysis (the paralyzed cord(s) cannot move laterally outward). In bilateral adductor paralysis, the cords are in the open paramedian position and the patient is aphonic. In unilateral adductor paralysis, the involved cord is in the paramedian position, making complete glottal closure impossible. There is much air wastage as the patient attempts to phonate, and the result is a breathy type of hoarseness with noticeable loss of voice intensity and pitch range. Voice therapy directed at increasing the sharpness of glottal attack, perhaps using pushing exercises, is sometimes useful in helping the patient with unilateral adductor paralysis to achieve a better, stronger voice. If the paralysis is permanent, however, about all that voice therapy can do is help the patient compensate for his loss by using the impaired mechanism as efficiently as possible; normal voice control is frequently an unrealistic goal for these cases. Medical management of adductor paralysis includes such approaches as the use of electrotherapy to stimulate the involved cord, as described by Böhme (18), or the surgical use of teflon injected into the paralyzed cord to increase its girth and thus make approximation with the normal cord possible, a procedure used and described by Kirchner and Toledo (93). For bilateral adductor paralysis, despite the patient's being almost aphonic, voice therapy is rarely very effective. Medical management of the problem may be achieved by surgical repositioning of the folds in a more midline position (the airway must be

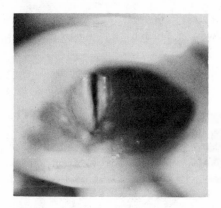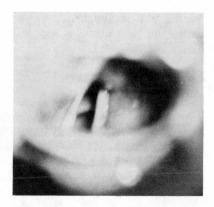

Fig. 17. A mirror view of a unilateral abductor vocal fold paralysis. (A) shows the full, wide normal right fold approximating at the midline with the paralyzed left fold. (B) shows the normal right cord abducting laterally for inspiration of air and the paralyzed left fold remaining in its fixed midline position.

kept open), teflon injection, and electrostimulation. Arnold (5) writes that many patients with vocal cord paralysis spontaneously recover, with no specific treatment required; the recovery occurs "within the first 3 months and is complete no longer than 6 months following the onset of nerve lesion."

Unilateral abductor paralysis would result in the paralyzed cord lying near the midline as shown in figure 17. The involved cord can in some cases abduct laterally to the intermediate position, but never to the full lateral position required for deep inspiration. The patient with abductor paralysis complains less about dysphonia and more about shortness of breath. Because of the decrease of the glottal opening, the patient experiences some actual decrease in inhaled air volume. While cord approximation may be sufficient for phonation and not cause any voice change, the heavy user of voice, such as the lecturer or singer, may develop dysphonia because of inadequate breath. The primary symptom of the disorder, however, is some impairment in respiration, often with little or no change in voice. The respiration problems become most dramatic if the patient experiences bilateral abductor paralysis, with the cords relatively fixed in the adducted midline position. In this case, the compelling need for an adequate airway requires an immediate surgical operation, such as a *tracheotomy* (the creation of an opening into the trachea, just below the level of the larynx), with this emergency procedure perhaps followed by surgical repositioning of the folds to create an open glottal airway. After this primary treatment by corrective surgery, the laryngologist may prescribe voice therapy so that the patient can learn to use his reconstructed phonatory mechanism as efficiently as possible. The desired goal in abductor paralysis, whether unilateral or bilateral, is for the patient first to have an adequate airway, and then to reestablish optimum phonation.

## VENTRICULAR DYSPHONIA

This condition—in which the false cords, the ventricular bands, adduct together over the true cords below—may develop as a purely functional disorder or it may be the substitute voice of the patient who has a severe disease of the true folds (such as severe papilloma or large polyps). The ventricular voice is usually low pitched because of the large mass of vibrating tissue of the ventricular bands (as compared to the smaller mass of vibrating tissue of the true folds). In addition, the voice has little pitch variability and is therefore monotonous. Finally, since the ventricular bands have difficulty in making a good, firm approximation for their entire length, the voice is usually somewhat hoarse. This combination of low pitch, monotony, and hoarseness makes most ventricular voices sound unpleasant. If there is no persistent true cord pathology which continues to force the patient to use his ventricular voice, this disorder will usually respond well to voice therapy. Sometimes, however, the patient's prolonged use of the ventricular bands will result in his developing *hypertrophy* (enlargement) of the ventricular bands, which makes their normal full retraction somewhat difficult.

Ventricular phonation is difficult to diagnose by the sound of the voice alone. On laryngoscopic examination during phonation, the ventricular folds are seen to come together, covering from view the true cords which lie below. Some ventricular dysphonias display a special form of *diplophonia* (double voice), where the true folds and ventricular bands phonate simultaneously. Identification and confirmation of what vibrating structures the patient is using for phonation can best be made by frontal tomographic X ray (coronal) of the sites of vibration. In true venticular phonation, the true vocal folds will be slightly abducted, with the ventricular bands above in relative approximation. In normal phonation, the opposite relationship between the true folds and the ventricular bands occurs; that is, the true folds are adducted and the ventricular bands are positioned laterally from the midline position. Once ventricular phonation is confirmed by laryngoscopy or X ray, any physical problem of the true cords which might make normal phonation impossible should first be eliminated. Once this is done, normal phonation can be resumed. There are some patients, however, who use the ventricular bands for phonation for no physical reason; these patients require voice therapy, as we shall discuss in chapter 6. It should be remembered that some patients who experience severe and permanent true cord pathology should be taught (if necessary), and encouraged to use, ventricular phonation as a substitute voice. The monotonous, low-pitched voice of ventricular vibration will tire easily and not be wholly satisfactory to the patient, but in the absence of true cord phonation, a ventricular voice is better than no voice at all.

### LARYNGOFISSURE, CORDECTOMY, AND LARYNGECTOMY

The most severe of all approximation difficulties is the removal of one or both cords or the removal of the larynx itself. The usual reason for such an extensive surgical approach is to treat a malignancy. In *laryngofissure*, the surgeon directly exposes the involved larynx by dividing the thyroid cartilage in the midline, and then retracts the lateral thyroid walls so that a direct exposure of the glottis is possible. After the intralaryngeal operation is completed, the divided thyroid cartilage is "sprung" back in place. Such a direct procedure is rarely used, and only considered when a superior, oral approach is not adequate for the surgical task required. A typical part of the laryngofissure approach is a *cordectomy* (removal of one vocal cord, sometimes including the arytenoid cartilage). A cordectomy is indicated when the malignancy involves only one of the cords, in which case the malignancy is usually a focal and small lesion. After the cordectomy, the voice is usually very weak and breathy. Any scar tissue that grows in to fill the defect may serve as a structure for the normal cord to approximate against. Saunders (*141*) recommends "small injections of Teflon in glycerin . . . to help fill out the scar tissue and strengthen the voice." Voice therapy for patients who have undergone a cordectomy is deferred in most cases until after surgical attempts are made to achieve some kind of approximating surface for the normal cord. Voice therapy is aimed at helping the patient use his impaired mechanism as optimally as possible, and experimentation with varying degrees of loudness and pitch level will often find a voice that is satisfactory to the patient.

Most problems of laryngeal malignancy require the total removal of the larynx (*laryngectomy*), which may include removal of all laryngeal cartilages, including the epiglottis and the hyoid bone. This surgery frequently requires a *radical neck dissection* as well, when there are suspicions that the lymphatic system in the neck is also involved. By definition, a laryngectomy will require that the patient develop a new voice source, which we shall call *alaryngeal speech* (to use the title of a recent book by Diedrich and Youngstrom [49], which deals in some depth with the processes of such speech). The new phonation source may be developed through esophageal speech, (described in chapter 8) or through the use of an artificial larynx. We shall consider all the possible voice approaches for the laryngectomy patient in chapter 8.

SUMMARY

The normal voice is highly dependent on optimum mass-size adjustments of the vocal folds and on the right degree of approximation of the two folds. We have considered specific disorders of mass-size and approximation which interfere with normal voice, producing various kinds of dysphonia and aphonia. We must not forget specific etiologies and possible medical treatments of these disorders in the overall context of voice rehabilitation. For some problems, e.g., papilloma, voice therapy is not indicated. For many problems of vocal hyperfunction, such as nodules or functional dysphonia, the approach of identifying and eliminating vocal misuse or abuse is warranted. Some problems, such as ventricular dysphonia, require special kinds of voice therapy. Whatever the kind of voice therapy required, its success will depend on an adequate diagnostic evaluation; in other words, it is crucial to first find out "what is going on."

*chapter four*

# The Voice Evaluation

*Sometimes as a result of a speech screening program, such as those in public schools, the speech pathologist discovers children with voice problems. These children are subsequently seen for diagnosis and treatment by the laryngologist before beginning voice therapy. Or often the speech pathologist sees voice patients on direct referral from the laryngologist. Sometimes voice patients come directly to the speech pathologist, at which time the patient is only evaluated and then referred to a laryngologist; if voice therapy is then recommended, the patient comes back to the speech pathologist. We shall consider the procedures used by the speech pathologist in his attempt to evaluate the patient's voice.*

Successful voice therapy is highly dependent on how well the voice clinician can identify what the patient is doing vocally. The typical voice evaluation is completed after someone else, such as the laryngologist, has already made the diagnosis of what the problem is and what may be causing it. The speech pathologist usually concentrates on making a detailed analysis of what the patient is doing with regard to respiration, phonation, and resonance. To do this, he makes good use of whatever medical descriptions of the problem may be available, he takes a detailed history, he observes the patient closely, he uses those testing tools and instrumentations necessary to make an accurate assessment, and he introduces to the patient various therapeutic approaches to obtain clues as to what direction the voice therapy should take.

Effective voice therapy requires a thorough initial voice evaluation and some amount of voice assessment at each subsequent therapy period. Evaluation and therapy are highly overlapping: what is found at the evaluation and "fed back" to the patient may be highly therapeutic; similarly, the constant probing for the right combination of factors to produce the "best" voice is an evaluative part of every therapy session. Because the voice evaluation and the voice therapy which may follow are so related, the reader should remember that many of the evaluational instruments described in this chapter are also appropriate as therapeutic tools.

### THE VOICE EVALUATION AND MEDICAL INFORMATION

No patient should receive voice therapy from the speech pathologist unless the voice problem has been diagnosed by a physician competent in the field of laryngology. Unfortunately, in some areas of the country there are no laryngologists, and it is not uncommon for speech pathologists in these areas to report that there are no medical doctors available who can perform *indirect laryngoscopy* (mirror view of the vocal folds). The speech pathologist in such a situation should confer with the patient's local physician, saying, for example, "Robbie seems to be hoarse every day. Could you please see that his vocal folds are examined?" It is the rare physician who will not appreciate such a request. If he feels he does not possess the skills required for indirect laryngoscopy, he will see that the patient is referred to a laryngologist. It is not unusual for patients living in remote areas of the United States to travel several hundred miles for an examination by a laryngologist. A laryngeal examination must be made before any kind of voice therapy is undertaken. Otherwise, the voice therapy might have serious consequences if the patient's symptoms were related to such conditions as laryngeal papilloma or carcinoma. Another reason for deferring voice therapy until a medical diagnosis has been made is that voice therapy is not effective for all kinds of phonatory disorders. If the symptoms are related, in the laryngologist's opinion, to hyperfunctional use of the vocal mechanism, then voice therapy may well be the preferred method of treatment. On the other hand, if there is a serious alteration of the laryngeal structure, such as laryngeal web, voice therapy would not be the choice of treatment. And, in still another circumstance, if the patient demonstrates severe interpersonal maladjustment, voice therapy might be deferred. The decision of whether or not to provide voice therapy for the patient is made by the laryngologist, who may request evaluational data from the speech pathologist to aid him in making his decision. The type of voice therapy provided is decided upon by the speech pathologist.

Let us suppose that the speech pathologist makes his initial contact with the new voice patient as the result of a public-school screening program. The first thing he does is to make his observation and evaluation of the patient's voice known to the laryngologist, deferring voice therapy until after the results of the laryngoscopic examination are known. The physician will then describe the status of the vocal folds in a brief written report sent directly to the referring speech pathologist. Typical statements by laryngologists about public-school children referred to them with varying degrees of dysphonia might be:

While Jim has enlarged, hypertrophied tonsils and adenoids, there is no indication at this time that they should be surgically removed. Laryngeal structure and function appear normal. Maybe voice therapy could clear up his hoarseness.

Mirror laryngoscopy found Penny to have a slight bilateral cord thickening, which may well be related to misuse/abuse of her voice.

Fred was seen by me in the ENT Clinic last Friday, presenting at that time on laryngeal examination the following: slight posterior bowing of the cords with the early formation of bilateral screamer's nodules. I discussed with Fred and his mother the possibility of eventual surgery to remove these nodule growths. Since you are already familiar with Fred and his voice problem, you might start him on voice therapy, and we can see if this might reduce the nodules. I would like to examine Fred again in three months or so, after a trial period of voice therapy.

Such statements may range from a terse "normal vocal cords" to a comprehensive, multiple-page evaluation. For phonatory disorders, what the speech pathologist needs primarily is a statement on the general status of the laryngeal mechanism; for respiration or resonance problems, different kinds of medical information are obviously required.

Whenever the speech pathologist is in doubt about the adequacy or meaning of the laryngologist's report, a direct conversation with the laryngologist by phone or in person will usually clear the matter up: It should be remembered, however, that questions like "What kind of voice therapy should I give?" or "What do you want me to do?" are inappropriate. Once the laryngologist recommends voice therapy, he usually looks to the speech pathologist to determine its nature and direction.

It is in the public schools where most voice problems are "discovered" by the speech pathologist. The next largest group of voice patients are referred to the speech pathologist by the laryngologist. The laryngologist's examination includes an assessment of the larynx and related structures. The vocal folds are assessed, usually by indirect mirror laryngoscopy, and their color, configuration, and position noted. During the patient's quiet respiration, the laryngologist looks for the normal inverted-V position of the cords. For phonation, the patient is often asked to phonate a relatively high pitch, perhaps by extending an *e–e–e* for several seconds. The higher the pitch, the further the epiglottis is extended upward, permitting a relatively unobstructed view of the vocal folds. A judgment is made on the adequacy of fold approximation during phonation. Other structures examined may include the ventricular folds, laryngeal ventricle, pharynx, tonsils-adenoids, nasal cavities, velopharyngeal mechanism, glands and muscles of the neck, etc. The laryngologist's examination is directed at finding the cause of the patient's presenting problem and evaluating the overall status of the larynx and related mechanisms. If the laryngologist wants additional information as to how the patient uses his voice, or if he feels voice therapy may be needed, he refers the patient directly to the speech pathologist. Such referral usually requires a written statement by the laryngologist describing the patient's problem, and, in actual practice, the written referral may be supplemented by a telephone conversation further describing the problem. The laryngologist's referral usually includes an abbreviated statement of the patient's history, a descriptive statement of the presenting problem, what was told to the patient, and a statement indicating treatment direction and probable prognosis. Taken from a clinic file is the following letter of referral from a local laryngologist who placed strong and continued emphasis on voice therapy for most of his patients with hyperfunctional voice problems:

I have asked Mrs. Pearl _____ to see you for a voice evaluation at the earliest opportunity. This 44-year-old woman works as a secretary to an insurance executive, a position which requires much talking on the telephone. In the past six months she reports continued hoarseness, usually worse at the end of the day, and she complains of occasional pain in the general hyoid region after prolonged speaking. She is married, the mother of three young adult sons. Until six months ago, there was no history of vocal distress.

On mirror laryngoscopy, I found the patient to have small bilateral nodes at the anterior one-third junction. Areas immediately adjacent to the nodes were characterized by increased vascularization, suggesting much irritation at this site. On cord adduction, there is noticeable open chinking on each side of the approximated nodes. Her voice, as you might suspect, is quite breathy with an audible escape of air, probably escaping through the open chinking. Inadequate voice loudness, also, appears to be a problem for her.

I am referring her to you for your ideas on what she may be doing wrong with her voice. If you feel she would benefit from voice therapy, please schedule her. I told Mrs. _____ that if you felt voice therapy were indicated, we would begin there. If not, we might attempt surgical removal of the nodules and then instruct her on proper voice usage to prevent their recurrence. She apears strongly motivated to improve her voice and will, I'm sure, gladly accept whatever you recommend.

While this letter lacks the details of the patient's history and examination, it contains the basic information typically required by the speech pathologist. For laryngologists and speech pathologists working side by side in a medical setting, such a letter would not be needed, since thoroughgoing information on the patient's history would be readily accessible to the speech pathologist.

Community health centers and university clinics routinely obtain medical information and some case history data from patients when the initial appointment is made, and, if a voice problem is indicated, schedule the patient first for a medical diagnostic evaluation. It sometimes happens, however, that a voice patient will make the initial appointment without identifying his problem as one of voice. If, for whatever reason, a patient arrives to be treated for some form of dysphonia, but has not had a previous medical examination, the speech pathologist must defer his final disposition of the patient until the medical information is obtained. The voice evaluation by the speech pathologist may begin, however, even in the absence of the medical information. The case history can be taken, respiration-phonatory-resonance observations and test data obtained, and only the decision about voice therapy need be deferred.

The ethics and efficacy of speech pathologists themselves doing indirect laryngoscopy might be discussed at this point. Some speech pathologists are trained to perform mirror laryngoscopy, a procedure which is not difficult to master; these persons use indirect laryngoscopy primarily as a method of teaching students laryngeal function and to observe the folds directly to determine any progress during therapy. No speech pathologist, however, should use laryngoscopy as a diagnostic device. Primary identification of laryngeal pathology is the clear responsibility of the laryngologist, who is equipped also with the medical techniques required for the treatment of the pathology, once it is identified. It would appear, therefore, for the ethical and legal protection of the speech pathologist, that the voice patient who comes in for evaluation without prior medical examination should *never* at this first visit be subjected to indirect laryngoscopy by the speech pathologist. To repeat, the diagnostic examination of the vocal cords belongs to the laryngologist. After the laryngologist has made a diagnosis, the speech pathologist trained in laryngoscopy may occasionally use mirror laryngoscopy to view the cords indirectly; this will facilitate his treatment of the patient by allowing him to make judgments about vocal cord adequacy.

No voice therapy should begin in any setting, with any aged patient until a laryngologist has examined the patient's vocal apparatus and recommended such therapy.

THE VOICE EVALUATION AND THE CASE HISTORY

To understand the patient with a voice disorder, it is necessary to collect background information about him. The techniques of good history-taking for voice disorders, and for other communication disorders, are well described in Johnson, Darley, and Spriestersbach's *Diagnostic Methods in Speech Pathology* (*89*) and Darley's *Diagnosis and Appraisal of Communication Disorders* (*44*), and need not be elaborated upon here. The list of questions developed in Moore's chapter on organic voice disorders in Travis' *Handbook of Speech Pathology* (*113*) will be useful in helping the voice clinician organize the questions he wishes to ask.

Relevant questions to explore with the voice patient may be seen on the first page of a typical voice evaluation form, shown in figure 18. Any case history will include general identifying information on the patient—details about his family, his schoolwork situation, his health, his habits, etc. Let us consider separately some of the more important questions usually explored with patients with voice disorders.

### DESCRIPTION OF THE PROBLEM AND CAUSE

One of the most valuable sections in the case history is the patient's own description of what he thinks his problem is and what he thinks is its cause. His description reveals much about his own conceptualization of the problem and the degree of insight he may have. What the patient feels is his problem may not be consistent with the opinions of the referring physician or the speech pathologist—a discrepancy which may be due to what we call the patient's "reality distance." This distance may be the result of the patient's lay background and his inability to understand adequately what had been explained to him. Often we hear highly discrepant reports of "what the doctor said" as the patient recounts the diagnoses of previous clinicians. More often this distance is the result primarily of his inability to accept and cope with the real problem. His defenses may force him to describe his problem in terms that are not consistent with the perceptions of others. What the patient says about his problem may provide the clinician with insights that no amount of observation or testing can match. This sort of reality distance is well illustrated by the following excerpts from the clinic records of a 39-year-old minister:

[Physician's referral statement]   This minister is extremely tense and finds it difficult to relate to people conversationally. His conversational voice sounds almost like spastic dysphonia at times while his ministerial sermon voice is resonant and of normal quality. On laryngoscopic examination he shows early polypoid thickening on the free margin of each vocal cord. His primary problem, however, appears to be one of vocal strain probably during times of conversation.

FIGURE 18

---

UNIVERSITY OF DENVER
Speech and Hearing Center
VOICE EVALUATION

| | |
|---|---|
| Name: | Date: |
| Address: | Birthdate: |
| Phone: | Age: |
| Referred by: | SHC #: |
| Examiner: | Occupation: |

---

*CLIENT INFORMATION:*
  *Specific*

  1. Description of the problem and cause:


  2. Onset and duration of the problem:


  3. Variation of the problem:
       Consistency—


       Better situations—


       Worse situations—


  4. Description of vocal use (daily use, misuse):



*Related*
1. Surgery:


2. Family speech and voice problems:


3. Previous voice therapy:


4. General health (serious illnesses, chronic conditions, drug or hormone therapy, excessive smoking or drinking):

[Speech pathologist's statement]  During conversation this man at times has no voice at all, closely resembling the phenomenon of spastic dysphonia. By laughing or joking, the phenomenon clears up and normal quality is restored. During moments of over-adduction of his cords, he pushes and demonstrates much physical effort to produce phonation. Symptomatic therapy might well be deferred for psychotherapy.

[Patient's statement of the problem]  I have trouble getting my voice out at times. The doctor says I have these little growths on my vocal cords that stick together preventing the escape of air. Apparently, I need some breathing exercises.

The patient's statement provides the clinician with obvious clues. The patient's need to blame his voice problem on his organic pathology will serve him well during the initial phases of voice therapy, but eventually the clinician will have to develop the patient's insight into the possible relationship between his tension during conversational situations and his fluctuating dysphonia. How and in what way the patient describes his problem is most illuminating, especially when the interviewer transcribes the response in the patient's own words.

### ONSET AND DURATION OF THE PROBLEM

How long the patient feels he has had the voice problem is important. A problem of acute and sudden onset usually poses a severe threat to the patient, that is, it keeps him from carrying out his customary activities (acting, singing, selling, preaching, or whatever). The aphonia or dysphonia of sudden onset deserves thorough exploration by both the laryngologist and the speech pathologist. Long-term chronic dysphonia usually has existed for so long because the patient has never been particularly disturbed by his voice problem. He very seldom comes to the speech pathologist of his own accord, but rather on the insistence of a friend or an examining physician. Voice therapy, like other forms of remedial therapy, is usually more successful with those patients who are motivated to overcome their problem. The patient with a long history of indifference toward his dysphonia usually presents a more unfavorable prognosis than the one who has recently acquired his disorder, depending, of course, on the kind and relative extent of the pathology involved.

### VARIABILITY OF THE PROBLEM

Most voice patients can provide rather accurate timetables with regard to the consistency of their problem. If the severity of the voice problem is variable, the clinician may be able to identify those vocal situations in which the patient experiences the best voice and the worst voice. In some voice problems, the patient reports that the disorder varies little with either the extent of voice usage or the time of day. The typical patient with vocal hyperfunction reports a better voice earlier in the day, with increasing dysphonia the more the voice is used. For example, a high-school social-studies teacher reported a normal-sounding voice at the beginning of the day; towards the end of a day, after six hours of lecturing, he reported increasing hoarseness and a feeling of "fullness and dryness in the throat." Voice rest and then dinner at the end of the day would usually restore his voice to nearly its normal level. Obviously, such fluctuations in the daily quality of the voice enabled the clinician easily to identify the situations contributing to the patient's vocal abuse. Another patient, whose dysphonia was closely related to an allergy and postnasal drip experienced during sleep, presented this kind of variation in hoarseness: severity in the morning upon awakening, decrease in severity with usage of the voice, complete disappearance by late afternoon, and severity again the next morning.

The variation of the voice problem can provide even more specific clues as to what situations most aggravate the disorder. A night-club singer reported that she had no voice problem during the day in conversational situations or while practicing her repertoire. She would develop hoarseness only at night, and only on those nights she sang. Further investigation of her singing act revealed that the adverse factors were the cigarette smoke around her, to which she was unusually sensitive, and the noise of the crowd, above which she had to increase her loudness level in order to be heard. Her singing methods were found to be satisfactory. A change of jobs to a summer-tent theater provided her with immediate, but temporary, relief.

Voice patients themselves can often isolate the particular situations in which their voice problems are heightened. Wolpe (*171*) and Rachman (*136*), in their use of *desensitization therapy,* asked patients with various adjustment problems to attempt to identify a hierarchy of situations in which they felt no tension, little tension, more tension, and so on, to extreme tension. In desensitization therapy, the patient starts out by using desirable behavior in the created "no tension" situation, and then attempts deliberately to create varying degrees of tense situations, at the same time maintaining the desirable behavior. The same approach is useful with some voice patients. First, the clinician tries to identify those situations in which the patient experiences a normal voice; next, a hierarchy of situations is determined in which the patient experiences increasing amounts of dysphonia; finally, the information thus gleaned is used therapeutically, with the patient attempting to maintain the "good" voice during successive episodes of recreated anxious moments. The voice patient often easily recalls his "better" and "worse" voice situations, providing good clues for the clinician as to what situations the therapy should focus upon.

Closely related to the topic of voice consistency is the kind of daily vocal use the patient experiences. It appears that only a small amount of vocal misuse daily is required to keep a vocal problem "alive" once it has developed. The mother who yells after school to her school-aged children would not have to do a lot of prolonged yelling to keep her inflamed vocal folds irritated. It is necessary for the voice patient to recall or demonstrate the kinds of phonation he uses in various daily situations if the clinician is going to uncover abusive forms of vocal behavior. Usually the office-visit voice of the patient in no way represents the kind of voice he uses in the many situations of his everyday life. In some cases it is necessary for the clinician, after identifying a possible situation of vocal abuse, to make an on-site visit to observe the patient using his voice. Often the patient can recreate his "pulpit voice" or his "auctioneer voice" in the voice clinic, but sometimes the most productive observation can be obtained only by visiting the church or the auction and observing the patient in that environment.

With children, special attention must be given to the identification of playground screaming and yelling. Here the clinician must enlist the observations of the teacher, the parents, classroom peers, etc. And a search for possible moments of voice abuse at home must also be made. Such information is a vital part of the case history for the child with dysphonia. Often the most effective voice therapy for children is the identification of abusive situations, followed by counseling and direct instruction to the child.

### ADDITIONAL CASE HISTORY INFORMATION

The case history forms of many school districts and various clinics include many other areas which may have relevance to the clinician's quest for more information about his voice patient. Of obvious importance are questions concerning previous voice problems, how they were treated (medically or by voice therapy); and, if the patient received previous voice therapy, how much and of what type was it. Possible family speech and voice problems should be explored with the patient. The general health history of the patient may be important, particularly with regard to serious past illnesses, surgical procedures, chronic conditions such as allergies, drug or hormone therapy, excessive smoking and drinking, etc.

### THE VOICE EVALUATION AND OBSERVATION OF THE PATIENT

Observation of the patient and close listening to his voice are important but often neglected parts of the voice evaluation. The beginning voice clinician often puts too little value on his own observations of the patient, giving primary importance to the medical information, case history, and his own quantifiable testing data. The clinician should value his own impressions of the client, although he must be mindful that such impressions, when conveyed to others, may be more meaningful if they describe what the patient did, rather than label the patient's behavior with terms from the clinician's own private vocabulary. For example, "The patient appeared nervous and over-controlled" is a highly personalized value judgment. The clinician could have accomplished more by writing: "John sat rigidly in his chair. He maintained an unchanging facial expression, characterized by a permanent smile and by eyes fixed on the floor." The reader (or the clinician) gets a much truer picture of John if his posturing is described rather than labeled. But even our descriptions will be strongly colored by our training and clinical background. Therefore, since some observational description of the voice patient adds to our understanding of him as an individual, these descriptions of the patient's behavior must be clearly separated from case history information and labeled "Clinician's Observations." Darley warns the clinician strongly about clinical biases:

*Beware of a priori conceptions.* The continuing occupational hazard of the clinician is letting his biases and preconceptions do his thinking for him. Each of us is prone to ride certain hobbies, to see what he wants to see, to rationalize behavior in terms of a notion he is devoted to. The scientific method abhors such slanting; it insists, rather, that one observe dispassionately, hypothesize coldly, test hypotheses disinterestedly, and accept inevitable conclusions unreservedly. [*44*, p. 9]

Since voice difficulties are often symptomatic of the patient's inability to have satisfactory interpersonal relationships, it is imperative that the clinician consider the patient's degree of adequacy as a social being. The patient who exhibits extremely sweaty palms, who avoids eye contact with the person to whom he is speaking, who uses excessive postural changes or sits with a masked, nonaffective facial expression, who exhibits obvious shortness of breath, may be displaying some of the behaviors frequently considered as symptomatic of anxiety. His struggle to maintain a conversational relationship may be accompanied by much struggle to phonate. Such observed behavior in the voice patient may be highly significant to the voice clinician as he plans a course of voice remediation. The decision on whether to treat the problem symptomatically (i.e., by voice therapy) or by improving the patient's potential for interpersonal adjustment (perhaps by psychotherapy) is often aided by a review of the observations of the patient. The patient who demonstrates friendly, normal affect is telling the clinician, at least superficially, that he functions well in a two-person relationship; such information may well have clinical relevance.

While the focus of voice analysis is on the testing phase of the voice evaluation, the clinician must make determinations of voice quality by listening to the patient talk. Once the clinican gets beyond using the word "dysphonia" and attempts to describe the voice he hears, he is in immediate difficulty. A useful illustration of the futility of describing a voice may be found in this bit of prose lifted from a patient's case history: "Mrs. _____ spoke with a breathy, almost metallic, strident voice, which at times seemed most nasal." Such a description undoubtedly had meaning to the clinician who wrote it—and, just as undoubtedly, a variety of meanings to all those who have read it since. Other dimensions than quality per se, such as loudness, pitch level, no voice at all, and nasality, lend themselves much more

FIGURE 19

---

*OBSERVATIONS OF CLIENT:*

*PHYSICAL MECHANISM:*
   *Types of Breathing Observed*
   Clavicular ___ Abdominal ___ Thoracic ___ Shortness of Breath ___
   Audible Breathing ___

   *Breath Control*
   Counts on One Breath _____ Sustains: s-s-s ___ z-z-z ___ ah ___ /i/ ___

   *Peripheral-Oral Examination*
      1. Lips:
      2. Teeth:
      3. Mandibular Movement:
      4. Hard and Soft Palate:
      5. Pharynx:
      6. Tongue: Size
                 Tonus (tremor or fasciculation)
                 Movement
                    Vertical:
                    Lateral:
                    Diadochokinesis:
   *Tension Sites*
      1. Face:
      2. Mandible:
      3. Neck:
      4. General Body:

   *Hearing Acuity*
                    Left              Right              Comments
      Air:
      Bone:

---

easily to verbal description, since their meanings are more generally agreed upon. Page three of our voice evaluation form includes some judgments on voice quality to be made by the clinician as part of his overall testing of the voice patient (fig. 20).

FIGURE 20

---

*PHONATION:*

Loudness

Normal ___ Too loud ___ Too soft ___ Varies ___

*Quality*

Breathy ___ Harsh ___ Hoarse ___ No Voice ___

Hypernasal ___ Denasal ___ Assimilative Nasality ___ Normal Resonance ___

*Related Observations*

Pitch Breaks ___ Phonation Breaks ___ Hard Glottal Attack ___ Glottal Fry ___
Spastic Dysphonia ___ Aphonia ___ Articulation Problems ___
Other:

*Pitch*

Pitch Range: Lowest Pitch ___ Highest Pitch ___ Habitual Pitch ___
Natural Optimum Pitch: (Yawn, Cough, Laugh, Uh-uh, ⅓ range) ___
Ability to Discriminate Pitch Differences:
Ability to Imitate a Sequential Pitch Pattern:
Ability to Carry a Tune:          Singing Experience:

---

CLINICAL IMPRESSIONS OF CLIENT:

---

MEDICAL DIAGNOSIS:

---

SUMMARY AND RECOMMENDATIONS:

---

                                        Examiner

---

THE VOICE EVALUATION AND TESTING OF THE PATIENT

While voice testing continues throughout the course of voice therapy, we shall consider the specific testing procedures and various kinds of test equipment that might be used at the initial visit. In no way do the following procedures represent a recommended testing battery; rather, the clinician should select from among them those that are appropriate for his assessment of the respiration, phonation, and resonance behaviors of the specific patient.

RESPIRATION TESTING

Since the vocal folds are activated for phonation by the outflowing air stream passing through the closed glottis, some observation and measurement of respiratory adequacy is a necessary part of the voice evaluation. The early phoniatrist placed much emphasis on breathing adequacy, particularly with regard to adequacy of singing; such a view has been most prominently advocated by Tarneud (*157*) and frequently cited by Luchsinger and Arnold (*101*) and Brodnitz (*24*). Most speech pathologists, but certainly not all, continue to show interest in how well the voice patient breathes, and particularly in how well he is able to extend and use his exhalation for phonation. It is commonly recognized, for example, that shortness of breath or speaking after most of the tidal breath is exhaled will have noticeable effects on phonation. We shall consider separately those instruments that can be used for measuring various aspects of respiratory movement and, finally, those observations and tests that we can use to assess the patient's use of respiration as it applies to phonation.

THE MEASUREMENT OF RESPIRATORY CAPACITY. The basic capacity dimensions which are quantifiable in respiration are: vital capacity, tidal capacity, supplemental air, and complemental air.

Many of the normal respiration values reported in chapter 2 were obtained by various investigators using either *wet spirometers* or *dry spirometers,* both of which are used to make capacity measurements (*153*). In the wet spirometer, a container floats in water placed in a larger container. As air is introduced to the smaller, floating container, it floats higher in proportion to the volume of air introduced. The distance or rise of displacement is measured in terms of cubic centimeters (cc) or liters. Typical capacity measurements using a wet spirometer obtained from a hospital respiratory-function laboratory are presented in figure 21.

Dry spirometers are usually smaller in size than wet spirometers and, according to Steer and Hanley, less "reliable and more dependent upon the force with which the breath is exhaled" (*153,* p. 183). Respiratory capacity measurements are made more frequently in the medical setting than in the speech clinic, particularly for such problems as emphysema, pneumonia, and after thoracic surgery, etc.

There appears to be little relationship between adequate respiratory capacity measures and adequacy of phonation. Obviously, for some clinical

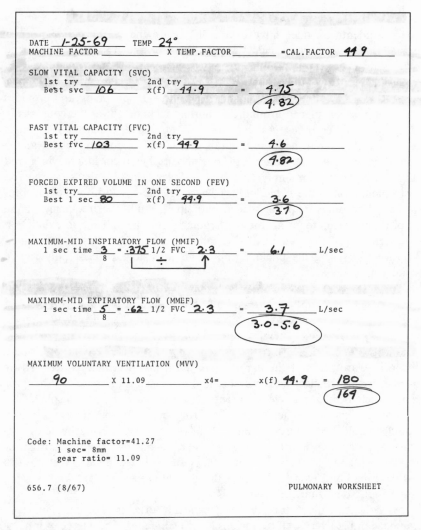

DATE _1-25-69_    TEMP _24°_
MACHINE FACTOR _____ X TEMP.FACTOR_____ =CAL.FACTOR _44 9_

SLOW VITAL CAPACITY (SVC)
    1st try_____ 2nd try_____
    Best svc _106_    x(f) _44·9_    = _4.75_
                                        _4.82_

FAST VITAL CAPACITY (FVC)
    1st try_____ 2nd try_____
    Best fvc _103_    x(f) _44.9_    = _4.6_
                                        _4.82_

FORCED EXPIRED VOLUME IN ONE SECOND (FEV)
    1st try_____ 2nd try_____
    Best 1 sec _80_    x(f) _44.9_    = _3.6_
                                         _3.7_

MAXIMUM-MID INSPIRATORY FLOW (MMIF)
    1 sec time _3_ = _.375_ 1/2 FVC _2.3_    = _6.1_    L/sec
               8

MAXIMUM-MID EXPIRATORY FLOW (MMEF)
    1 sec time _5_ = _.62_ 1/2 FVC _2.3_    = _3.7_    L/sec
               8                               _3.0-5.6_

MAXIMUM VOLUNTARY VENTILATION (MVV)
    _90_    X 11.09_____    x4=_____ x(f) _44.9_ = _180_
                                                            _169_

Code: Machine factor=41.27
      1 sec= 8mm
      gear ratio= 11.09

656.7 (8/67)                                    PULMONARY WORKSHEET

Fig. 21. A pulmonary laboratory report. The patient was tested on several spirometric devices to determine several aspects of vital capacity, inspiratory and expiratory flow rates. Such pulmonary studies are useful for patients with obvious problems in respiratory function, particularly for the emphysema patient.

patients, aberrations in breathing capacity may have a direct relationship to various voice problems. Of more clinical practicality, however, is how well the patient uses the respiratory mechanism, which can be measured by several devices recording muscle movement and various dimensions of respiration timing.

THE MEASUREMENT OF RESPIRATORY MOVEMENT AND TIMING. For many years, students of voice have been able to use the *pneumograph* for the measurement of thoracic and abdominal movements during inhalation and exhalation. The pneumograph is usually connected to a recording device, of which there are two main types, the *kymograph* and the *polygraph,* both of which provide graphic measurement write-outs. The pneumograph provides straps, which are placed around the thorax or abdomen; at the ends of the straps are rubber tubes. As the tubes are stretched, a partial vacuum is created within them, and the amount of vacuum is communicated to the recording instrument. Pictures of pneumographic recording devices and illustrative descriptions may be found in Steer's and Hanley's chapter on instrumentation in the *Handbook of Speech Pathology (153).* The pneumographic recordings help the speech pathologist study the frequency of the respiration cycle, focusing on the regularity of the inhalation-exhalation ratio. How well the patient can sustain his exhalation can be determined very well by using the pneumograph with a kymographic or polygraphic write-out.

The experimental use of the *electromyograph* (EMG) in investigating the use of particular muscles in breathing during speech has been explored in several studies reported by Hoshiko *(83),* but there has been little regular use of the electromyograph as a clinical tool for respiration assessment. Which muscle is doing what may be determined by the clinical EMG, where recordings are made of the variations in electrical potential as detected by needle or surface electrodes inserted into or placed on a muscle. Whenever that muscle becomes active (contracts), its electrical activity is displayed on a graphic write-out. The differential firing of inspiratory and expiratory muscles could be important diagnostically; however, the mechanical difficulty of implanting needle electrodes in the various overlapping muscles of respiration, and the many problems encountered in using surface electrodes (as described by Eblen [51]), make the clinical use of the EMG for assessing respiration somewhat impractical.

Movement of the thorax and the downward excursion of the diaphragm can be identified very well by various Xray techniques. The degree of inflatability, as seen by thoracic expansion and downward movement of the diaphragm, has been evaluated with convenience by *still Xray.* We have found still Xrays taken at moments of maximum inhalation and exhalation to be helpful in identifying those sites of respiration (apical versus base of lungs) which show the most deflation or inflation, providing us with knowledge as to the type of breathing the patient employs: abdominal-diaphragmatic, mid-thoracic, or clavicular. Similar information can be obtained by viewing the respiratory mechanism in action, assessing actual movement by the use of other Xray techniques, namely, *fluoroscopy* and *cinefluorography.*

THE MEASUREMENT OF RESPIRATION FUNCTION. Page two of the voice evaluation form lists several techniques for evaluating breathing adequacy (fig. 19). The type of breathing can sometimes be determined accurately by visual observation of the patient. The most inefficient type of breathing, *clavicular*, seems to be the easiest to identify. The patient elevates his shoulders on inhalation, using the neck accessory muscles as his primary muscles of inhalation. This upper chest breathing, cnaracterized by noticeable elevation of the clavicles (hence the name, clavicular breathing), is unsatisfactory for good voice for two reasons: first, the upper, apical ends of the lungs, when expanded, do not alone provide an adequate respiration, and second, the strain in using the neck accessory muscles for respiration is often visually apparent, with individual muscles "standing out" (particularly the sternocleidomastoids, as they contract to elevate the upper thorax). While there is little research evidence that clearly identifies the negative effects on speech of clavicular breathing, no serious singer would waste his time developing such a shallow, upper-lung reservoir of air. Clavicular-type breathing requires too much effort for too little breath. *Diaphragmatic-abdominal* breathing may well be the preferred method of respiration, especially if the patient has heavy vocal demands placed upon him, as in singing or acting-speaking without electronic amplification. If the patient is employing diaphragmatic-abdominal breathing, this should be noted on the voice evaluation form. This use of lower thoracic breathing is usually identifiable by the presence of abdominal and lower thoracic expansion on inhalation, with a gradual decrease in abdominal–lower thoracic prominence on exhalation. When asked to "take in" a deep breath, the patient will demonstrate, upon inhaling, a relatively active expansion of the lower thorax and little noticeable upper-chest movement. As Greene (67) points out, however, the words we use in instructing the patient may influence the type of respiration he uses: "The simple instruction to breathe in and breathe out generally produces the exact reverse of the action desired, pulling in of the abdomen on breathing in and pushing it out on breathing out" (p. 93). We can perhaps obtain a more accurate assessment of how the patient breathes for speech when we ask him to demonstrate his various voices, such as his pulpit voice, his calling-the-kids voice, his talking-to-superiors voice, etc. Diaphragmatic-abdominal breathing does seem to produce a quicker, more efficient inhalation and to provide the individual with some conscious control over the expiratory phase of the respiration, the phase most vital for speech; the quick distention of the abdominal viscera by the descending diaphragm can be followed by a conscious and volitional gradual contraction of the abdominal muscles, providing a continuous, sustained exhalation. It may well be the relatively available volitional control of the abdominal muscles which makes diaphragmatic-abdominal breathing an attractive method for singers and actors. Most voice patients exhibit breathing patterns which are somewhere in between clavicular and diaphragmatic-abdominal breathing, and for these persons we use the somewhat nondescript term, *thoracic,* on our voice evaluation form. The thoracic breather is the patient who exhibits no noticeable upper thoracic or abdominal expansion on inhalation. For the typical voice patient, *how* he breathes (clavicularly, diaphragmatic-abdominally, or thoracically) will provide the clinician with only gross clues as to the adequacy of his respiration for phonation; there are times, however, when the identification of breathing type proves useful.

The general mode of breathing can often be assessed if the clinician observes the patient closely as he speaks. *Shortness of breath* is sometimes noted, and appears more often than not to be a symptom of nervousness, perhaps a signal that the patient is uncomfortable in his two-person relationship with the clinician. There are physical causes of shortness of breath, such as emphysema or the limited vital capacity of the patient with bulbar involvement, where the patient is forced to speak in short phrases in order to accommodate to his respiratory inadequacy. Sometimes the clinician hears a *vocal tremor* which is produced by tremors of the diaphragm or thorax, usually as part of the symptomatology of some kind of neurological dysfunction, such as Parkinson's disease, amyotrophic lateral sclerosis, or multiple sclerosis. Sometimes he sees a patient who obviously *struggles to breathe* in any kind of phonatory context; the struggle may be observed visually as the patient works to speak, emitting audible gasps and sighs. Such breathing struggles should be noted as part of the evaluative description of the patient. Speaking on *residual air* is a breathing behavior we often observe. Here the voice patient does not attempt to talk until most of his tidal expiration has ended; such an inadequately produced phonation can inflict unnecessary strain on the vocal mechanism.

There are several respiration-phonation tasks we can give the patient which will provide us with some information about his efficiency in using the respiratory system for phonation. One is to *ask the patient to count as far as he can on one breath.* (Such a task is in part a measure of the speed with which the patient is able to move his articulators, particularly when he is asked to count as fast as he can in a fixed period of time, such as 10 or 15 seconds; but this is of less relevance to voice problems.) We usually provide the patient with a rate-of-count model, somewhere close to about three digits per second. The typical patient takes what he considers to be a big breath (usually elevating his shoulders), and his beginning phonation for the first few numbers will usually be more adequate in loudness and quality than his phonation for the numbers that follow. We take a measure of both how far he can count and how long in seconds he is able to count. Beyond the obtained measures—e.g., a count of 54 in a total time period of 17 seconds, for an adult—we have his total performance to evaluate. How does the patient proceed in "getting a big breath," how does he sustain his exhalation, how does he view the task (overly important, silly, etc.), and does he feel a need to try to do it again and better his scores?

Another respiration-phonation task is to ask the patient to take a breath and sustain a hissing, non-vocalized "*s-s-s*" as long as he can. The typical prepubertal child can sustain the voiceless exhalation for about 10 seconds; the average adult in the voice clinic can do so for about 20 seconds. Such a measure gives some clue as to how well the patient can sustain his exhalation independent of phonation. We then ask the patient to sustain a voiced exhalation, prolonging the /s/ cognate, *z-z-z*. The dysphonic patient without vocal fold pathology will typically be able to extend the voiceless *s-s-s* and the voiced *z-z-z* for about the same length of time. So will the normal subject. Patients with vocal fold pathology, however, such as thickening or polyps or nodules, will generally perform normally on the voiceless task, but give evidence of real difficulty in prolonging the exhalation when they add voice. Their relative time ratio will often be around two to one in favor of the unvoiced production. The problem, it would appear, is less one of respiration control than of difficulty in producing phonation. The voiceless-voiced sustained exhalation ratio is a quick, useful device in attempting to sort out how much of the phonation problem is related to poor respiration control. Further determination of the ability to sustain exhalation can be made by seeing how long the patient can sustain various vowels, such as *ah,* or how long he can read a particular passage aloud without stopping to renew his breath.

THE MEASUREMENT OF ASPECTS OF PHONATION. Of the various aspects of phonation, the pitch level of the voice is perhaps the most measurable. It is possible to measure the patient's speaking and singing range, to determine his habitual speaking pitch level, and to make some prediction about his optimum pitch level, or the speaking pitch which appears to be most compatible with his overall vocal mechanism. It should be remembered, however, that what pitch level the patient happens to use may have only a tenuous relationship to his developing and maintaining a voice problem. Of greater relevance may be how the patient uses his voice, that is, his loudness, method of glottal attack, use of vocal inflection, the amount of tension in his vocal tract, and the quality of his voice. We shall discuss separately these various phonatory usage parameters and how we test for them, following our discussion of measurement of pitch.

*The Measurement of Pitch.* In our early observation of the patient's conversation, we observe the appropriateness of his pitch level with regard to his age and sex. A general observation of "too high" or "too low" serves as a rough guide for determining which areas of pitch level will require specific testing. The third page of our voice evaluation form is concerned with observations and measurements of pitch (fig. 20). Once the general appropriateness of pitch level has been determined, attempts may be made to determine the patient's *habitual pitch level,* the fundamental frequency used most often in his everyday voice or, as Fairbanks has described it, "the central tendency of the pitches used" (*55*). Habitual pitch level will vary in different settings, depending upon such factors as the role of the speaker, etc., and must never be thought of as a fixed, static value. The pitch level the patient habitually uses in the clinic may not be the pitch level he uses in his everyday experiences elsewhere.

Perhaps the easiest and most valid method of measuring habitual pitch level is to record some conversational speech and oral reading by the patient. The initial voice recording made at the time of the patient's first clinic visit will provide a useful tool for analyzing the patient's habitual pitch level. This analysis can be made after the patient has left the clinic. One method we have used is to stop the recorder at random points and attempt to match the voice pitch level with a *pitch pipe.* After some experience with a pitch pipe, such as the type shown in figure 22, it is possible to match pitch levels between the pitch pipe frequency and the patient's voice. This feat is facilitated by remembering key pitch values for average voices; that is, in cycles per second, the typical adult male voice will be somewhere near $C_3$ (128 cps), and therefore not very different from the $C_3$ note on a pitch pipe. Using the pitch pipe, we would start at $C_3$ and then go by gradations (sharps and flats) until we got "near" the recorded level of the patient's voice. With an adult female we might select as our beginning pitch $A_4$ (213 cps) and go up or

Fig. 22. A typical one-octave pitch pipe is frequently of value to the clinician and the patient in determining pitch level as part of voice therapy.

down to match the patient's voice. A typical starting place for a prepubertal child would be middle C, C₄ (256 cps). In a two- or three-minute sample from the voice recording, we might select seven or eight voice samples for analysis of pitch level. Our fundamental frequency values will be more or less gross, depending upon our skill in using the pitch pipe, but this need not concern us, since we are only looking for relative pitch usage. After we have determined the approximate pitch of the patient's voice samples, we then count the various pitch levels and look for the *modal pitch value* (the pitch level that occurs most often), recording this as the patient's habitual pitch level. Using the modal pitch probably gives us a more valid habitual pitch than averaging the obtained sample values and using the mean.

There are instruments available which may help the clinician determine more exactly the patient's habitual pitch level. One is the *PAD Pitch Meter* (*125*), which can use any continuous tone, such as the prolonging of a vowel, and provide a fundamental frequency reading. To determine habitual pitch level, one would select representative vowels from the patient's voice recording and feeding their playback directly into the PAD Pitch Meter. This instrument sometimes focuses on a harmonic of the fundamental, giving a harmonic value on the frequency dial. The clinician should once again remember the relative appropriateness of pitch to age and sex. Should he obtain a fundamental frequency value of 256 cps for an adult male voice, he should convert this value down by one-half, to 128 cps, remembering that the harmonics are but continuous multiples of the true fundamental frequency. Since the determination of habitual pitch level requires the selection of various voice samples from connected speech, devices like the PAD Pitch Meter are somewhat cumbersome because they can only analyze selected vowels and not running speech; they are far more useful in determining pitch range and as therapeutic devices for patients working on pitch level. Probably the best instrument for extracting the fundamental frequency out of connected speech, and, therefore, ideally suited for determining the habitual pitch level, is the Fundamental Frequency Indicator (FFI) developed by Hollien and his colleagues (*78; 80*). Here, a running fundamental is extracted from the patient's connected speech sample, fed into a computer, and then analyzed and averaged into the average fundamental frequency used for that specific passage. While such a device provides the precision in fundamental frequency analysis that is vital to research and the development of our understanding of the vocal mechanism, its cost makes its clinical application at this time somewhat impractical.

The patient's *pitch range* should be determined. This may be done by asking him first to match a pitch level provided to him by the clinician. It is usually easier for the patient to match his own voice with another person's voice than to a generated pitch level from some instrument such as a piano, a pitch pipe, etc. For this reason, it is most useful to have on hand some recordings of normal voices (adult male, adult female, several children's voices) producing vowels, prolonging each vowel for about three seconds. These samples can be recorded on small cartridge tapes, discs, or on blank Language Master cards (98). On playing the sample voice, which should be "close" to the patient's observed pitch level, we ask the patient to say "ah" with the sample voice, matching it as closely as he can. This allows us to provide the patient with a model, showing him how we want him to sing down to the lowest note he can make, descending by one full note on the musical scale for each production. In our model sample, we prolong each note for about three seconds. The patient's performance should be recorded on tape, whenever possible, and the actual frequency analysis done later in the laboratory. He then attempts to sing down to the lowest note he can produce. The patient is then instructed to sing up, one full note at a time, until he reaches the highest note he can produce, including the falsetto, and then to sing down, one note at a time, until he reaches his lowest note again. Finally, when the lowest note is reached, he is asked once again to sing up to the highest note of his range. This pitch-range task is usually easiest for the patient if he is instructed to sing one note at a time, taking a breath between each three-second production. Many voice patients, and perhaps the population in general, have real difficulty in matching their own voices to a pitch model and in producing a range of their lowest to their highest pitch productions. It may be impossible for some patients with vocal fold pathology, such as nodules or polyps, to vary much the pitch of their voice. By providing various models and encouragement at the right times, the experienced voice clinician can usually obtain some pitch-range information.

Pitch-range analysis can be performed by the experienced clinician by using either the pitch pipe or the piano. Once again, instrumentation offers precise frequency information useful in plotting voice frequency range. The PAD Pitch Meter, which is designed for the analysis of the fundamental frequency of vowels, is best used in determining pitch-range values if the patient is asked to sing his "ahs" up and down the scale; the instrument provides ongoing frequency values as the patient produces the various pitches. The Purdue Pitch Meter (46), which also permits frequency analysis, gives the clinician the choice of three frequency ranges: 50–250, 100–500, and 200–1,000 cps. The best way to use the Purdue Pitch Meter for pitch-range analysis is to feed into the instrument a tape recording of the patient's pitch productions, usually vowels sung at one-note intervals up and down the scale. We have employed a version of the *stroboscope* to measure the pitch range of an individual, using the audio oscillator to generate various frequencies and asking the patient to match what he hears with his own vowel productions. Any oscillator capable of generating exact cycles-per-second gradations in the frequency range of 50 to 1,500 cps, such as the B and K Beat Frequency Oscillator (11), can be used for the patient to match his own voice productions and serve as an objective index of the patient's vocal pitch range.

For each individual, there appears to be a voice pitch level that can be produced with an economy of physical effort and energy. This relatively effortless voice production is known as *optimum pitch* and is apparently that pitch level at which the thyroarytenoids and other intrinsic muscles of the larynx can produce vocal fold adduction with only minimal muscular effort. The vibrating frequency emitted from the approximated vocal folds is directly related to the natural length and mass of the thyroarytenoids, without much lengthening or shortening. It is doubtful, however, that optimum pitch represents any exact cycles-per-second value. Optimum pitch is more often found in two or three notes somewhere at the bottom of the individual's pitch range, several notes higher than his lowest possible pitch production.

A standardized method of determining optimum pitch, described very well by Fairbanks in his *Voice and Articulation Drillbook* (*55*), is to require the subject to phonate his entire vocal range, including the falsetto, from his lowest production to his highest. The total range of full-step musical notes is then counted. For adult males, the optimum pitch level is considered to be the one located one-fourth of the way from the bottom of the total pitch range; for female adults, it might be one or two notes lower than the one-fourth level. Other writers, such as Hahn et al. (*69*), maintain that optimum pitch is determined by assessing the total pitch range, excluding falsetto, and taking the pitch value one-third of the way up from the bottom. Our experience with several patients, using both the one-fourth and the one-third method with each patient, indicates that the same note generally emerges as the optimum pitch, regardless of the method used. What is important is that most persons should avoid speaking at the very bottom of their pitch range; their phonation will feel more comfortable and sound better if they stay a few pitches higher. Speaking at a pitch level more than one-third higher from the bottom of one's total pitch range will also be tiring, and may be somewhat irritating to the listener. For each individual there does appear to be a voice pitch level that is most compatible with his physiological mechanism, and which is as easy to phonate and pleasant to listen to as any of his other pitch productions. One investigator, Thurman, found no validity to the concept of optimum pitch in normal speakers when testing pitch level by singing techniques (*159* and *160*; see also, Johnson, Darley, and Spriestersbach, *89;* and Darley, *44*). Clinically, however, it does seem to have been well demonstrated that there are pitch levels (as well as intensity levels) where the patient's voice functions best and seems to sound best.

Optimum pitch is often a useful concept in therapy. Since so many voice patients seem to have problems of vocal hyperfunction, an attempt to have the patient produce easy, relatively effortless phonations has obvious diagnostic and therapeutic implications. If the patient can produce a good voice easily, such a voice can become an immediate therapy goal. When an optimum pitch has been determined, by either the one-fourth or one-third method, the patient should be asked to produce various other vowels and words at that general pitch level. A qualitative judgment should then be made as to how the voice sounds at that level. Other validating methods of optimum pitch determination may be used, including these methods succinctly described by Murphy:

(a) the loud-sigh technique: take a deep breath and intone *ah* on expiration; (b) the grunt method: grunt *ah* or *o,* gradually prolonging the utterances until a passage is chanted at the original grunt pitch level; (c) the swollen tone technique: stop up the ears, sing *ah* or hum *m* up and down the scale until the pitch level at which the tone swells or is loudest is identified; (d) cough sonorously on an *ee* sound. [*119,* p. 95]

We might add to Murphy's list two other brief methods which aid in determining optimal pitch: ask the patient to yawn and sigh (the relaxed phonation of the sigh is often the optimum speaking pitch) and also to say "uh-huh" (this somewhat automatically produced, affimative utterance often approximates the optimum pitch level). The six methods—these two and Murphy's four—will usually yield pitch levels that are close to one another, even if not the same. It is the general pitch area, not an exact pitch value, that is important.

*Variations in pitch as a diagnostic aid.* An inappropriate pitch level may at times contribute to the development of a voice disorder. Some vocal fold pathologies, on the other hand, produce an aberration of voice pitch, often because of the weighting or increased mass-size of the involved fold(s). Many functionally produced low-pitched voices may be called "the voices of profundity." The young professional person may employ an artificially low voice to assert his authority and knowledge; a preacher may try to "hit the low ones" in his sermon; a young woman may think a low-pitched voice is more sexually attractive. Conversely, the high-pitched voice is often symptomatic of general tension and difficulties in relaxation. Or, the postmutational falsetto of the postpubertal male may be the result of serious psychological problems of identity, or may serve the patient little or not at all, persisting out of habit or set. If the patient's pitch appears uncongruous with his chronological age and sex, the clinician should first determine if the patient has the functional ability to speak at a pitch level more compatible with his overall organism. Determination of an optimum pitch should be followed by therapeutic techniques designed to establish the optimum pitch as part of the patient's regular vocal repertoire. If pitch variation is impossible, it might be the result of cord paralysis, or of certain virilizing drugs which have permanently changed the vocal folds, or of glandular-metabolic changes.

*Variations in loudness.* Some patients are observed to speak too loudly or too softly for particular vocal situations. There is no optimal loudness level for any one individual, as voice loudness will vary according to the situation in which the individual finds himself. In the evaluation session, the clinician can make a judgment about the loudness of the patient's voice. If it appears to be impossible for the patient to speak in a loud enough voice, the dysphonia may be related to vocal fold paralysis, or to increases in the mass of the folds (such as with problems of vocal nodules), or to bowed vocal folds worn out from continuous use. Soft voices may be heard also in patients who feel relatively inadequate and inferior, their softness of phonation being consistent with their overall self-image. There are some neurological disorders, such as Parkinson's disease and bulbar palsy, where the patient characteristically speaks in a voice that may be barely audible. At the other end of the spectrum, there are patients who speak with voices that may be perceived as uncomfortably loud; the deaf occasionally speak like this. Some dysphonic patients, particularly those who speak with hyperfunction, may have inappropriately loud voices as part of their total problem. Another intensity variation which may be observed at the time of the voice evaluation is the patient who speaks with little or no fluctuation in loudness, also, perhaps, with no variation in pitch. Not only is this controlled, bland method of speaking (the monotone) unappealing for the listener, but there is some evidence that such speakers expend unnecessary energy maintaining their vocal sameness.

*Variations in Vocal Fold Approximation.* One of the early diagnostic signs of a voice problem is the emergence of some kind of vocal quality disorder, such as hoarseness or breathiness. It is usually some form of *dysphonia* (the term used throughout this text for all disorders of voice quality) that signals to the patient that he has a voice problem. At the time of evaluation, the clinician should listen closely to how the patient speaks and make an attempt to describe what he hears. The verbal description of dysphonia is extremely difficult. Until the state of our art improves, the voice clinician will simply have to grope for the terms he wants to use to describe the voice he hears. Fairbanks (55) lists three quality conditions, *breathiness, harshness,* and *hoarseness,* which may well be related to difficulties in optimal approximation of the vocal folds on phonation. In breathiness, we can usually observe an audible escape of air as the approximating edges of the glottis fail to make optimum contact. Breathiness may be related to the patient's functional inability to bring his folds firmly together—he has the functional capability of firmer vocal fold approximation, but, for whatever reason, prefers speaking with the breathy voice. Sometimes the breathiness is related to growths on the folds, such as nodules or polyps, which prevent optimum adduction; or it may be the result of cord paralysis, which prevents

optimum fold adduction. Or, as Brodnitz describes the problem of hypofunction:

*Hypofunction* appears as the end-stage of prolonged hyperfunction. The bowing
of the cords denotes the weakening of the thyroarytenoid muscles. Or one sees
on phonation a gap between the cords in the posterior third, due to weakness of
the interarytenoid muscles. The voice becomes breathy because of the escape of
non-vibrating air between the imperfectly closed cords. [*24*, p. 46]

The presence or absence of breathiness should be noted at the time of the
voice evaluation.

Overadducted vocal folds may produce the deviation known as *harshness*.
The harsh voice, which sounds unpleasant, is probably related to aperiodic-
ity of the laryngeal vibration. It is frequently characterized by hard glottal
attack—the abrupt initiation of phonation heard in the "Bette Davis" type of
voice. There is a forced, "hard" quality to the voice. The patient sounds as
if he were working hard to speak. A harsh voice may be described as strident,
metallic, grating, etc., but whatever the adjective, it usually carries an
unpleasant connotation. In addition to firm vocal fold approximation and
possible hard glottal attack, the patient may speak with a closed mandible,
with his tongue retracted toward the pharynx. The pharynx itself may be in
an unusual state of hypercontraction. The general picture, then, is one of
tightness and hypertonicity. If such a patient is observed at the time of the
initial evaluation, the clinician should attempt to describe what he sees
and hears. This description of a patient with a harsh voice tells us far more
than the label "harsh" ever could:

Mr. T. speaks relatively rapidly. However, each word seems to stand out as a
separate entity, as he uses almost a staccato phonation with abrupt initiation of
tone. He appears to speak at the bottom of his total pitch range and at an inappropriately loud level. His overall voice resonance appears to be somewhat
nasopharyngeal in focus.

More often than not, voices described as harsh have the same characteristics as those described above: hard glottal attack, low voice pitch, inappropriate voice loudness, harsh nasal resonance.

Perhaps the most common dysphonia is *hoarseness*. Anything that interferes with optimum vocal fold adduction can produce the symptom of
hoarseness. Many patients exhibit it on a purely functional basis; that is,
because they approximate the vocal folds too tightly or too loosely together,
they produce hoarseness. Darley writes that "hoarse voice quality combines
the acoustic characteristics of harshness and breathiness and usually results
from laryngeal pathology" (*44*, p. 57). The typical dysphonic patient dis-
plays the kind of hoarseness we hear in the patient who has some form of

laryngitis. The hoarse voice heard in the patient with bilateral vocal nodules includes a breathy escape of air, and is often accompanied by hard glottal attack as the patient attempts to compensate for his phonation difficulties. This patient clearly demonstrates the validity of Darley's statement that hoarseness combines the acoustic characteristics of harshness and breathiness. Moore, in his chapter on organic voice disorders in the *Handbook of Speech Pathology* (*113*), differentiates between three types of hoarseness: (1) *dry,* characterized by relatively loud breathiness; (2) *wet,* similar to the voice we hear in laryngitis; and (3) *rough,* a complex vocal disorder characterized by two voice pitches produced simultaneously. Fairbanks writes of hoarseness:

The harsh element predominates in some hoarse voices, the breathy element in others, and the same kinds of variations may be heard within a given voice. Most hoarse speakers, in fact, have periods of simple harshness and breathiness. [*55*, pp. 182–183]

It should be possible to make a judgment of hoarseness at the time of the evaluation, and to relate the judgment to conditions of harshness and breathiness. A notation that wet hoarseness has been observed would imply that the patient has the typical kind of hoarseness, the kind we often hear in persons with infectious laryngitis. It would appear that the poorer the degree of vocal fold approximation, the greater the probability that the patient will have a quality voice disorder: breathiness, harshness, or hoarseness. Contributing to any diagnostic observation on voice quality would be, of course, some analysis of vocal resonance, which will be described in chapter 9.

Other variations in vocal fold approximation may produce symptoms of *glottal fry, register variations, pitch breaks,* and *phonation breaks. Glottal fry* is a lot easier to hear than to describe. Cleeland (*32*), in an unpublished dissertation on glottal fry, described the fry as a rhythmic beating, scraping noise. The phenomenon of fry is usually observed as a slight hoarseness that comes into the individual's voice toward the bottom of his pitch range. It has been described as sounding like an outboard motor boat, a creaking door, popcorn popping, etc. Moore and von Leden (*114*) termed glottal fry "dicrotic dysphonia." Others have described the vocal folds during the production of fry as thick, with the ventricular bands in close contact with the superior surface of the true vocal folds. It is undoubtedly this thickness of folds which produces the lower fundamental pitch that usually accompanies glottal fry. With some elevation of voice pitch, the fry will often decrease. By asking the patient to speak at a slightly higher voice pitch, the glottal fry will sometimes disappear. In fact, we frequently observe glottal fry in the patient who is attempting to add a little authority to his voice, speaking at the bottom of his pitch range and using the fry as an additional component of authority and maturity.

*Register variations,* rarely mentioned in American speech pathology texts, do appear to exist as clinical problems in some voice patients. The concept of vocal register comes from the organ stop, which in German is called "register." Luchsinger and Arnold write this on the subject of register:

In chest voice, the cords vibrate over their entire breadth, whereas the falsetto voice reveals vibration limited to the inner cord margins. When phonating low tones, the cords appear rounded, full, and relaxed, while they are sharp-edged, thin, and taut for falsetto tones. These differences may readily be seen on frontal laryngeal tomograms. [*101*, p. 97]

Occasionally we observe voices that seem incompatible with the resonating bodies of the patient. Certain patients may produce variations by attempting to speak at their lower pitches with vocal folds approximated in the manner typical of high-pitched head register. Conversely, sometimes higher pitches are produced with the folds approximated in their fullest broad dimension, the typical pattern of the low-pitched chest register. Register variation (fold approximation incompatible with the desired pitch level) can best be confirmed by frontal X ray of the approximating glottal surfaces, as seen in frontal tomograms. Typical tomographic configurations for varying registers were seen in figure 13 (chapter 2).

When *pitch break* is observed, it is usually in a voice that is pitched too low. As the patient is phonating, his pitch level will suddenly break upward to a falsetto level, often exactly one octave above the pitch level he was using. Pitch breaks may be observed in a voice pitched too high, also, and the break then is downward, usually a full octave below the previous pitch level. In an adult patient, voice breaks can be extremely embarrassing. Sometimes the pitch break is the patient's primary, and perhaps sole, reason for seeking voice therapy. Pitch breaks in children are much more common, but are rarely considered to be clinical problems. Curry *(41)* found in his voice studies of adolescents that while voice breaks in males can occur in pre-puberty, they are much more common at around the age of fourteen, when rapid pubertal changes take place. In eighteen-year-olds, Curry found virtually no pitch breaks. It would appear that pitch breaks in children, particularly in males at around the time of puberty, are fairly common and usually disappear with continuing physical maturation. In adults, pitch breaks are relatively rare and appear most often to be a symptom of inappropriate habitual pitch level—too low a pitch with an involuntary pitch break upward, or too high a pitch with the break occurring downward.

The *phonation break* is a temporary loss of voice which may occur for only part of a word, a whole word, a phrase, or a sentence. The individual is phonating with no observable difficulty when suddenly he experiences a loss of voice or phonation break. Patients who experience voice breaks usually exhibit some degree of vocal hyperfunction as they speak. They work to talk. The typical patient with voice breaks may be someone who uses his voice a lot, perhaps a teacher. After prolonged speaking, he begins to experience vocal fatigue. He begins to do something to improve the sound of his voice, such as raising or lowering his voice pitch or speaking through clenched teeth. The result is increased vocal tension. Finally, while he is phonating, his vocal folds spontaneously abduct and he temporarily loses his voice. By throat clearing, coughing, swallowing water, or whatever, phonation is restored until the next phonation break. Most voice patients, even if they have occasional phonation breaks, will not exhibit this temporary voice loss during the evaluation session. Therefore, at that time the patient should be asked if he ever experiences a temporary loss of voice when he is speaking. Phonation breaks are not serious problems in themselves, but may be considered as symptomatic of an unnecessary amount of effort directed toward phonation.

*Sites of vocal hyperfunction.* The normal peripheral oral evaluation used with all speech and voice patients should be used with children and adults with voice disorders. There are many excellent, widely used texts on the systematic evaluation of parts of the speech mechanism; the reader is referred to Johnson, Darley, and Spriestersbach's *Diagnostic Methods in Speech Pathology (89)* and to Darley's *Diagnosis and Appraisal of Communication Disorders (44),* to name but two. The usual examination of the speech mechanism will check such structures as the lips, teeth, tongue, hard and soft palate, velopharyngeal closure, etc.

For the voice patient, we should add particular anatomical sites of possible hyperfunction to this check list. Beyond observing obvious problems in breathing, some attention should be given to the amount of *neck tension.* The accessory neck muscles and the supralaryngeal strap muscles in some patients literally stick out as the patient speaks. Often closely associated with neck tension is *mandibular restriction,* where the patient speaks with clenched teeth, with little or no mandibular movement. Such restricted jaw movement places most of the burden of speech articulation on the tongue, which, to produce the various vowels and diphthongs in connected speech, must make fantastic adjustments if no cavity-shaping assistance from the mandible is forthcoming. As we shall see in the next chapter on therapy, mandibular restriction greatly increases the overall tension in the vocal tract. Reduction of this speaking-through-clenched-teeth by, say, the chewing method of therapy has been found to be an effective therapeutic approach to the reduction of such hyperfunctional voice problems as vocal nodules. Another externally observable hyperfunction of the vocal tract is unusual *downward* or *upward* excursion of the larynx during the production of various pitches. Any unusual movement upward while phonating higher pitches, or unusual movement downward while phonating lower ones, should be noted. The *angle of the thyroid cartilage* may be digitally felt as the patient sings a number of varying pitches; typically the fingertips will feel little discernible change in thyroid angle as the patient sings up and down the scale. Sometimes, however, the thyroid cartilage can be felt to rock forward slightly in the production of high pitches, as it sweeps upward to a higher position toward the hyoid bone. Any really noticeable amount of lifting or lowering of the larynx, as well as the tipping forward of the thyroid cartilage in the production of high pitches, should be noted as possible hyperfunctional behavior.

It is more difficult to observe hyperfunctional vocal behavior within the pharynx and oral cavity themselves. To determine tongue position in relation to the pharynx and the velum with any degree of accuracy, we probably have to depend on lateral view cineradiography. Or, after an acoustical analysis of the voice, we can perhaps use spectrographic analysis to make inferences about what parts of the vocal tract contribute to the resonance patterns being studied. By use of both cinefluorography and spectrographic analyses, Boone (*19*) and others (*38, 106, 158*) found that deaf children in general seem to retract their tongues posteriorly, creating alterations of vocal resonance. It would appear that during moments of tension, some individuals talk with the tongue retracted unnecessarily toward the pharynx, sometimes creating *cul de sac* pharyngeal resonance (a resonance of the voice that appears to have a pharyngeal focus). Other patients may be observed to create by tongue retraction an acoustic "bottleneck" in the pharynx, which absorbs and mutes the laryngeal tone in such a manner that the voice lacks little supralaryngeal resonance, suffering in both quality and loudness. In these patients with tongue retraction (usually functional in origin), when the patient is asked to open his mouth wide and phonate an /a/, consistent with the standard doctor's office procedure, the tongue is seen to retract severely under the uvula, often occluding completely any possible view of the pharynx. Such obvious tongue retraction may be one of the things the patient is doing unnecessarily, adding tension and effort to the total functioning of the vocal tract. In our discussion of clinical problems of resonance in chapter 9, we shall describe various velopharyngeal posturings which may serve as further hyperfunctional behaviors.

## THE MEASUREMENT OF RESONANCE

One of the most common disorders seen by the speech pathologist is some deviation from expected voice resonance. Sometimes there is excessive nasal resonance, *hypernasality*. Sometimes the normal nasal resonance for the nasal phonemes /m/, /n/, and /ŋ/ may be lacking; this is *denasality*. Or the patient's nasality may be excessive only for that voice signal which is immediately adjacent to one of the nasal phonemes, which is *assimilative nasality*. Sometimes consonant distortion may be heard in the air stream escaping from the nasal cavities during the subject's production of certain high-pressure consonants, and such airflow distortion is known as *nasal emission* or *nasal escape*. The behavioral distinctions between these alterations of nasality will be discussed in chapter 7, and to prevent duplication of description, we shall defer our discussion of resonance-measuring instruments and techniques until that chapter.

### SUMMARY

The voice evaluation is the necessary beginning of all voice therapy. Moreover, it continues as a part of every therapy session as the voice clinician searches for new vocal behaviors that the patient may be able to employ in his quest for a better, more efficient voice. Voice therapy is deferred until the patient's laryngeal mechanism and related structures have been evaluated by the physician. Another prerequisite for voice therapy is that the speech pathologist get to know the voice patient as a person. He should be thoroughly familiar with the patient's feelings about his voice problem, when he thinks it started, what he thinks caused it, when he thinks his voice is better, etc. The speech pathologist must make observational judgments on the adequacy of the patient's respiratory, phonatory, and resonance behaviors. By using various instruments and testing techniques, he must make measurements which will add to the knowledge of how well the patient uses his various vocal mechanisms. When all this information has been assembled, the speech pathologist attempts to derive from it a valid impression of what the patient may be doing to contribute to his voice problem. If any harmful vocal behaviors are identified, the pathologist will attempt to eliminate or reduce them through therapy. From the initial evaluation, an actual plan of therapy may evolve. Or additional evaluational procedures may be required. Or it may be decided that the patient should be referred to another type of professional person—a plastic surgeon, say, or a psychiatrist. Finally, the speech pathologist must establish some target dates for improvement and some target vocal behaviors to serve as realistic goals for the patient.

# chapter five

# Voice Therapy for Problems of Vocal Hyperfunction

Many voice problems are related to vocal hyperfunction, that is, to the patient's using too much force and tension while speaking or singing. Most of them are attended by an inappropriate approximation of the vocal folds and inappropriate changes in the mass and size of the folds. Voice therapy requires of the clinician continuous searching for those vocal behaviors the patient can produce with relatively little effort. These basic "can do" vocal behaviors of the patient then serve as target models in the patient's therapy. Twenty techniques are described which may be applied in this search for good "can do" vocal behaviors.

In the many voice problems related to vocal hyperfunction, the patient, usually over a period of time, uses the vocal mechanisms (respiration, phonation, resonation) in a forceful, tense manner, eventually producing some form of dysphonia. This dysphonia may be related wholly to functional misuse with no structural change of the mechanism, or perhaps, after prolonged functional misuse, actual tissue change will occur. No matter what the basis of the dysphonia, functional or organic, there is little difference in the kind of voice therapy indicated.

The voice therapy we would use with a child with a functionally dysphonic voice would not vary in kind from the voice therapy we would recommend for a child with bilateral vocal nodules. Many adult problems of dysphonia and vocal fatigue demonstrate no structural change of the laryngeal mechanism, either as a cause of the problem or as a result. Functional voice problems usually respond to the same techniques of voice therapy as dysphonias related to cord thickening, vocal nodules, polyps, contact ulcers, etc. A differential therapy approach—i.e., a certain method for nodules, a different one for polyps—is not needed for each voice disorder. Rather, our therapy might be more effective and relevant if, after analyzing the voice disorder along the dimensions of pitch, loudness, and quality, we then applied a therapy appropriate to those dimensions.

It would be easy, and very wrong, to identify for the patient the various things he is doing wrong vocally and then provide him with a series of specific remedial therapy techniques. Rather, the voice therapist must continually search for the patient's best and most appropriate voice production. This searching is necessary because so much of our vocal behavior is highly automatic, particularly the dimensions of pitch and quality. The patient cannot volitionally break vocalization down into various components and then hope to combine them into some ideal phonation. Our therapy techniques are primarily vehicles of facilitation; that is, we try a particular therapy approach and see if it facilitates the production of a better voice. If it does, then we utilize it as therapy practice material. If it does not, we quickly abandon it. As part of every clinical session, we must probe and search for the patient's best voice. When an acceptable production is achieved, we use it as the patient's target model in therapy. The patient's own best voice becomes his goal. This requires, of course, the continuous use of auditory playback equipment, such as a tape recorder, a Language Master (*98*), a Phonic Mirror (*132*), an Echorder (*52*), or a similar feedback loop tape device. It would appear, then, that voice therapy for hyperfunctional voice problems is basically the search for the patient's own best voice, a voice essentially free from unnecessary force and strain. Once this comparatively effortless voice is achieved, the therapy focuses on techniques to facilitate its production. This search is best illustrated by the following case history of a 41-year-old man who was successfully treated by voice therapy for a problem of contact ulcers.

Mr. F., aged 41, was a successful plant manager, happily married and the father of three children. At the time of the voice evaluation, he was found to have a one-year history of recurring dysphonia, with particularly aggravating pitch breaks while speaking before various management groups. On mirror laryngoscopy, he was found to have bilateral contact ulcers on both vocal processes, "surrounded by injected, edematous tissue." Prominent findings at the voice evaluation were that the patient spoke very near the bottom of his tested voice range ($G_2$ to $G_4$), with his habitual pitch at $B_3$. At the $B_3$ level he experienced frequent one-octave pitch breaks and much glottal fry. The voice clinician also thought that the patient spoke with a noticeable hard glottal attack and with excessive mandibular restriction. From his interview, the examiner attached some significance to the patient's statement that a colleague at work had a beautiful deep voice and that "ever since he's worked with me I've tried to deepen my own voice to get a voice like his." Subsequent voice therapy quickly revealed that when the patient spoke at a slightly higher pitch level ($D_3$), his pitch breaks and glottal fry disappeared. By using a pitch pipe as a cue, this patient was able to reestablish rather quickly a slightly higher pitch level that apparently caused him far less vocal strain. Attempts at overall relaxation and some work on breath control quickly proved to be nonproductive. At his third therapy visit the patient was introduced to the chewing method, as outlined by Brodnitz and Froeschels (26), and this resulted in a reduction of his hard glottal attack and a natural increase in his mandibular movement. The chewing method and a slight elevation of pitch level, the only therapy techniques practiced by this patient, both produced an easier mode of phonation and noticeably improved the sound of his voice. The balance of his sixteen voice therapy sessions (twice a week for eight weeks) was devoted to laboratory practice in using the higher pitch level and chewing; some exploration was done on the patient's attitudes towards himself, his family, and his work, with the patient giving ample evidence of relative psychological health. Mirror laryngoscopy eight weeks after his original evaluation found him to be free of contact ulcers and further signs of irritation on both vocal processes.

Talking at a slightly higher pitch level with some use of the chewing method produced for this patient a good-sounding, easily produced voice and subsequently eliminated his contact ulcers. Many of the traditional approaches in voice therapy for contact ulcers (Peacher, G. and Holinger [129], Peacher, G. M. [127], and Baker [12]) offered therapy techniques which could have been tried with this patient. In analyzing what the man was doing, however, it appeared that his problem was less one of contact ulcers per se than of vocal fold mass/size (his low habitual pitch) and vocal fold approximation (his hard contact), with the contact ulcers a natural consequence of the mass-approximation problem. The clinician selected beginning exploratory techniques that have been found useful with mass and approximation problems, and, indeed, some slight manipulation of habitual pitch apparently enabled the patient to use his vocal folds more optimally, while the chewing approach helped him approximate his folds with less posterior slamming of the vocal processes. The selection of what to do in voice therapy with any particular patient is related to what *the patient is doing* and what we can give him to do to produce a "good" voice.

Before detailing particular voice therapy approaches which are helpful in making pitch levels more natural, altering loudness of voice, and improving overall quality, we must describe differences in therapy approaches to young children and adolescents-adults.

## VOICE THERAPY FOR YOUNG CHILDREN

The public-school speech clinician probably encounters more children with hyperfunctional voice problems than any other voice specialist. Sometimes she finds children with various dysphonias in her school screening program; sometimes they are referred to her by concerned parents and teachers. As emphasized in the last chapter, before providing any child with voice therapy, she must first secure a medical evaluation of the child's vocal apparatus, preferably by a laryngologist. This information will guide her in her voice therapy attempts. Cord thickening and vocal nodules are the most common laryngoscopic findings in children with dysphonia related to vocal hyperfunction. Many children, of course, despite their dysphonias, are free of any laryngeal pathology, including that large group of boys, 10 to 13 years of age, who undergo the prepubertal laryngeal changes that may produce hoarse, husky voices. With regard to voice therapy for children's vocal problems resulting from nodules, Wilson (*168*) has written that considerable improvement may be achieved in a three-to-six-month period by focusing on reducing intensity of voice, reducing vocal abuse, and lowering the habitual pitch level.

Probably there is no more effective thing the clinician can do than isolate for the child those situations in which he is vocally abusive, such as yelling at a ball game, screaming in the playground, crying, imitating noises below or above his speaking pitch range, etc. Many children maintain their vocal pathologies simply by engaging in abusive vocal behavior for just brief periods each day. The old adage, "a little vocal abuse each day will keep a voice problem alive," is particularly relevant to the voice problems of children. It is usually not possible to identify these vocal abuses through interview methods or by observing the child in the therapy room; rather, the child must be observed in various play settings, in the classroom, and at home. This need for extensive observation requires that the clinician solicit the help of the child himself to determine where he might be yelling or screaming. The teacher will provide some helpful clues about the child's vocal behavior both on the playground and in the classroom. A meeting with parents will often reveal further situations of vocal abuse, and the parents may be asked to listen over a period of time for abusive vocal behavior in the child's play or in his interaction with various family members. At times, we have had good luck in using the child's siblings or peers to help us determine what the child may be doing vocally in certain situations.

Once the abusive situations are isolated, the clinician should obtain baseline measurements of the number of times the vocal abuse is observed in a particular time unit (an hour, a recess period, a day, etc). Figure 23 shows a vocal abuse graph plotting the number of abuses the child himself has recorded over a period of two weeks.

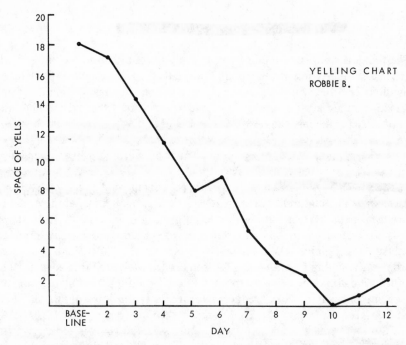

Fig. 23. An eleven year old boy was found at the time of his voice evaluation to do a lot of screaming and yelling. He was asked to count each day the number of times he found himself yelling. Fig. 23 charts the boy's daily tally of his yelling over a 12 day period. On the first day a baseline count of 18 yells was tallied. The general overall contour of the curve shows a marked decrement in the amount of yelling he recorded.

You will notice that the first plot on the abcissa is the first day's baseline measurement, which tells on the ordinate how many times the child caught himself yelling on that particular day—for this child, 18 separate yells. The overall contour shows a linear decrement in voice yelling, which is a somewhat typical curve for young children. Having to monitor his offensive behavior seems to motivate the child to reduce it. In his pocket he may keep a tally card on which he marks down each occurrence; at the end of the day, he tallies that day's occurrences and plots the total figure on his graph. The review of the plotting graph is a vital part of the therapy, and the child's pride in his graph (which will usually show a decrement in the behavior) helps him continue to curb the vocal abuse. Some children require assistance in making this kind of plot, and sometimes we ask the teacher, the parents, or a friend to also keep a tally card, recording the number of events they observed in a particular time period. It appears that if the child is given a proper orientation to the task and clearly knows why he must cut down his number of vocal abuses, his tally counts are higher, and perhaps more valid, than the counts of the external observers.

This tally method is a prominent part of voice therapy with children and cannot be underestimated for its importance in eliminating vocal abuse. If it is successful, often no other form of therapy is needed.

An important prelude to the tally method—indeed to any form of speech therapy, particularly voice therapy—is for the clinician to explain to the child what his problem is, what he seems to be doing wrong vocally, and what can be done about it. Obviously, the child must first know he has a voice problem (rarely does a child recognize such a problem independently) before he can develop any awareness of it or do anything about it. This explanation to the child is especially important when we remember that most children with voice problems are not self-referred. Their dysphonia has been discovered by someone else. To the child, there may be no problem. The clinician who uncovers a voice problem often has to do a selling job, not only to the child, but possibly to the parents, the teacher, the school nurse, and her supervisor. What must be sold is basically this: the child appears to have a dysphonia not typical for his age and sex, and he should be examined by a laryngologist.

Voice therapy is a highly individualized endeavor and does not lend itself well to group therapy. The public-school clinician who may work primarily with groups may not be in a position to help the child with a voice problem. Since the child's own best voice production is frequently the goal in therapy, grouping may well confuse the children, each of whom will have a different target in mind. If possible, the child with a voice problem should be seen individually for several sessions a week, each session being 20 to 40 minutes long. The clinician must be allowed some flexibility of schedule if she is to identify and quantify the number of vocal abuses the child is making.

Since it is difficult to define clearly the vocal behaviors of pubertal youngsters, with their continual changes of voice, it is doubtful if voice therapy for this age group is very effective. It would appear that voice therapy here should be deferred until the physiologic changes of the larynx and vocal tract are completed. When the adolescent appears to have achieved some voice stability, voice therapy can then begin according to the usual approaches for typical vocal fold mass/approximation problems.

## VOICE THERAPY FOR ADOLESCENTS AND ADULTS

The abusive vocal behaviors of adults are likely to be far more difficult to isolate than those of children. It is the relatively rare adult voice patient whose vocal abuses are bound only to particular situations, even though the preacher or the auctioneer whose voice problems appear only on the job may indeed be excellent examples of focal abuse. Generally, the dysphonic adolescent or adult has a hyperfunctional set toward phonation. He works to talk in most situations. Sometimes his exaggerated efforts are related to a generalized feeling of tension which becomes more acute in particular settings, such as when he speaks to authority figures or when he is trying to make a favorable impression on his listeners. It is this common observation—that many people with hyperfunctional voice problems exist in a milieu of tension—that has fostered the belief among laryngologists and voice clinicians that the symptomatic treatment of the voice disorder should be avoided in favor of a more comprehensive psychological approach. Gray, England, and Mahoney (65) have described an approach which combines some elements of traditional voice therapy with an emphasis on deconditioning the patient's anxiety and tensions by using the behavioral approach of reciprocal inhibition. It is the point of view of this text that while unresolved tension and anxiety contribute to the voice problems of some voice patients, most of our patients are fully capable of producing a good, optimum voice, providing someone (the clinician) will only help them "find" it.

Therefore, the primary task of the voice clinician is to explore with the patient the various therapy techniques which might produce that "good" voice. Once the patient is able to produce a model of his own best voice, this model and the techniques used to achieve it become the primary focus of the voice therapy. To be sure, the voice clinician also provides the patient with needed psychological support, and together they explore various facilitating techniques to be used in particular situations. Borrowing from the work of Wolpe (171) and of Gray and his associates (65), efforts are made to have the patient isolate those hierarchies of stress in which his phonation varies.

The voice clinician has an advantage in working with adolescents and adults in that most of them are self-referred and, at least to that extent, motivated to succeed. The average patient experiences some form of dysphonia for several months before seeking professional help from his physician or from the laryngologist to whom he has been referred. The physician, in turn, usually refers the patient to a speech pathologist. If the patient is disturbed enough by his voice problems he will seek help. In voice therapy, as in psychotherapy, if the problem makes the patient miserable enough, his motivation usually will be sufficient to enable him to participate in the therapy very well.

The average patient with a hyperfunctional voice problem will respond well to symptomatic voice therapy (4; 24; 67; 101; 119; 162; 169). The clinician should analyze what the patient is doing with regard to vocal fold mass/size and vocal fold approximation, relating these observations to the acoustic dimensions of loudness, pitch, and quality. Loudness disorders are usually characterized by voices which are too weak to be heard or inappropriately loud. Many problems of inadequate loudness are directly related to the patient's self-image, mirroring rather closely his inner psychic state. However, such patients sometimes respond well to respiration exercises designed to increase subglottal air pressure for relatively short verbal units;

by expending greater breath for short verbal segments, they can add considerably to their loudness. Some loudness problems may be related to inadequate vocal fold adduction and approximation, where much subglottal air pressure is wasted. We shall discuss several techniques which facilitate more optimum vocal fold approximation, which in turn helps produce more adequate loudness. Pitch problems are usually directly related to faulty mass/size adjustments of the vocal folds, although some pitch problems are the result of additive tissue to the vocal folds, a consequence of such problems as vocal nodules, polyps, cord thickening, etc. We shall also consider techniques which help the patient establish appropriate vocal pitch levels. Quality problems, always difficult to define, appear to be those departures in total voice sound that distinguish the patient from the normal speaker. Such voices may be described variously as hoarse, husky, breathy, harsh, etc. These quality problems are generally related to problems in fold approximation. Of the twenty facilitating techniques discussed below, many will be applicable to quality problems; that is, the technique will produce for the patient a good target voice. Once that voice is produced, it is the clinician's task to see that the patient practices the facilitating technique with some frequency, so that the target voice will be produced repeatedly. The best voice therapy appears to be to practice, under various conditions, the best voice one is able to produce.

## VOICE THERAPY FACILITATING TECHNIQUES

In the voice clinician's attempt to aid the patient in finding and using his best voice production, it is necessary to probe continually within the patient's existing vocal repertoire to find that one voice which sounds "good" and which he is able to produce with relatively little effort. A *voice therapy facilitating technique* is that technique, which, when used by a particular patient, enables him easily to produce a good voice. Once discovered, the facilitating technique and the resulting phonation become the symptomatic focus of therapy. After the patient has achieved a voice production that approximates the target model (the therapy goal), he requires systematic practice in using that phonation. This use of a facilitating technique to produce a good phonation is the core of what we do in symptomatic voice therapy for the reduction of hyperfunctional voice disorders. Such an approach involves the continuous search for "can do" vocal behaviors in each particular patient. What may work (or facilitate) for one person may well not work for another. While the clinician should be familiar with a number of voice facilitating techniques and know how to use them, his search for what works and what does not should not be based on arbitrary trial and error. Rather, each technique should be evaluated in terms of its possible effect on vocal fold mass/size and approximation as observed in changes of voice loudness, pitch, and quality. Figure 24 lists twenty facilitating techniques which have been found

FIGURE 24. TWENTY FACILITATING APPROACHES IN VOICE THERAPY

| Facilitating Approach | Phonatory Process Affected | | Parameter of Voice Affected | | |
|---|---|---|---|---|---|
| | Mass/Size | Approxi- mation | Loudness | Pitch | Quality |
| 1. Altering Tongue Position | | X* | | | X |
| 2. Change of Loudness | | X | X | X | X |
| 3. Chewing Approach | X | X | X | X | X |
| 4. Digital Manipulation | X | | | X | |
| 5. Ear Training | X | X | X | X | X |
| 6. Elimination of Abuses | X | X | | X | X |
| 7. Elimination of Hard Glottal Attack | | X | X | | X |
| 8. Establish New Pitch | X | | | X | |
| 9. Explanation of Problem | X | X | X | X | X |
| 10. Feedback | X | X | X | X | X |
| 11. Hierarchy Analysis | X | X | X | X | X |
| 12. Negative Practice | X | X | X | X | X |
| 13. Open Mouth Approach | X | X | X | X | X |
| 14. Pitch Inflections | X | | | X | X | X |
| 15. Pushing Approach | | X | X | | X |
| 16. Relaxation | X | X | X | X | X |
| 17. Respiration Training | | X | X | | X |
| 18. Target Voice Models | X | X | X | X | X |
| 19. Voice Rest | X | | | | X |
| 20. Yawn-Sigh Approach | X | X | X | X | X |

*"X" indicates the particular Facilitating Approach effective for that particular Phonatory Process or Parameter of Voice.

useful in producing easier phonation in children and adults with hyper-functional voice problems.

It should be noted that some techniques are applicable for facilitating both mass/size changes and approximation of the vocal folds. Others appear to be used primarily for promoting mass/size changes, and still others primarily for better vocal fold approximation. Similarly, certain approaches have greater facilitating effects on loudness, others on pitch, and others on quality. Some techniques, such as number 20 (the yawn-sigh approach), appear applicable to most problems. Many techniques may be used in combination with one another, and the basic rule of application (when to apply) is to use that approach which works best with the individual patient.

For each of the twenty techniques which follow, the reader will find these areas developed:

A. Kinds of problems for which the approach is useful
B. Procedural aspects of the approach
C. Typical case history showing utilization of the approach
D. Evaluation of the approach

## I. ALTERING TONGUE POSITION

*A. Kinds of problems for which approach is useful.* The position of the tongue within the mouth and pharynx is a primary shaping factor of resonance. The distinguishing characteristics of vowels and consonants are produced by tongue positioning, and any group of people speaking the same language will make basically the same tongue movements; that is, if one's vowels or consonants are to be intelligible to his listeners, he must make them in the same way the listeners do. In the faulty positioning of tongue that contributes to voice disorders, it is not the individual phoneme placement that is in error, but the overall carriage of the tongue. Some patients carry the tongue backward, almost occluding the pharynx, which contributes to a hollow-sounding *cul de sac* resonance; the focus of the voice appears to be pharyngeal. I have pointed out elsewhere (*19*, p. 691) that "deaf boys and girls, regardless of age, have a tendency for a pharyngeal focus in their vocal resonance." Some voice patients retract their tongues into the pharynx during moments of tension, reporting problem voices only at these times. Other patients have the opposite problem, carrying their tongues too far forward, creating what Fisher (*57*) describes as a "thin quality." This is the baby-talk voice; lacking the full resonance of back vowels, it sounds immature or pathologically meek and submissive. Both the muffled voice with posterior resonance focus and the weak, thin voice with anterior carriage can sometimes be favorably improved by direct work in modifying tongue position.

*B. Procedural aspects of approach*

1. For the patient with posterior tongue carriage, these activities will help promote a more forward tongue positioning:

*a.* Preface any exercises with a discussion and demonstration of pharyngeal tongue positioning and its effect on voice. Check the posture of the patient and be sure that the chin is neither tucked in toward the chest nor excessively extended.

*b.* Begin practice with the whispered production of tongue tip–alveolar consonants, such as /t/, /d/, /s/, and /z/. Require that the patient whisper a rapid series of "ta" sounds, perhaps ten per breath. After several minutes of using "ta," go on to the next front-of-the-mouth phoneme. Each practice series of several minutes should be followed by some analysis with the patient of what he just did, e.g., "What does the front-of-the-mouth production feel like?" Keep the early practice confined to whispered productions. Other front consonants which lend themselves well to practice are: /w/, /wh/, /p/, /b/, /f/, /v/, /θ/, /ð/, and /l/. The following vowels have a relatively high oral focus and lend themselves well to joint practice with the above consonants: /i/, /I/, /e/, /ɛ/, and /æ/.

*c.* After some success with whispered productions, add voice lightly. Select for oral reading those exercises that are heavily loaded with tongue-tip consonants and front vowels. Practice contrasting this new front resonance with the old posterior resonance. On recorded playback, listen to the difference critically; evaluate the difference in the "feeling" of the two productions.

2. For excessive anterior carriage of the tongue, these activities will help develop a more normal tongue position:

*a.* After explaining the problem, determine whether the patient is using an appropriate pitch level (often he is not).

*b.* Instruct the patient that he does not have to shape his tongue in any particular way. By saying the back vowels aloud in as full a voice as he can, he has usually already brought the tongue back to where it should be. These vowels should be practiced first in isolation, with some effort given to sustaining each one for a period of about five seconds: /a/,/ɔ/,/o/,/ʊ/, and /u/.

*c.* Practice the reading of materials heavy with the back consonants /k/ and /g/, and heavy also with the back vowels. When the patient has achieved some success in posterior productions, ask him to contrast the old method of speaking with the new, perhaps using both methods for each work or phrase read aloud. Spend some time listening to the two and discussing the difference in sound and feeling between them.

*C. Typical case history showing utilization of approach.* F. D., a 27-year-old male teacher, found himself in situations where his voice would become muffled and almost inaudible. The voice evaluation found him to have a normal larynx and a "tendency to withdraw his tongue posteriorly into the pharynx during moments of stress." By using hierarchy analysis, facilitating technique XI, he was able to identify those situations which produced the most stress—situations in which he would almost reflexively draw his tongue back in his pharynx. The patient was taught to alter his tongue carriage to a more anterior position by practicing, in whispers, front-of-the-mouth consonants and vowels. He then practiced using this anterior tongue carriage in various situations in the hierarchy of stress, maintaining optimum tongue position with good voice production in increasingly tense situations. The patient maintained this success in most situations; he reported that only occasional situations, such as speaking up at a teacher's union meeting, were characterized by the old voice.

*D. Evaluation of approach.* Many voice patients appear to develop faulty tongue positioning as part of their overall problem of dysphonia. Altering the main carriage of the tongue, whether it be excessively posterior or anterior, can be achieved to some degree by most patients. A slight alteration of position toward a more normal carriage usually has a profound influence in improving the quality and resonance of the voice. It would appear that proper positioning of the tongue enables the oral resonance cavities to function more naturally in their amplification of the laryngeally produced fundamental frequency. The relatively normal positioning of tongue appears to be an important component of a normal voice.

## II. CHANGE OF LOUDNESS

*A. Kinds of problems for which approach is useful.* Some patients have voices that are either too soft or too loud. The prolonged use of inappropriate loudness levels can result in organic pathologies of the vocal folds, such as nodules or polyps. Many of the vocal pathologies of children are related to such excesses of loudness as screaming and yelling. Weak, soft voices may develop as a consequence of the prolonged hyperfunctional use of the vocal mechanism that results in the eventual breakdown of glottal approximation surfaces, e.g., the patient with vocal nodules who loses much air flow around the nodules and is unable to produce an intense enough vocal fold vibration to achieve a sufficiently loud voice. Some speaking environments require a loud voice, and the untrained speaker or singer may push for loudness at the level of the larynx rather than adjust his respiration. Inappropriate loudness of voice is most often not the primary causative factor of a voice problem, but rather a secondary, if annoying, symptom. Reducing or increasing the loudness of the voice lends itself well to direct symptom modification through exercise and practice, and often, if other facilitating techniques are being used, does not even require the use of loudness techniques per se.

*B. Procedural aspects of approach*
1. For a decrease in loudness:
   *a.* See that the patient has a thorough audiometric examination to determine adequacy of hearing before any attempt is made to reduce voice loudness. Once it has been established that the patient has normal hearing, the following steps may be taken.
   *b.* Discuss with the patient the observation that he has an inappropriately loud voice. The patient may be unaware of his loud voice, and, if this is the case, he should be asked to listen to tape-recorded samples of his speech. The best demonstration tape for loudness variations would include both the patient's voice and the clinician's, to provide contrasting levels of loudness. Then ask the patient, "Do you think your voice is louder than mine?"
   *c.* Focus on making the patient aware of his problem. Once the patient becomes aware that his voice is too loud, the clinician might ask him, "What does a loud voice in another person tell you about that person?" Loud voices are typically interpreted to mean that the speaker feels "overly confident," or "sure of himself," or that he is putting on a confident front when he's really scared, or that he is mad at the world, impressed with his own voice, trying to intimidate his listeners, etc. For the average patient, some discussion of these negative interpretations is usually sufficient to motivate him to learn to speak at normal loudness levels.
   *d.* For practice materials, have the patient read aloud at varying loudness levels from such practice sources as Akin's *And So We Speak* (*1*), Eisenson's *The Improvement of Voice and Diction* (*53*), Fairbanks's *Voice and Articulation Drillbook* (*55*), and Fisher's *Improving Voice and Articulation* (*57*). Instruct the patient to contrast loudness levels for certain words and phrases

and to listen back to tape-recorded samples of his practice reading. While most of the loudness practice procedures developed in the above references are for increasing voice loudness, the clinician can, with a little effort, adapt the materials for the purpose of decreasing loudness.

2. For an increase in loudness:

   *a.* Determine first that the inappropriate softness of the voice is not related to hearing loss, general physical weakness, or a severe personality problem; for these cases, a symptomatic approach is not indicated. The steps that follow are for voice patients who are physically and emotionally capable of speaking in a louder voice.

   *b.* Discuss with the patient his soft voice. A tape-recorded playback of the patient's and clinician's voices in conversation will usually illustrate for the patient the inadequacy of his loudness. After the patient indicates some awareness of his soft voice, the clinician might ask, "What does a soft, weak voice tell us about a person?" Inadequately loud voices are typically interpreted to mean that the speaker is afraid to speak louder, is timid and shy, is unduly considerate of others, is scared of people, has no self-confidence, etc. Some discussion of these negative interpretations is usually helpful.

   *c.* By exploring pitch level and fundamental frequency, try to achieve a pitch level at which the patient is able with some ease to produce a louder voice. If the patient habitually speaks near the bottom of his pitch range, a slight elevation of pitch level will usually be accompanied by a slight increase in loudness. Isshiki (*85*) has reported that at very low pitch levels, glottal resistance is dominant in controlling intensity, but as pitch levels rise, voice intensity is controlled almost entirely by air-flow rate. A voice pitch somewhere around one-fourth of the way from the bottom of the total range (including falsetto) will often provide a pitch level suitable for loudness practice. When the patient finds his "best" pitch level, he should practice sustaining an /a/ at that level for five seconds, concentrating on good voice quality. He should then take a deep breath and repeat the same pitch at a maximum loudness level. After some practice at this "home base" pitch level, ask the patient to sing /a/, up the scale for one octave, at one vocal production per breath; then have him go back down the scale, one note per breath, until he reaches his starting pitch.

   *d.* Explore with the patient his best pitch, i.e., the one which produces the best loudness and quality. Auditory feedback devices (such as loop-tape recorders) should be employed, so that the patient can hear what he is doing. Some counseling may be needed with regard to the practice pitch used, since the patient may be resistant to using a new voice pitch level. It should be pointed out that the practice pitch level may well be only a temporary one, and not necessarily the pitch level the patient will use permanently. The exercises and reading materials in the previously cited voice and diction references will be useful as practice material. It is important that the work be pursued both in and out of therapy. A change in loudness cannot be achieved simply by talking about it. It requires practice.

   *e.* Sometimes respiration training (facilitating technique XVII) is necessary for the patient with a loudness problem. It should be remembered, however, that while loudness is directly related to the rate of air flow through the approximated vocal folds, there is little evidence to indicate that any particular way of breathing is the best for optimum phonation. Any respiration exercise that produces increased subglottal air pressure may be helpful in increasing voice loudness.

*f.* Particularly effective in functional voice loudness problems is the pushing approach (facilitating technique XV). When pushing is coordinated with phonation, there is little air wastage and firm vocal fold approximation, both of which result in louder phonation; Van Riper and Irwin write that "pressing or lifting strongly with the hands or arms while phonating can raise both pitch and intensity levels" (*162*, p. 259). However, if the patient can achieve adequate loudness through initial counseling, "best" pitch practice, and some help in respiration, the pushing approach and other techniques requiring physical effort can be avoided.

*g.* For the patient who appears to resist increasing the loudness of his voice, it might be necessary to introduce loud noise as a competing sound to the feedback of the patient's own voice. The Lombard effect (speaking at louder voice levels during conditions of competing noise), lends itself well therapeutically to the demonstration of greater voice loudness. The clinician may use white noise, a pure tone (such as 125 or 256 Hz), the patient's own voice amplified on a simultaneous or delayed auditory feedback device, or any other sound. The procedures of the approach are as follows: (1) ask the patient to read aloud a passage of about 100 words; (2) tape-record the patient's oral reading; (3) at about word 30, introduce the loud competing auditory stimulus; the patient's voice will be heard to increase in loudness; (4) at about word 50, shut off the sound stimulus; the patient will immediately be heard to use a softer voice; (5) for the balance of the reading, alternately introduce and stop the sound source at about 15-word intervals; (6) complete the procedure by having the patient listen to the recorded playback, noticing the Lombard effect on the loudness of his voice. An extension of the approach might be to ask the patient to attempt to match his own loudness models.

3. A few patients demonstrate little or no loudness variation. To achieve such variation:

*a.* Have the patient listen to a tape recording of his voice. Then, after making appropriate comments, ask him how he likes his voice, whether he thinks he should change it, etc. People who become aware of the monotony of their voices, and who are concerned about it, can usually develop loudness inflections with practice.

*b.* The maintenance of an unvarying level of loudness seems to require a great deal of energy. There appears to be less work in speaking naturally, which means speaking with a mouth well open and with pitch-loudness variations. The rare patient with hyperfunctional voice problems who speaks in a loudness monotone should be encouraged to increase his loudness variation. Any good voice and diction book will include useful practice materials for developing such variation; the reader is referred particularly to chapter 5 of Eisenson's *The Improvement of Voice and Diction* (53), or to chapter 13 of Fairbanks's *Voice and Articulation Drillbook* (55).

*C. Typical case history showing utilization of approach.* A 31-year-old teacher, C. T., complained for over a year of symptoms of vocal fatigue, i.e., pain in the throat, loss of voice after teaching, etc. Laryngoscopy revealed a normal larynx, and the voice evaluation found the man to speak at "a monotonous pitch and low loudness level, with pronounced mandibular restriction, at times barely opening his mouth." Early efforts at therapy included the chewing approach, with special emphasis given to varying pitch level and increasing voice loudness. The patient was highly motivated to improve the efficiency of his phonation; he requested voice therapy three times a week and supplemented the therapy with long practice periods at home. After nine weeks of therapy, pre-therapy and post-therapy recordings were compared, and the patient agreed with the therapist that he sounded "like a new man." Speaking in a louder voice for this patient seemed to have an immediate effect on his overall self-image, resulting in an almost immediate increase in his total communicative effectiveness. Not only did the patient achieve a better-sounding speaking voice, but he reported no further symptoms of vocal fatigue.

*D. Evaluation of approach.* Inappropriate loudness of voice penalizes the patient. Happily, however, many of the facilitating techniques described in this chapter have some influence on voice loudness, and when inadequate loudness constitutes part of the patient's vocal symptomatology, it is often a variable that is highly modifiable. In fact, more often than not the use of various other facilitating techniques will have an indirect effect on voice loudness, obviating the need for loudness techniques per se.

### III. CHEWING APPROACH

*A. Kinds of problems for which approach is useful.* The method is helpful in reducing generalized vocal hyperfunction, in that it promotes more optimum vocal fold size/mass adjustments and better fold approximation. It can influence loudness, pitch, and quality in hyperfunctional disorders without vocal fold pathology, and is useful in such organic disorders as cord thickening, vocal nodules, polyps, contact ulcers, chronic laryngitis, etc.

*B. Procedural aspects of approach*
1. First of all, explain to the patient that he is speaking with unnecessary tension. If appropriate, point out that he is speaking with an approximated mandible, through clenched teeth, with so little mouth opening that he "speaks like a ventriloquist." Use a mirror to show the patient what he looks like when he talks. Let him see his relatively restricted mandibular movement. An explanation should follow of how relatively relaxed the jaw, throat, tongue, and lips are when one chews, and how chewing and talking simultaneously often result in a more relaxed voice. Instruct the patient that he will be using the chewing method in order to promote the greater oral movement which produces a more relaxed

voice. Emphasize that the chewing method will only be a means to an end. That is, make sure the patient understands that he will be chewing in an exaggerated manner only temporarily, to get the feeling of vigorous action, and that he need not worry that you want him to speak permanently with such exaggerated, open-mouthed postures. If patients are sufficiently warned that the method is but a temporary way of introducing a more relaxed phonation, and that it will eventually be brought down to a more normal way of talking, few will be resistant to learning it.

2. With both the clinician and the patient facing a mirror, ask the patient to pretend that he is opening his mouth wide, about to bite into a handful of four or five stacked crackers, and then to pretend that he is chewing them. (Usually this imagery is sufficient. Occasionally, however, the crackers are actually introduced and the patient is asked to chew them in an open-mouthed, exaggerated fashion, observing himself closely. This is followed immediately by having the patient imitate the chewing he just did.) Point out to the patient the degree of his mouth opening, and the movement of his jaw. Several minutes should be spent in establishing a natural and exaggerated motion of chewing.

3. Demonstrate the chewing for the patient and add a very soft phonation. Have the patient imitate you. Brodnitz warns that "at this stage, many patients will go through the motions of opening and closing the jaws but the tongue is left flat and motionless on the floor of the mouth. A monotonous 'yam-yam' will result" (24, p. 80). It is therefore important for the clinician to point out early that the tongue must be kept moving so that a variety of sounds will emerge. The patient should stay with this exercise until he is able to produce chewing and voicing simultaneously, with an ever-changing number of different sounds. For the method to be effective, the natural movements of the tongue, as experienced when actually chewing food, should be retained.

4. After the patient has performed the chewing-voicing exercise satisfactorily, introduce some actual words and phrases, such as "lampshade"; "peaches and cherries,"; "candy chunks." Either stay with such words until the patient demonstrates that he can say them well, or explore other words with him, starting with those that he is able to produce while still maintaining good chewing.

5. When a few nucleus words are established with the chewing method, ask the patient to count from one to ten, using the same technique. Some practice at this is usually necessary. If the numbers appear to reduce the patient's ability to use the method correctly, go back to an earlier level and reestablish more appropriate chewing. If the patient is able to voice well while chewing and saying numbers, have him listen to himself doing it (using some kind of feedback device, such as a loop auditory tape, an Echorder, or a Phonic Mirror). It is critical that the patient not only experience the relaxed "feel" of the method but that he also receive some immediate auditory feedback showing the effect of the method on the sound of his voice.

6. After the patient has demonstrated that he can chew and say numbers satisfactorily, he can usually tackle more extensive, connected speech. Provide him with verbal material to say or passages to read aloud. This chewing–connected speech should usually not begin with true conversation, but rather with neutral verbal material, such as a passage from a book.

7. The last practice step is to use the approach during conversational speech. If the patient experiences difficulty at this level, and in the beginning he usually will, have him go back to the highest successful level and guide him forward from there. When he has some success in using the method conversationally in therapy, have him use it also outside of therapy in comfortable verbal settings, that is, in situations in which he will have no fear that the exaggerated method will evoke negative reactions from his listeners. Good listeners in the beginning might be his parents, a friend, or his wife.

8. The great advantage of the chewing method, once it is learned, is that the patient can practice it many times, for a minute or so each time, throughout the day. The average patient's phonation will be noticeably more relaxed when he uses the chewing method, and because it facilitates a better voice so well, he will use it extensively outside of therapy. A great deal of daily practice, maybe as often as five times an hour, should be established.

9. Finally, after several weeks of practicing the method, the patient should be taught how to diminish the exaggerated chewing to a more normal jaw movement. It is important, however, as chewing is deemphasized, that the patient retain the same feeling and the same sound in his voice. If, when the chewing is minimized, the patient reverts to earlier faulty phonation patterns, have him go back to an earlier chewing level where optimum performance was achieved, and proceed forward again from there.

10. Ultimately, the patient just "thinks" the method. By this time he has developed an awareness of what oral openness and jaw movement feel like, and has experienced the vocal relaxation that accompanies the feeling.

*C. Typical case history showing utilization of approach.* Mrs. M. L. was a 52-year-old housewife who, after experiencing persistent dysphonia for over six months, was referred by her physician to a laryngologist. On mirror laryngoscopy, the laryngologist found "a unilateral vocal nodule on the anterior third of the left vocal cord." Subsequent evaluation of the patient by the speech pathologist found her to have "a moderately severe dysphonia accompanied by severe mandibular restriction and hard glottal attacks." The initial phase of voice therapy began with an explanation of the observed mandibular restriction and how this seemed to contribute to the patient's general strain in speaking. The clinician's preferred facilitating technique for this woman was the chewing method. It took the patient four weeks to master the chewing approach well enough to use it in conversation. When she used the chewing method, and at the same time lowered her head down toward her chest, her dysphonia would clear markedly. She reported to the clinician that she used the chewing approach about 50 times daily, usually with good results. At the end of the sixth week of voice therapy, a reexamination of the larynx found no evidence of the vocal nodule, and the patient experienced no dysphonia. It should be stated, however, that approximately nine months later the nodule and the dysphonia reappeared; both were again successfully treated by voice therapy, and, at the time of this writing (two years after treatment), they had not reappeared.

*D. Evaluation of approach.* The chewing method is not a panacea for all voice problems, but its effectiveness in helping patients reduce vocal hyperfunction is frequently observed (Brodnitz and Froeschels, *26*). When involved in the somewhat automatic function of chewing, the oral structures seem to become capable of more synergic, relaxed movement. Relaxing the components of the vocal tract in this way appears also to relax the phonatory functioning of the larynx. By employing a commonly used action, chewing, the patient is able to achieve some relaxation of the vocal tract from a holistic, or *gestalt,* point of view, without having to fulfill such impossible directions as "relax your throat" or "relax your voice"; since no individual has volitional control over the vegetative functions of the throat and larynx, compliance with such instructions is quite impossible. More often than not, however, the patient can achieve such relaxation by combining chewing with phonation. As Brodnitz writes, "The main advantage of using the chewing approach in vocal practice seems to lie in the fact that it treats vocal function as a whole" (*24*, p. 81). The chewing approach appears to be one of the most effective facilitating techniques for producing good voice in patients with hyperfunctional voice disorders.

*IV. DIGITAL MANIPULATION*

*A. Kinds of problems for which approach is useful.* External pressure on the patient's thyroid cartilage by the clinician is sometimes effective in helping the patient establish a lower voice pitch. The external pressure tilts the thyroid cartilage slightly backward, toward the vocal processes, shortening the vocal folds; this increases the size and mass of the vocal folds, producing a lower fundamental voice pitch. Another facet of digital manipulation is for the patient to feel the movement of his larynx with his fingers; as he goes up and down his pitch range with his fingers placed externally on the thyroid cartilage, he will feel his larynx rise with the high pitches and descend with the low ones. This method of feeling the upward and downward excursion of the larynx is used for persons who may be phonating at either too low or too high a pitch level; it will help develop their awareness of the inappropriateness of their pitch.

*B. Procedural aspects of approach*
1. With the exception of some men with falsetto voices, patients will respond to digital pressure by producing a lower voice. Ask the patient to phonate and to extend his phonation by "hanging on to an *ah.*" As the phonation is prolonged, apply slight finger pressure to the thyroid cartilage. The patient's voice pitch will lower instantly.
2. Then ask the patient to maintain the lower pitch, even when your fingers are removed. If he can do this, he should continue practicing the lower pitch. If he quickly reverts to the higher pitch, the digital-pressure method of producing the lower pitch should be repeated. If this method is used for giving the patient

some experience with the feeling and sound of a lower pitch, some time should be spent in practicing the production of the lower pitch and in providing the patient with auditory feedback of what his voice sounds like.

3. A variation of the digital-pressure technique is to begin by pressing the fingers on the thyroid cartilage and then asking the patient to phonate. Once the lower pitch is produced, release the finger pressure suddenly. There will be an immediate rise in voice pitch. This rise should be monitored by the patient with his own fingers, and he should be instructed to bring his voice back to (i.e., acoustically match) the lower pitch. Most patients can do this almost instantly. Only at the second of release will a break in pitch be heard. Practice with this technique is most helpful for the patient desiring to lower his pitch.

4. A few falsetto patients may not be particularly interested in lowering their pitches, and the effect of digital pressure may be to make their pitches even higher. In some cases this pitch elevation is due to the patient's segmental mode of vocal fold approximation, the effect of pressure being to shorten the fold segments even further. By using digital manipulation at the lower end of the patient's falsetto range, it is usually possible to obtain the lower pitch response. If this method does not work, for whatever reason, it should be abandoned for another type of facilitating technique.

5. For a completely different kind of digital manipulation, show the patient how to place his fingers on his external larynx and feel the upward and downward movement of the larynx. Then ask him to phonate a pitch level which you feel is close to his optimum one, and to place his fingers to the thyroid cartilage to feel the vibration. Keeping his fingers in place, the patient should then phonate one musical note at a time until he reaches his lowest comfortably produced pitch. The lowest pitches are usually accompanied by downward laryngeal movement. If this occurs, the movement should be demonstrated again and pointed out to the patient. The patient should then be asked to phonate successive one-note steps until he reaches his highest note, exclusive of falsetto; he will usually experience a continuous elevation of the larynx as he goes successively higher up the scale. This movement should be clearly described to and experienced by the patient; if pronounced movement does not occur, the method should not be used.

6. Around the level of his optimum pitch, the patient should feel that there is little or no upward-downward laryngeal movement. If the clinician is attempting to establish a new pitch level, whether it be lower or higher, the finger monitoring of laryngeal movement for the faulty pitch, and the absence of movement for the desired pitch, will help the patient discriminate between the two.

C. *Typical case history showing utilization of approach.* J. F. was a 17-year-old male who had been raised exclusively by his mother until her sudden death about a year before. Since that time he had lived with a maternal uncle who was concerned over the boy's effeminate mannerisms and high-pitched voice. Laryngeal examination revealed a normal adult male larynx. The boy was found to have a habitual pitch level of around 200 cps, well within the adult female range, but below the level of falsetto. The most effective facilitating technique for producing a normal voice pitch was to apply digital pressure on the external thyroid cartilage. The young man was able to prolong the lower pitch levels with good success, but any attempt at conversation would be characterized by an immediate return to the higher pitch. After three therapy sessions, he was able to read aloud using the lower pitch, but was unable to use the lower voice in conversation except with his male clinician. Subsequent psychiatric evaluation and therapy were initiated for "identity confusion and schizoidal tendencies." Voice therapy was discontinued after two weeks, when it was clearly demonstrated that the patient could produce a good baritone voice (125 cps) *whenever he wanted*. Unfortunately, follow-up telephone conversations several months after therapy with the young man revealed that he was using his high-pitched, pre-therapy voice exclusively.

D. *Evaluation of approach.* With some problems of vocal hyperfunction, particularly cord thickening and vocal nodules, it is sometimes necessary to work toward lowering the child's or adult's (but not the adolescent's) pitch level, as suggested convincingly in the writings of Tarneaud (*157*) and Wilson (*168*). Elevation of pitch may be needed for such problems as contact ulcers, which are well defined by Peacher (*127*). Digital pressure on the thyroid cartilage is an excellent facilitator for many patients in developing a lower voice pitch. If the method does not produce a lower pitch level, as it may not do for certain cases of falsetto, the method cannot be used. Even though the method may produce an immediate change of voice to a more desired, lower pitch level, as illustrated in our case history example, it may not be able to effect a permanent voice change without some counseling or psychotherapy. Digital pressure, while effective in lowering pitch level, will rarely bring about permanent success unless other therapeutic approaches are used as well.

A well-trained singing or speaking voice is produced with a minimum of physical effort, with relatively little upward-downward movement of the larynx. Some patients with habitually inappropriate pitch levels may demonstrate unnecessary laryngeal excursion as they speak. An excellent method of pointing this out to the patient, and of helping him establish a more optimum phonation with only minimal vertical laryngeal movement, is to have him place his fingers lightly on the laryngeal thyroid cartilage, feeling the downward movement as the pitch lowers and the upward movement as it rises.

*V. EAR TRAINING*

A. *Kinds of problems for which approach is useful.* Most voice therapy involves the identification and elimination of faulty vocal habits, and their replacement by more optimum ones. The basic input modality in developing appropriate phonation is the auditory system, particularly the patient's self-hearing. No one has much awareness of what he is doing laryngeally, whether he is approximating his folds or shortening or lengthening them, except as he hears his voice. The surprise nearly always evoked in people at hearing their own voices on recordings is one indication of how gross our self-hearing is. This lack of voice feedback has always presented problems to the clinician, as the patient literally does not know what he is doing when he phonates. Music teachers have historically attempted to circumvent the problem by using imagery in their training attempts, since the voice will often respond appropriately to psychological-anatomical instruction—e.g., "put your voice forcefully down in your chest"—even though the physiology of the described event is in error. In voice therapy, we are concerned with making the patient a critical listener. He may need practice in learning to listen to his own voice. Davis and Boone (45) report that some voice patients, like some people in the normal population, demonstrate difficulty in pitch discrimination and tonal memory as measured by subtests of the Seashore Tests of Musical Aptitude (142). Such patients may have serious problems in voice therapy in making pitch discriminations and in remembering the sound of their own model voices. Up to a certain point, gross pitch discrimination and tonal memory can be taught by ear-training practice, wherein the patient learns how to listen critically to his own "good" and "bad" voices and to the voices of others. Through the use of auditory feedback devices, such as loop tape recorders, he learns to hear and monitor auditorily his own phonation. For patients who have defective listening skills, voice training must include instruction in making pitch discriminations, improving tonal memory, and learning to hear one's "good" and "bad" voices. But the clinician should first assess the patient's listening skills, for many voice patients have no problem in this area; for others, just as for some people in the normal population, listening abilities may be surprisingly deficient. It is the latter group that may profit from ear training.

### B. Procedural aspects of approach

1. Take a baseline measurement of how well the patient can make pitch discriminations. The Seashore pitch discrimination subtest, or a piano or pitch pipe, may be used. Present to the patient a pair of tonal stimuli, asking if the stimuli are the same as one another or different. This should be followed by voiced pitch discriminations, either produced by the clinician or prerecorded. If the patient is unable to discriminate between one whole note and its flat or sharp the indication is that his pitch discrimination is not normal, but not necessarily that pitch discrimination therapy is needed. In gross departures, however, such as the patient's being unable to discriminate between notes that are more than a third apart (say, between a $C_4$ and an $E_4$), some discrimination training may be needed if he is ever going to match a target model voice successfully.

2. Pitch discrimination training should begin at the baseline "can do" performance of the patient. When he makes correct discriminations at this level,

his performance should be positively reinforced. Pitch stimuli can come from a piano, a pitch pipe, or the voice itself; it is often better therapy to mix all three types of pitch stimuli into the practice sequence, rather than to use one type only. The clinician should continue this activity for as long as necessary, until the patient is able to discriminate between pitches that are one full musical note apart (e.g., $C_4$ and $D_4$). This pitch discrimination approach can effectively be practiced alone, without the clinician, with the patient listening to prerecorded practice materials and making his "same-different" choices as he listens. To learn the correctness of his responses, he can mark his choices down on paper and then check them against a master sheet. Simple programming equipment has also been used successfully; here, the patient indicates his "same-different" choice, and a light goes on when the choice is correct.

3. Tonal memory therapy also begins where the patient is. That is, if the patient can remember a two-note sequence (via piano, pitch pipe, or voice), the therapy should begin by presenting him with two two-note sequences and asking him to identify which note varies between the two presentations. It does not appear to be necessary for the patient to work beyond remembering a four-note series. When he can hear a four-note melody, remember it, and compare it successfully with a second four-note melody (with only one note varying between the first and second presentation), his tonal memory is probably good enough for him to remember various voice-model presentations. Tonal memory therapy is also well suited to self-practice, with the patient listening and responding to prerecorded sequences.

4. If a target model voice has been produced by the patient himself, can he discriminate between this good production and his faulty one? It is essential in voice therapy that the patient use his own "best" voice as his therapy model whenever possible. He may need some practice in learning to listen for his own "best" and "bad" voices. The clinician should capture the patient's voice productions on recordings, editing and splicing them into contrasting pairs, and the patient should listen discriminatively to these pairings so as to learn to identify his better phonations quickly and correctly. Recordings of other people's voices with similar problems, also paired for discrimination listening, make excellent practice materials. When the patient is able to demonstrate a consistent ability to hear his "good" voice, whether or not he is able to produce that voice, there is little need to emphasize ear training. For some patients, just a little listening to their own voice helps; for others, even a great deal of practice is useless. For the rare patient who shows no improvement after trial ear-training, further such training might just as well be abandoned.

*C. Typical case history showing utilization of approach.* C. M., a nine-year-old girl with functional hypernasality, was evaluated by a local cleft-palate team and found to have adequate velopharyngeal closure (as demonstrated by cinefluorography), normal manometric pressure ratios, and normal stimulability for producing good oral resonance in isolated words repeated after the examiner. Voice therapy on a twice-weekly basis was recommended. The focus of therapy was on ear training, helping the patient to discriminate between her nasal resonance and oral resonance. The first seven weeks of therapy were spent both in this discrimination listening, which in the beginning was very defective, and in producing contrasting oral and nasal resonations. In the early phases of therapy, orality was stressed only in the therapy and practice sessions, with no attempt at any outside carry-over. Eventually, carry-over phrases and sentences were practiced in situations outside the clinic setting. As the therapy progressed, the girl showed excellent auditory self-monitoring and was able to develop normal oral voice quality in all situations. Voice therapy was judged a success and terminated after eleven weeks.

D. *Evaluation of approach.* In voice therapy, the patient must become a critical listener to his own voice. Some voice patients, like some people in the normal population, have real difficulty in making pitch discriminations and judgments of tonal memory. Of these patients, some will profit from ear training. The patient must learn to hear, if possible, how he is phonating. As Sommers and Brady have written, "improvements in phonation and resonance are heavily dependent upon the subject's ability to detect desirable changes as a function of specific voice therapy activities" (*150*, pp. 3–7). If the patient's listening abilities are poor, ear training should be initiated. If there is no problem in listening, ear training should be avoided.

## VI. ELIMINATION OF ABUSES

A. *Kinds of problems for which approach is useful.* Some vocal abuses are relatively focalized and easily identifiable. They include crying, screaming, yelling, throat-clearing, grunting, coughing, and focalized cases of inappropriate pitch, loudness, or quality. It appears to require only a minimal amount of vocal abuse each day to maintain a dysphonia or to develop and maintain a laryngeal pathology. By the same token, and this is especially true for children, the elimination or reduction of the vocal abuse will often be remarkably effective in eliminating the dysphonia and its accompanying laryngeal pathology. For any voice patient with approximation or mass/size problems of the vocal folds, vocal abuse, if present, should be eliminated or at least reduced. It appears, also, that a patient who has once had dysphonia, with or without an accompanying laryngeal pathology, can no longer tolerate vocal abuses as well as someone in the normal population. For example, the child who once had a vocal nodule may develop symptoms of dysphonia after periods of abuse or misuse much sooner than will his normal peer performing the same abusive vocal act. Therefore, not only are the identification and elimination of vocal abuses essential in voice therapy, but the avoidance of abuse must continue after therapy is over. The patient may have to avoid unnecessary vocal excesses for the rest of his life.

B. *Procedural aspects of approach*
1. By evaluating and observing the patient, identify the offensive vocal act.

Then determine its baseline rate of occurrence. For instance, if the vocal abuse is throat-clearing, try to observe the patient in various settings, such as the classroom, the playground, the therapy room, etc., and count the number of times he clears his throat.

2. Discuss the identified vocal abuses with the patient, emphasizing his need to reduce their daily frequency. Assign to the patient the task of counting the number of times each day he finds himself engaged in a particular abuse. Perhaps a peer or sibling could be brought in, told about the situation, and asked to join in on the daily count; or, depending upon the age of the patient, a parent or teacher, or spouse or business associate, might be asked to keep track of the number of abuses occurring in their presence. At the end of the day, the abuses should be tallied for that day.

3. Ask the patient to plot his daily vocal abuses on a graph, similar to the one shown in figure 23. Along the vertical axis, the ordinate, he should plot the number of times the particular abuse occurred, and along the base of the graph, the abscissa, the individual days, beginning with the baseline count of the first day. Instruct the patient to bring these graphs with him to his voice therapy sessions. Keeping a graph usually increases the patient's awareness of what he has been doing and results in a gradual decrement of the abusive behavior. The typical vocal abuse has a sloping decremental curve, indicating its gradual disappearance. Any decrement in the plots of the people observing the patient, but particularly in those compiled by the patient himself, should be greeted with obvious approval by the clinician.

C. *Typical case history showing utilization of approach.* R. B., a nine-year-old little league baseball player, began the school year with marked hoarseness. His school speech clinician referred him for laryngoscopy, which found "early bilateral nodule formation." Both his teacher and one of his parents reported that he made an unusual screeching sound on the playground and while playing little league baseball. Observation by the speech clinician confirmed his high-pitched staccato yell on the playground. A baseline measurement was made by the playground supervising teacher. The problem was discussed with the boy, and he was told that his severe problem of hoarseness might well be related to his ball-playing screech. The boy and a close friend were each asked to keep track of the screeches daily and to plot a "screech curve." The friend was unable to do this with any regularity; the patient, however, kept daily plots for about a week, and by the time of his next appointment with the clinician, his screeching behavior had been completely extinguished. No formal voice therapy was ever scheduled, and within a period of several weeks the boy's voice quality sounded normal. In this particular case, just calling the boy's attention to his screeching appeared to be all that was needed (and the clinician was especially fortunate because it happened to be the end of the baseball season).

D. *Evaluation of approach.* Identifying vocal abuses and attempting to eliminate them by plotting their daily frequency on a graph appears to be a most effective method of helping young children with voice problems. Adolescents are equally guilty of vocal abuses and profit greatly from keeping track of what they are doing. Typical adult abuses, such as throat-clearing, are often eliminated in a week or two by graph plotting by motivated patients. The effectiveness of this approach, in fact, appears to be highly related to the skill of the clinician in motivating the patient to eliminate his abusive behavior. Such daily graph plotting by the patient himself is a most useful therapy device in stuttering therapy as well, but it is particularly effective in eliminating focal abuses of the voice.

## VII. ELIMINATION OF HARD GLOTTAL ATTACK

*A. Kinds of problems for which approach is useful.* Hard glottal attack (the glottal stroke) is frequently among the abusive vocal behaviors of patients with hyperfunctional voice disorders. In hard glottal attack, the patient adducts his vocal folds, but does not initiate phonation until the outgoing air flow is strong enough literally to blow the glottis open. The acoustic result is an abrupt staccato initiation of phonation. This crisp style of phonation will usually take a toll on the glottal structures, and particularly on the arytenoid cartilages, whose only covering on the glottal margins is a relatively thin mucosal membrane. Hard glottal stroke is, therefore, particularly common among patients with posterior glottal pathologies, such as contact ulcers. When employed in a prolonged performance by a singer or lecturer, the hard glottal stroke will often result in generalized glottal edema (swelling), which will have noticeable effects on the quality of the voice. Any patient with a dysphonia related to hyperfunctional voice usage should be suspected of employing hard glottal stroke in some situations, even if he does not do so at the time of the clinical evaluation.

*B. Procedural aspects of approach*
1. Hard glottal attack is a fairly common phenomenon among actors, politicians, and untrained singers. Recordings of the voices of such people, and of the patient, should be played for the patient, and a contrasting demonstration should be made of the soft, easy glottal attack. The length of the demonstration will be dependent on the insight of the patient.
2. The yawn-sigh approach (facilitating technique XX) is particularly effective in eliminating hard glottal attack.
3. The chewing approach (facilitating technique III) almost always reduces the glottal stroke. It is nearly impossible to produce abrupt phonations while chewing.
4. Use the whisper-phonation technique. Here, a few monosyllabic words are chosen, each beginning with a vowel. The patient's task is to whisper very lightly the initial vowel, prolonging it by gradually increasing the loudness of the whisper until phonation is introduced and, finally, the whole word is said. The whisper blends into a soft phonation.
5. Select monosyllabic words beginning with the aspirate /h/ for soft-attack

practice. When the /h/ words are produced correctly, introduce other words beginning with unvoiced consonants for similar practice.

6. Record for the patient both his hard-glottal-stroke speech and his soft-attack words. Have him listen to the contrast. He should study the difference between the two approaches in both sound and feel. Most patients will agree that using the hard glottal attack is a much more difficult way to speak.

*C. Typical case history showing utilization of approach.* M. C., a 34-year-old single woman, had a two-year history of vocal fatigue after every day of teaching high-school social studies. The discomfort gradually increased, until she suffered severe pain in the hyoid area. Laryngoscopy found her to have bilateral contact ulcers, and the voice evaluation found that she had "an inappropriately low voice pitch for her total pitch range, and pronounced hard glottal attack." From the beginning of voice therapy, she was able to use a slightly higher pitch level and reduce her hard glottal attack, producing good phonation of generally pleasant quality. She succeeded in permanently reducing the hard glottal attack by listening and learning to discriminate between hard and soft attack, by chewing, by using the yawn-sigh and whisper-phonation techniques, and by practicing word lists beginning with various unvoiced consonants. After twenty weeks of twice-weekly individual voice therapy, the patient reported no further symptoms of dysphonia and vocal fatigue, and a post-therapy laryngeal examination revealed "no further posterior pathology."

*D. Evaluation of approach.* There is probably no way of singing or speaking that is more vocally fatiguing than using hard glottal attack. Singing teachers, who have long been concerned with eliminating hard glottal stroke, have generally relied on teaching general body relaxation as a means of inducing greater vocal tract relaxation. Although the effort and force required to speak with glottal attack makes it a common symptom of patients with hyperfunctional voice disorders, many voice clinicians do not focus directly on modifying the hard glottal stroke. The reason for this is that once the patient becomes aware of his hard glottal attack and its contrast with normal ways of beginning phonation, the old abrupt manner of phonating is usually spontaneously reduced. It is a common clinical observation that the reduction of hard glottal attack results in a corresponding improvement in voice quality.

*VIII. ESTABLISHING NEW PITCH*

*A. Kinds of problems for which approach is useful.* Problems of mass and size of the vocal folds resulting in inappropriate voice pitch levels are sometimes helped by direct attempts to change the pitch level. A change of pitch level will often have audible effects, also, on the loudness and quality of the voice. A common characteristic of hyperfunctional voice disorders is inappropriate pitch level, the maintenance of which often requires much effort. Sometimes patients with vocal fold problems of additive mass (cord thickening, nodules, polyps) will speak at a lower pitch because of the increased amount of vibrating tissue. Other patients will use low-pitched voices purely on a functional basis, while still others will use inappropriately high-pitched ones merely as a faulty habit. Elevating or lowering the voice pitch, if this is needed in therapy, can usually be accomplished by direct symptom modification through exercises and practice.

*B. Procedural aspects of approach*

1. If, as a result of the diagnostic evaluation, it is apparent that there is a discrepancy between the patient's habitual pitch level and his tested optimum pitch, this discrepancy should be explained and demonstrated to the patient. The methods of determining habitual and optimum pitches described in chapter 4 can be applied here. A tape recording should be made while the patient is searching for his pitches, and when the habitual and optimum pitches have been recorded, they should be played back. The playback should always be followed immediately by a discussion comparing the sound and feel of the two pitches.

2. Most voice patients will be able to imitate their own pitch model, once it has been produced with the appropriate facilitating techniques. An excellent model can be produced by having the patient extend an /a/ at the desired pitch level for about five seconds, recording the phonation on a loop tape recorder, such as the Phonic Mirror or the Echorder. If the loop is set for a two- or four-second playback, the patient's phonation will come back to him on playback while he is still producing it. This will provide him with a continuous model of his own preferred pitch level. There appear to be distinct advantages in using the patient's own voice as the model, in that he will already have had the experience of producing the sound he is trying to duplicate. The clinician should stay on the loop model of /a/ for considerable practice before introducing a new stimulus.

3. In practicing the new pitch level, proceed cautiously from the simple /a/. Have the patient work at first on single words, preferably those beginning with a vowel, repeating each word in a pitch monotone. The /a/ may be used to initiate the word, blending the word into the end of the /a/. It will occasionally be observed that the patient has more difficulty in using the new pitch with certain words. Any of these "trouble" words should be avoided as practice material, for what is needed at this stage of therapy is practice in rapidly phonating a series of individual words at the new pitch level.

4. Once the patient does well at the single-word level, introduce phrases and short sentences. It is usually more productive at this stage to avoid practice in actual conversation, since the patient is better able to use the new phonation in such neutral situations as reading single words, phrases, and sentences. When success is achieved at the sentence level, assign the patient reading passages from various voice and diction books.

5. After reading well in a monotone, the patient may try using the new pitch in some real-life conversational situations. In the beginning he may have more success in talking to strangers, say, store clerks; patients often find it difficult

to use the new pitch level with friends and family, since their previous "set" may prevent them from utilizing their new vocal behavior. Whatever conversational situation works best for the individual should be the one initially used. The desired goal at first is successful phonation practice, regardless of whom one is speaking to or what one is saying.

6. There will be a few voice patients who will not be able to produce the new pitch level voluntarily. Here, the facilitating techniques discussed elsewhere in this chapter—coughing, yawning, clearing the throat, singing up and down the scale—will be useful. Whatever the method used, it is important to record the phonation so that the patient will have a playback model of his own "best" voice. Aphonic patients, of course, and patients with a mutational falsetto, will not be able to make pitch changes volitionally, and pitch productions should not be directly solicited from them.

7. A few patients will best develop a new pitch level by inflecting from their habitual pitch down or up to the desired level. Ask the patient to say a number of words in series, inflecting each word toward the desired pitch level. Once the lower or higher pitch is achieved with some regularity, proceed with steps 3, 4, and 5, as described.

*C. Typical case history showing utilization of approach.* J. K., a ten-year-old boy, was referred by his public-school speech clinician for a laryngeal examination because of a six-month history of hoarseness. The findings included a normal larynx and a "low-pitched dysphonic voice." The youngster could readily demonstrate a higher phonation, which was characterized by an immediate clearing of quality. In the discussion which followed the tape-recorded playback of his "good" and "bad" voice, the boy stated that he thought he had been trying to speak like his older brother. The clinician pointed out to him that his better voice was more like that of other boys his age, and that the low-pitched voice he had been using was difficult for others to listen to. In subsequent voice therapy with his public-school clinician, the boy focused on elevating his voice pitch to a more natural level. His success was rapid, and therapy was terminated after six weeks.

*D. Evaluation of approach.* Pitch level changes constantly according to the situation in which the speaker finds himself. In some voice patients, however, the pitch level appears to be too high or too low for the overall capability of the laryngeal mechanism. In other persons, an aberrant pitch level is but one manifestation of the total personality. In fact, Moses (*118*) has so successfully espoused the view that pitch and personality are entwined that pitch level is sometimes considered best changed by changing the personality of the speaker, rather than by working on pitch per se. Voice clinicians, however, who modify what appear to be inappropriate pitch levels, find that pitch change can be accomplished quickly and permanently with most patients. It would appear that the only patients who are sometimes found to be psychologically resistant to pitch change are those adults, men and women, who speak at fundamental frequency levels typical of members of the opposite sex. And even many of these patients can develop pitch levels compatible with their physical mechanisms, often after only minimal therapy. If the voice patient is able to produce an optimum phonation by using facilitating approaches (chewing, yawn-sigh, etc.) other than those directly aimed at pitch change, these other approaches should be used. This is true also for working on loudness. However, if it becomes necessary in voice therapy to work directly on the pitch change, the clinician will usually find the child or adult (but not the pubertal) patient able to comply.

## IX. EXPLANATION OF PROBLEM

*A. Kinds of problems for which approach is useful.* Most therapy for speech, language, or voice, if it is to be effective, begins with some kind of explanation to the patient of what the problem is and what can be done about it. This is particularly true in voice therapy. As a prerequisite to therapy, the patient with a hyperfunctional voice problem needs to know what he is doing incorrectly and what he should do to change. In the case of those dysphonias that are related wholly to functional causes (such as hyperfunction), it is important that the clinician not confront the patient with the implication that he "could talk all right if he wanted to." Instead of saying, "You are not using your voice as well as you could," we might say, "Your vocal folds are coming together too tightly." The latter statement absolves the patient of the guilt he might experience if we indicated that he was doing things "wrong." The patient will be much more receptive to a statement that puts the blame on his vocal folds. For patients with structural changes of the vocal folds, such as nodules or polyps, it may be necessary to explain that the organic pathology may well be secondary to prolonged misuse, and that by eliminating the misuse, the patient will eventually experience a reduction of vocal fold pathology.

*B. Procedural aspects of approach.* In problems of the voice related to vocal hyperfunction, it is important to identify for the patient those behaviors of his which help maintain his dysphonia. No exact procedure for this can be laid down; each case will have its own rules. For problems related to abuse and misuse of the voice, it is important that the clinician identify the inappropriate behavior and demonstrate to the patient some ways in which it can be eliminated. For truly organic problems, such as unilateral adductor paralysis, the same explanations must be made, but in terms of inadequate and adequate glottal closure. Most voice patients want to understand what their problem is and what they can do about it. The clinician must make use of his medical and diagnostic information, but formulate his explanations to the patient in language the patient can understand. Such imagery as "your vocal cords are coming together too tightly," or "you seem to place your voice back too far in your throat," may lack scientific validity, but may very well help the patient understand his problem. While explanations should be brief and to the point, the clinician must take care that he does not put the patient psychologically on the defensive at the first visit. If, after the evaluation, it appears that some psychological or psychiatric consultation is necessary, further diagnostic/therapy sessions may have to be held before the patient is able to agree with the clinician's statements that "we need to find out more about our feelings" or "find out more about ourselves." The explanation of the problem does not have to be completed before voice therapy begins; indeed, it might well be an important part of every therapy session. The explanation should always hint at the general direction of immediate and future therapy, and it should give the patient some indication of the prognosis.

*C. Typical case history showing utilization of approach.* Doris L., a nine-year-old-girl with a one-year history of dysphonia, was found on mirror laryngoscopy to have "a nodule on the left cord at the anterior-middle third, with a corresponding thickening on the right cord." Prolonged discussion with her teacher and parents revealed that Doris was an extremely verbal, active child who made many loud and noxious noises while at play. The voice clinician was able to observe the girl on a school playground and confirm her screaming, screeching play noises. The explanation which the voice clinician gave the child described the vocal fold thickenings which were taking place, probably as a direct result of all that screaming on the playground. Doris was told:

We are concerned about your voice getting increasingly hoarse. Often people can't understand what you are saying because they cannot hear your speaking voice. Your bad voice is the result of your screaming. The more you scream and screech, the bigger the bumps on your vocal cords will get. If they get much bigger, you won't have any voice at all. If you cut down on your screaming, those bumps will start to get smaller. If you can stop screaming altogether, the bumps will go away, and I think then your voice will become just as good as anyone else's.

Pictures of nodules, some description of the effects of vocal abuse, and recordings of the "before-after" voices of other children who had been successfully treated for vocal nodules convinced Doris of the need to reduce her screaming. In this case, the explanation of the problem proved to be a most effective motivator. The girl plotted the number of screams she made each day on a weekly graph, and succeeded in almost completely extinguishing her screaming behavior. There was a concomitant reduction in the thickening of her glottal margins, and an obvious improvement in the quality of her voice. No formal voice therapy was required.

*D. Evaluation of approach.* An explanation of the problem is an important part of voice therapy, particularly for children with dysphonia related to particular vocal abuses. And if the clinician can tell the patient which vocal behaviors will produce a better voice, this too, should be done. Because the patient-clinician relationship is so important in voice therapy, it is vital that the clinician be honest with the patient in explaining what the problem appears to be and what can be done about it.

## X. FEEDBACK

*A. Kinds of problems for which approach is useful.* Once the patient is able to produce a model voice, his own or one that matches some external model, it is important that he make an attempt to study what the voice feels like and how it sounds. Tactual and proprioceptive feedback are common modalities through which we get some information about our voices as we speak, but it is primarily the auditory feedback system that we use in monitoring our own phonation. We have little awareness of what our muscles are doing in the larynx, throat, palate, or tongue, which is why voice therapy relies heavily on the auditory feedback mechanism. Many voice patients are virtually unaware of how they sound. Yet the success of almost any kind of voice therapy is dependent on the patient's matching some kind of auditory model. Patients with some problem in auditory monitoring may benefit from practice in simultaneous auditory feedback, using some kind of amplifying system which provides ongoing amplification of their own voices. The patient is often able to produce a better voice when he has learned to listen to his own ongoing phonation as a result of some practice in auditory feedback.

*B. Procedural aspects of approach*
1. Discuss with the patient the general concept of feedback. Tactual feedback might be illustrated by moving the finger tips lightly over the surface of a coin. Proprioception can be demonstrated by having the patient close his eyes, extend an arm, and slowly raise the arm, bending it at the elbow joint. Muscle and joint proprioceptors tell us where our arm is in space and that it is moving. But in the larynx, such proprioceptive feedback is essentially lacking; we must rely on hearing our voices as we phonate to monitor what we are doing laryngeally.
2. The conventional tape recorder has never been particularly useful as a training device for auditory feedback. All it can do, essentially, is serve as an amplifying system. By the time the clinician rewinds the tape and find's the precise recording segment, the patient has already lost his focus on that particular stimulus. Today, however, there are many auditory tape devices available— Language Master (*98*), Phonic Mirror(*132*), Echorder (*52*), Artik (*10*), etc.— which provide an immediate auditory stimulus of an event just recorded. A loop recording device, for example, set on a two-second delay, will give the patient an immediate playback of what he has just said. By using such a device, the patient can immediately match what he thought he sounded like with the actual playback of what he sounded like externally. Vowel prolongations, single words,

and phrases are used as the stimuli in this delayed feedback practice. The clinician should remember that this practice in self-listening will be much more effective if coupled with commentary and questions about what was heard, what was different between the old voice and the new, etc.

3. Introduce the patient to simultaneous feedback. Any amplifying device can be used for this kind of practice—a tape recorder with an external monitoring system, an auditory trainer, a hearing aid. As the patient speaks into a microphone, his voice is amplified and fed back to him simultaneously either through a speaker or headset earphones. In the beginning, it is wise to use those words with which the patient is best able to produce his best target phonations. Vowels extended for several seconds, single words, phrases—all these are good stimuli for feedback practice. After the patient has made several productions with simultaneous and amplified feedback, he should be asked questions about what quality deviations he has heard.

*C. Typical case history showing utilization of approach.* A ten-year-old boy, C. M., had a six-month history of bilateral vocal nodules when voice therapy was initiated. Much of his voice problem was believed to be related to his speaking at an inappropriately low voice pitch and to his excessive screaming and yelling on the playground. The latter situation was clearly identified for the boy, and he was able gradually to reduce his screaming and yelling by writing down and graphing his daily number of such vocal abuses. An elevation of his voice pitch (from $D_3$ to a $B_4$) was accomplished with ear training, particularly through the use of auditory feedback. Once the boy was able to produce an optimum phonation ($B_4$), he learned to listen for it critically by first using .2-delayed auditory feedback with the Echorder loop tape device. Eventually he was able to employ simultaneous auditory feedback, using the amplifying system of a clinic tape recorder. For both the delayed and simultaneous auditory feedback training, the clinician found that the boy focused better on what he was doing when he wore earphones rather than when he listened to free-field speakers. After an initial demonstration by the clinician, this child was able to use the auditory feedback equipment alone, after school without a supervising clinician; he spent many hours during the first few weeks learning to use his "new" voice. By the end of one academic semester, follow-up laryngoscopy revealed a normal larynx, and the boy's voice quality was considered normal by his teacher, his public-school correctionist, and his parents.

*D. Evaluation of approach.* As Van Riper and Irwin have written, "Unlike articulation training, in which visual, tactual, and kinesthetic cues can be used to guide the revision of phonemes, vocal training relies primarily on the ear" (*162*, p. 283). If the voice patient is to be successful in identifying and producing his target phonation, it is important that he develop his capacity for self-hearing. In the beginning, to make the task easier, the clinician should introduce the patient to the delayed auditory feedback of his own phonations. After the patient has had some success in monitoring these delayed reproductions, he should try to work with simultaneous feedback. If a voice patient appears to have some difficulty in monitoring his own phonations, auditory feedback practice of this sort will often help him develop his self-hearing skill. As in the case of the ten-year-old boy, most patients need only a brief demonstration by the clinician in order to proceed in practicing alone with various electronic auditory feedback devices. In the typical outpatient voice clinic, the patient first has a half hour of voice therapy with the clinician and then practices alone, perhaps with a loop tape feedback device, with exercise material designed to make him a more critical self-listener.

*XI. HIERARCHY ANALYSIS*

*A. Kinds of problems for which approach is useful.* In hierarchy analysis, the patient constructs lists of various situations in his life which ordinarily produce some anxiety, arranging the situations in a sequential order from the least to the most anxiety-provoking. Or he may prepare a hierarchy of situations ranging from where he finds his voice best to where he finds it worst. This technique is borrowed from Wolpe's method of reciprocal inhibition (*171*), wherein the patient is taught relaxed responses to anxiety-evoking situations: after identifying a hierarchy of anxiety-evoking situations, the patient begins by employing the relaxed responses in the least anxious of them, and, in therapy, works his way up the hierarchy, eventually deconditioning his previously established anxious responses. The identification of hierarchical situations (less anxiety-more anxiety; worst voice-best voice) appears to be a useful therapeutic device for most patients with hyperfunctional voice problems, which by definition imply excessive overreacting. Patients with functional dysphonia, or with dysphonias accompanied by nodules, polyps, and vocal fold thickening, frequently report that their degree of dysphonia varies with the situation. Such patients may profit from hierarchy analysis.

*B. Procedural aspects of approach.*
1. Begin by developing in the patient a general awareness of the hierarchical behavior to be studied. If, for example, the patient is to be asked to identify those situations in which he feels most uncomfortable, discuss with him the symptoms of being uncomfortable. Or if he is going to develop a hierarchy of situations in which he experiences variation of voice, discuss and give examples of what is a good voice, and a bad voice. Explain to the patient that he must develop a relative ordering of situations sequencing them from "good" to "bad." Some patients are initially resistant to this sort of ordering, perhaps never before having realized that there are relative gradations to their feelings of anxiety or relative changes in their quality of voice. They may not be aware that the degree of their anxiety or hoarseness is not constant.
2. While the majority of voice patients are soon able to arrange situations into a hierarchy, a few require some practice with the clinician in sequencing

some neutral stimuli. On one occasion, a woman was taught the idea of sequential order by arranging five shades of red tiles from left to right, in the order of light pink to the darkest red. Having done this, she was then able to sequence her voice situations, proceeding gradually from those in which her voice was normal to those in which it was extremely dysphonic.

3. As a home assignment, have the patient develop several hierarchies with regard to his voice. One hierarchy might center on how his voice holds up with his family, another on how it is related to his work situation, and a third on what happens to it in varying situations with his friends. An excellent example of hierarchical situations developed by a woman with vocal nodules is given in an article by Gray, England and Mahoney (*65*). After these hierarchies have been developed by the patient at home, review them in therapy.

4. In therapy, use the "good" end of the hierarchical sequence first. That is, begin by asking the patient to recapture if he can the good situation. It is the goal of therapy to duplicate the feeling of well-being or the good voice which the patient experienced in the situation he rated best. Efforts should be made in therapy to recall the good factors surrounding the more optimum phonation. If the patient is successful in re-creating the optimum situation, his phonation will sound relaxed and appropriate. The re-created optimum situation thus serves as an excellent facilitator for producing good voice. When the patient demonstrates some success in re-creating the first situation on the hierarchy, capturing completely his optimum response (whether this be relaxation or phonation or both), he will then be able to move on to the second situation. There, again, the goal will be to maintain his optimum response. The rate of movement up the hierarchy will depend entirely on how successfully the patient can re-create the situations and maintain his optimum response. By using the relaxed response in increasingly more tense situations, he is conditioning himself to a more favorable, optimum behavior.

5. While some patients can re-create situations outside the clinic with relative ease, some cannot. As soon as possible, have the patient practice his optimum response outside the clinic under good conditions, so that he will be able eventually to use it in his real world in more adverse situations. The patient must not lose sight of his goal of maintaining the good response in varying situations outside the clinic.

6. Some patients succeed in going just so far up the hierarchy, only to reach a situation in which they continuously have a maladaptive response. When this occurs, the patient should drop back to a lower hierarchical level and attempt once more to capture the optimum response under more favorable conditions. When a good response is again maintained, efforts at the next level should be resumed. For some individuals, however, there are certain situations which seem to preclude an optimum response, and for these people in those situations, the approach may have to be abandoned for other facilitating techniques.

*C. Typical case history showing utilization of approach.* Miss L. L. was a 24-year-old forest conservationist who worked in an office with ten male conservationists. For six months she had experienced recurring dysphonia, particularly when on the telephone at work. Laryngoscopic examination found her to have an "early nodule formation on her left vocal cord"; during the voice evaluation she demonstrated a relatively normal voice. The patient's dysphonia appeared to fluctuate, becoming particularly severe, she reported, in certain anxiety-provoking situations. As part of her three months of voice therapy, she was asked to develop several hierarchical scales, listing the situations in order of those in which she experienced a normal voice to those in which she became all but aphonic. Here is the hierarchy she developed for her vocal responses at the office:

BEST VOICE

1. Calling mother on the phone every day from the office.
2. The female secretary at the office is easy to talk with, particularly when the older men in the office are not around.
3. Dictating on the dictaphone and talking to the secretary are about the same.
4. Bill W. talks to me a lot at the office and on dates.
5. The younger men kid me about going out with them on field trips.
6. The older conservationists at the office keep reminding me that I have only school and no field experience, which always makes me clear my throat.
7. Talking about forestry projects on the phone is hard.

WORST VOICE

8. I lose my voice entirely when talking to our regional manager, and if I can't get over this, I will lose my job.

As voice therapy developed, hierarchy analysis and counseling with the speech pathologist gave this patient greater insight into her difficulties in various interpersonal relationships. Her varying dysphonia was but a symptom of the discomfort she felt with certain people. Voice therapy was terminated after three months in favor of psychotherapy in a psychiatric clinic.

*D. Evaluation of approach.* Voice patients typically report marked inconsistencies in the severity of their dysphonias. In one situation they will phonate with relative ease, and in other situations, usually those in which they feel some stress, their voice may break down completely. These vocal inconsistencies can be studied effectively through hierarchy analysis. This use of hierarchy analysis differs considerably from Wolpe's (*171*), although the principle of maintaining an optimum response under varying conditions of stress is the same. Wolpe teaches his patients relaxation techniques to apply during various hierarchical situations, beginning with low-on-the-hierarchy situations where the patient is relatively free of stress. The relaxation response is established at the lower levels and gradually conditioned to occur at higher ones. With voice patients, we establish optimum phonation at lower levels and gradually condition it to occur at higher levels. In one sense, we are teaching the patient to react optimally to various situational

sense, we are teaching the patient to react optimally to various situational cues, a method advocated by Murray (*120*) for establishing and maintaining effectiveness of communication under varying situations. By analyzing the hierarchical situations in which he becomes more anxious and more dysphonic, the voice patient learns what situational cues trigger for him an ineffective response, a poorer voice. By using various facilitating techniques and recapturing the relaxed phonation he may use in low-on-the-hierarchy situations, he conditions himself to produce more relaxed phonation at all levels of the hierarchy.

### XII. NEGATIVE PRACTICE

*A. Kinds of problems for which approach is useful.* In voice therapy we use various facilitating techniques to develop new, desirable, target voices. While it is comparatively easy to produce optimum phonation in therapy, the patient is often resistant to using the new phonation outside in his everyday world. Negative practice, the intentional use of a previously incorrect response, is a helpful method for facilitating the carry-over of new voice patterns to out-of-clinic situations. Negative practice of an old voice is relatively easy for most voice patients and appears to be particularly useful for patients attempting to change voice pitch and loudness.

*B. Procedural aspects of approach.*

1. Once the patient is able to produce target phonations freely in the clinical situation, ask him to voice deliberately an old phonation pattern. Make a tape recording contrasting the new phonation with the old, perhaps no more than 20 seconds in total length. Then evaluate the playback with the patient, having the patient analyze what the two phonations "feel" like in contrast to one another and how they differ in sound.

2. Ask the patient about those situations in which he is best able to produce his new voice, and, after he has identified them, have him make specific plans to use the old voice pattern deliberately at certain times within them. It appears to be most useful to confine negative practice to those situations where the patient is comfortable and where he can use his new phonation pattern any time he wishes. Negative practice should always be accompanied by some analysis by the patient of his contrasting vocal behaviors.

*C. Typical case history showing utilization of approach.* A 35-year-old teaching colleague of the writer had a long history of vocal fatigue (pain and dysphonia) after prolonged lecturing. His laryngoscopic examination was normal. His only observed faulty speaking habit was pronounced mandibular restriction—most of the time he literally talked through clenched teeth and with a closed mouth. The chewing approach was used successfully with this man, and shortly after establishing good chewing behavior, he began to use negative practice. In situations where he found chewing an easy and relaxing aid to maintaining good phonation, he would deliberately revert to his previous style of speaking with little or no jaw movement. The effort required to speak in this old way became apparent to him immediately, and in only a few weeks he developed a lasting enthusiasm for the open-mouthed, relaxed, chewing method. His problem of vocal fatigue after lecturing was greatly reduced.

*D. Evaluation of approach.* Negative practice is a useful approach for anyone attempting to establish a new behavioral response in place of an old one. In the case of the voice patient, the old response is a faulty one and generally requires a great deal of hyperfunctional effort; the patient works to talk. When a more optimum method of phonation is established, negative practice reinforces for the patient how much easier it is to talk in the new way. Negative practice, a useful approach with such problems as articulation defects and stuttering, is equally beneficial with various voice problems.

### XIII. OPEN MOUTH APPROACH

*A. Kinds of problems for which approach is useful.* Encouraging the patient to develop more oral openness will often reduce generalized vocal hyperfunction. Opening the mouth more while speaking, and learning to listen with a slightly open mouth, both allow the patient to use his vocal mechanisms more optimally. The open mouth approach promotes more natural size/mass adjustments and more optimum approximation of the vocal folds, aiding in problems of loudness, pitch, and quality. The approach is particularly effective in developing a better voice for persons with dysphonia in the absence of any organic pathology. Development of greater oral openness should be a part of any voice therapy program where the patient is attempting to use his vocal mechanisms with less effort and strain.

*B. Procedural aspects of approach.*

1. Have the patient view himself in a mirror (or on a videotape playback, if possible) to observe the presence and absence of open mouth behavior. Any lip tightness, mandibular restriction, or excessive neck muscle movement should be identified for the patient by the clinician.

2. Develop an awareness of oral openness when listening. Demonstrate to the patient that it is possible to listen or to read with the teeth slightly apart and the lips gently parted. Have the patient try to do this. Many patients with hyperfunctional voice problems are so "tight" orally that they find it difficult initially to relax their mouths. These patients should be instructed that what they are attempting to do will at first feel foreign and inappropriate. The initial stages of letting the jaw relax are frequently anything but relaxed.

3. To establish further this oral openness, ask the patient to drop his head toward his chest and let his lips part and his jaw drop open. Once he can do this, have him practice some relaxed /a/s. When the head is tilted down and the jaw is slightly open, a more relaxed phonation will often be achieved.

4. In order for the patient to develop a feeling of openness when listening and as a pre-set to speaking, he must in the beginning develop a conscious awareness of how often he finds himself with a tight, closed mouth. One way to develop this awareness is to have the patient mark down, on a card he carries with him, each time he becomes aware that his mouth is closed unnecessarily. The marking task itself is often enough to increase his awareness, and his number of mouth closings over a period of a week will decrease notably. Another way of developing an awareness of greater orality is to have the patient place, in his living environment (on a dressing table, desk, car dashboard, etc.), a little sign that says "OPEN" or perhaps has a double arrow ( ↕ ) or any other code which might serve as a reminder.

5. Once the patient has achieved oral openness, such oral resonance practice materials as those set down by Fisher (57), Eisenson (53), Akin (1), and Fairbanks (55) will be helpful in establishing a carry-over between greater orality and the speech-voicing task itself. Practice in steps two and three under this open month approach will usually help produce a more optimum voice and should precede the reading of actual speech materials.

*C. Typical case history showing utilization of approach.* J. J., a 17-year-old high school girl, was examined by a laryngologist about one year after an automobile accident in which she had suffered some injuries to the head and neck. Laryngoscopic examination found all visible laryngeal structures normal in appearance and function, despite the fact that since the accident the girl's voice had been only barely audible. The speech pathologist was impressed "with her relatively closed mouth while speaking, which seemed to result in extremely poor voice resonance." Voice therapy combined both the chewing and the open mouth facilitating approaches. It was discovered in therapy that for three months after the automobile accident the girl had worn an orthopedic collar which seemed to inhibit her head and jaw movements. It appeared that much of her closed-mouth—mandibularly-restricted speech was related to the constraints imposed upon her by the orthopedic collar. When using the open mouth approach with her head titlted down toward her chest, she was immediately able to produce a louder, more resonant voice. The open mouth approach was initiated before beginning chewing exercises, and both achieved excellent results. Therapy was terminated after six weeks, with much voice improvement in both loudness and quality.

*D. Evaluation of approach.* It is commonly recognized by singing teachers that the best musical voice of any one individual is highly related to good mouth opening. Speaking with an open mouth is not only more relaxed, but the increased size of the oral cavity provides for better oral resonance. It requires relatively more muscle force to keep the jaws together than to let them hang open, an observation easily verified by looking at the typical cadaver with its characteristic gaping mouth. Not only is the open mouth approach an effective facilitator for producing more relaxed, efficient phonation, but it is a useful technique for the tense patient to employ at any time as a method of achieving oral relaxation.

### XIV. PITCH INFLECTIONS

A. *Kinds of problems for which approach is useful.* The normal voice will vary below and above its habitual pitch, which is the pitch level used most often. But in some voices this pitch variation is lacking. Such a monotonous pitch, which for the average speaker would be impossible to maintain, requires the inhibition of natural inflection and is observed usually in overcontrolled persons who display very little overt affect. Fairbanks, who describes pitch variation as a vital part of normal phonation, defines inflection and pitch thusly: "An *inflection* is a modulation of pitch during phonation. A *shift* is a change of pitch from the end of one phonation to the beginning of the next" (55, p 132). Voice therapy for patients with monotonic pitch seeks not only to establish more optimum pitch levels, but to increase the amount of pitch variability. Any voice patient with a dull, monotonous pitch level will profit from attempting to increase his pitch inflections.

B. *Procedural aspects of approach.*
1. Listen, with the patient, to recorded samples of the patient's voice, contrasting these perhaps with samples of a few voices with excellent pitch variation, and follow this listening with direct comment on the problem. The patient must be made aware of his lack of pitch variation.
2. Begin working on downward and upward inflectional shifts of the same word, exaggerating in the beginning the extent of pitch change. Akin (1), Eisenson (53), Fairbanks (55), and Fisher (57) provide excellent practice materials for enhancing inflection.
3. Using the same source material, have the patient practice introducing pitch shifts within specific words.
4. Record the patient's oral reading and conversation from time to time, critically analyzing these productions with regard to his pitch variability.

C. *Typical case history showing utilization of approach.* R. M., 52-year-old farm implement salesman, had a two-year history of recurring dysphonia with occasional aphonia. Laryngeal examination found him to have "an edematous larynx with early polypoid formation on the right vocal fold at the junction of the anterior third-middle third." His voice evaluation revealed an inappropriately low-pitched voice with almost no pitch variation. Trial voice therapy suggested that the patient experienced more relaxed phonation when he used pitch inflections and spoke at a higher pitch level ($D_3$ instead of $B_3$). The patient terminated voice therapy after four sessions, leaving behind recordings which clearly demonstrated that the use of pitch inflection helped him maintain a slightly higher voice pitch and noticeably improved his overall voice quality. It was the clinician's opinion that had the patient continued in voice therapy, practicing a slightly higher voice pitch and the use of pitch inflection, he would have experienced a marked reduction of his dysphonia and a gradual clearing of his polypoid formation.

D. *Evaluation of approach.* In voice therapy, anything that can be done to reduce the amount of effort used by the patient to speak usually has a positive effect on the laryngeal mechanism and its vocal product. Increasing pitch variability in a monotonic voice usually contributes to increased vocal relaxation. Patients are easily taught to increase their pitch inflections, and such an approach should be used in any case where pitch variability is lacking.

*XV. PUSHING APPROACH*

A. *Kinds of problems for which approach is useful.* Pushing exercises are useful for the patient with problems of vocal fold approximation, and may be helpful in increasing loudness and improving the quality of voice. Froeschels, who introduced the pushing approach, first used the method for increasing the strength of the soft palate, later adapting it with others *(62)* to problems of cord paralysis and to voices worn out from continued hyperfunction (hypofunctional voices). We have found the pushing approach useful with patients with weak voices related to such varied causes as generalized systemic fatigue, myasthenia, unilateral cord paralysis, and traumatic injury to the larynx, and especially effective with patients who have bowing of the vocal folds as a result, usually, of prolonged hyperfunctional use of the voice.

B. *Procedural aspects of approach*
1. First demonstrate the pushing method by raising the patient's fists to about shoulder height, and then pushing his arms down suddenly in a rapid, uninterrupted motion until his hands, fully extended, reach to just below his hips. Then instruct the patient to do the same thing by himself. Occasionally a patient may require some active assistance from the clinician to be sure he achieves the rapid, downward movement required.
2. After the patient can perform the pushing well, ask him to push and phonate simultaneously. It usually requires only short practice for the patient to synchronize the two actions. Phonations produced while pushing are usually louder and have better resonance.
3. Another variation of the pushing approach is to ask the patient to hang on to the seat of his chair, and, while gripping the chair, to push down firmly with his arms. Next, ask him to add phonation while pushing in this way. Short successive bursts of pushing-phonation should then be practiced.
4. Once better phonation has been produced through pushing, have the patient listen to it on some kind of auditory feedback loop system. While the

pushing may be the primary facilitator in producing the better voice, the patient should soon attempt to match the same loudness and quality of phonation without pushing. A useful approach would be to have him listen discriminatively to his two phonations, one with pushing and one without, and see how closely he can match them in subsequent imitative attempts.

5. Once the patient is able to extend the good voice into a series of practice phrases, the pushing should be stopped. It is generally advisable to terminate pushing as soon as the same voice loudness and quality can be achieved without it. The primary value of pushing is in its initial facilitating effect.

*C. Typical case history showing utilization of approach.* M. M., a 52-year-old attorney, had a two-year history of a "tired" voice that could not be heard during his courtroom appearances. On laryngoscopic examination, he appeared to have "severe posterior bowing of the cords, with the vocal processes in a fixed state of slight abduction." Voice therapy focused on a slight lowering of pitch level and on the pushing approach. On the first day of evaluation-therapy, the patient was able to produce a louder, more resonant voice by combining arm-extension pushing with the lowered phonation. In four therapy sessions, he was able to combine pushing with the more vigorous phonation of practice phrases. The patient continued in voice therapy for a total of eight weeks, seeing the clinician for thirty-minute practice sessions twice a week. He was soon able to produce good matching phonations without pushing. As for carry-over to the courtroom, the setting where his difficulty had been most penalizing to him, he was able to achieve this by occasionally pushing down hard on his chair while speaking. Laryngeal examination at the end of therapy found "normal vocal fold approximation, with no evidence of vocal process abduction." Voice loudness and quality appeared to be highly adequate at the time that therapy was discontinued, but no follow-up evaluation could be made to determine the permanence of these gains.

*D. Evaluation of approach.* One of the primitive functions of the larynx is its valve closing during particular physiologic states of the organism, such as during heavy physical effort. The pushing approach, which requires the person to use his upper extremities in a forceful pushing manner, is usually accompanied by glottal closing. This glottal closure is observed in heavy lifting efforts, which are frequently accompanied by primitive vocalizations, indicating relatively firm approximation of the vocal folds. When the patient employs intentional vocalization "on top of" primitive sphincteric closure, the result is often a phonation of good loudness and quality. Pushing exercises have been found useful for hyperfunctional voice conditions and paralytic conditions by Froeschels, Kastein, and Weiss *(62)* and Brodnitz *(24)*.

Pushing exercises should be thought of as only a facilitating approach for producing firmer vocal fold approximation, which will result in a louder, more resonant, voice. Once the patient is able to match his "push-ing" voice without pushing, the exercises should be progressively mini-mized. Continued pushing carries with it the unhappy possibility that the patient will revive, as Brodnitz warns, "the hyperfunctional use of the voice that preceded the hypofunctional phase" (*24*, p. 46). However, as a facilitator for producing a stronger voice, the pushing approach is excellent.

## XVI. RELAXATION

*A. Kinds of problems for which approach is useful.* Most dysphonias and laryngeal pathologies are related to prolonged and continued vocal hyperfunction, the reduction of which is a frequent goal in voice therapy. It does not necessarily follow, however, that with all these hyperfunctional problems we teach general body relaxation. Using such methods as the chewing approach or the yawn-sigh approach achieves vocal tract relaxa-tion without working on it directly. It is usually futile in therapy to imply to tense patients that if they would "just relax," all would be well. If the patient could relax, he would; if his tension did not in fact serve him in some way, he would get rid of it. A certain amount of psychic tension and muscle tonus is normal and healthy, of course, but there are individuals who overreact to their environmental stresses; instead of "running at a slow idle," they are like "fast idle engines," expending far more energy and effort than the situation requires. By relaxation, therefore, we mean a realis-tic responsiveness to the environment with a minimum of needless energy expended. Some voice patients, but certainly not all, profit from a therapy program designed to reduce unnecessary tension by using relaxation tech-niques. The clinician who chooses to use relaxation methods with particular patients should remember that these methods are usually best combined with other facilitating techniques designed especially for producing a better voice.

*B. Procedural aspects of approach.*
1. The classical method of differential relaxation, as outlined by Jacobson (*87*), might be explained to the patient and applied. Under differential relaxation, the patient concentrates on a particular site of the body, deliberately relaxing and tensing certain muscles, discriminating between muscle contraction and relaxation. The typical procedure here is to have the patient begin distally, away from the body, with the fingers or the toes. Once the patient feels the tightness of contraction and the heaviness of relaxation at the beginning site, he moves "up" the limb (on to the feet or hands, and thence to the legs or arms), repeating at each site the tightness-heaviness discrimination. Once the torso is reached, the voice patient should include the chest, neck, "voice box," throat, and on through the mouth and parts of the face. With some patients, we start the distal analysis with the head, beginning with the scalp and then going to the forehead, eyes, facial muscles, lips, jaw, tongue, palate, throat, larynx, neck, etc. Some

practice in this progressive relaxation technique can produce remarkably relaxed states in very tense patients.

2. Wolpe (*171*) combines relaxation, once it is taught, with hierarchy analysis (facilitating technique XI). The patient responds to certain tension-producing cues by deliberately employing a relaxed response, such as a feeling of heaviness in certain parts of the body, and this in turn enables him to maintain a degree of relaxation despite the presence of anxiety-provoking stimuli.

3. Head rotation might be introduced as a technique for relaxing components of the vocal tract. The approach is used in this way: the patient sits in a backless chair, dropping his head forward to his chest; he then "flops" his head across to his right shoulder, and then lifts it, again flopping (the neck is here extended), along his back and across to his left shoulder; he then returns to the anterior head-down-on-chest position; he repeats the cycle, rolling the head in a circular fashion. A few patients will not find head rotation relaxing, but most will feel the heaviness of the movement and experience definite relaxation in the neck. For this latter group, once the patient reports neck relaxation, he should be asked to phonate an "ah" as he rolls his head. The relaxed phonation might be recorded and then analyzed in terms of what it sounds like in comparison to the patient's other phonations.

4. Open throat relaxation can also be used. Have the patient lower his head slightly toward his chest and make an easy, open, prolonged yawn, concentrating on what the yawn feels like in his throat. The yawn should yield conscious sensations of an open throat during the prolonged inhalation. If the patient reports that he can feel this open throat sensation, ask him to prolong an "ah," capturing and maintaining the same feeling he experienced during the yawn. Any relaxed phonations produced under these conditions should be recorded and used as target voice models for the patient. Encourage the patient to comment and think about the relaxed throat sensations he may have experienced during the yawn.

5. Ask the patient to think of a setting he has experienced, or perhaps imagined, as the ultimate in relaxation. Different patients will use different kinds of imagery here. For example, one patient thought of lying in a hammock, but for another person the suggestion of lying in a hammock produced a set of anxious responses. Settings typically thought of as relaxed are lying on a rug at night in front of a blazing fire, floating on a lake, fishing while lying in a row-boat, lying down in bed, etc. The setting the patient thinks of should be studied and analyzed; eventually, the patient should try to capture the relaxed feelings he imagines he might have, or may actually have experienced, in such a setting. With some practice—and some tolerance for initial failure in recapturing the relaxed mood—the average patient will be able to find a setting or two which he can re-create in his imagination and use in future tense situations.

6. Additional methods for facilitating relaxation of the vocal tract can be found in Fisher's *Improving Voice and Articulation* (*57*), and in other books on voice and articulation, physical exercise and therapy, physical conditioning, and singing technique.

*C. Typical case history showing utilization of approach.* M. Y., a 34-year-old missile engineer, developed transient periods of severe dysphonia when talking to certain people. At other times, particularly in his professional work, he experienced normal voice. Mirror laryngoscopy revealed a normal larynx. During the voice interview, the speech pathologist was impressed by the man's general nervousness and apparently poor self-concept. In exploring the area of interpersonal relationships, the patient confided that in the last year he had seen two psychiatrists periodically, but had experienced no relief from his tension. Further exploration of the settings in which his voice was most dysphonic revealed that his biggest problem was in talking to store clerks, garage men, and persons who did physical labor; some of his more relaxed experiences included giving speeches and giving work instructions to his colleagues. Subsequent voice therapy included the Jacobson approach of progressive relaxation. Once relaxed behavior was achieved, the patient developed a hierarchy of situations, beginning with those in which he felt most relaxed (giving instructions to colleagues) and proceeding to those in which he experienced the most tension (talking with car mechanics). After some practice, the patient was able to recognize various cues which signaled increasing tension. Once such a cue occurred, he would employ a relaxation response, which more often than not enabled him to maintain normal phonation in situations which had previously induced dysphonia. As this consciously induced response continued to be successful, the patient reported greater confidence in approaching the previously tense situations, knowing he would experience little or no voice difficulty. Voice therapy was terminated after eleven weeks, with the patient reporting only occasional difficulty in phonating in isolated situations, and developing increased self-confidence in all situations.

*D. Evaluation of approach.* While many psychological and psychiatric therapists today advocate symptomatic therapy for the relief of psychological tension, there is the other view that symptomatic therapy treats only the symptom and not the true cause of the disorder. Representing the latter view, Murphy writes:

To focus therapeutic energy on the tensions as such does not bring us closer to the factors producing the tensions. Therefore, any effort to erase tension and to induce relaxation directly is likely to be only temporarily effective or to fail altogether. [*119*, p. 118]

Some of the thinking supporting the other view, direct symptom modification, is presented in chapter 1 of this text and need not be repeated here. It should be added, however, that there appears to be a growing body of clinicians who feel that direct symptom modification, such as teaching relaxed responses to replace previous tense responses, breaks up the circular kind of behavior that characterizes so much of what we do as human beings; that is, we respond in a certain way now because we responded in the same way before. Perhaps the basic cause of our original response is no longer present. But our continued response, such as becoming tense, has become so conditioned that it can be extinguished from our repertoire only by being replaced with a newly conditioned, more optimum, response. Regardless of the arguments or bias of the clinician, it does appear that the average tense voice patient can be taught some relaxed responses to use instead of his previous tense ones. It further appears that a slight decrease of unnecessary vocal tract tension replaced by some increase in relaxation has a positive influence in producing a more relaxed, optimum phonation.

## XVII. RESPIRATION TRAINING

*A. Kinds of problems for which approach is useful.* Back in the first part of the twentieth century, some of the earliest articles about voice therapy supported the view that most voice disorders were related to poor breathing patterns—and, indeed, the singing teacher and the dramatic coach to this day include breathing exercises and breathing technique as part of their instruction. The modern-day voice clinician, whether he be a laryngologist or a speech pathologist, places far less emphasis on faulty respiration than his predecessors did. However, there are some voice patients, described in earlier chapters, who profit from some attention given to improving their control of respiration, especially their control of the expiratory phase of the breathing cycle. While general improvement in total respiration, such as an improvement in vital capacity, appears to have little effect on the voice, any marked departure in the inspiratory-expiratory cycle may produce noticeable voice alterations. Some loudness and quality problems of the voice sometimes respond well to therapeutic techniques designed to help the patient increase and extend his expiratory air flow.

*B. Procedural aspects of approach.*
1. Give the patient a simple explanation of phonatory physiology, emphasizing that it is the flow of the outgoing air stream that trips the approximated vocal folds into vibration. If the patient demonstrates a problem in this area (and work on respiration should be avoided if no problem exists), the problem and what can be done about it should be described by the clinician.
2. Demonstrate a slightly exaggerated breath, as used in sighing. The sigh is characterized by a slightly larger-than-usual inhalation followed by a prolonged open-mouth exhalation. The type of breath used to produce the sigh can be described to the patient as the "breath of well-being," the kind of easy breath one might take when comfortable or happy—the proverbial sigh of contentment.
3. Demonstrate the quick inhalation and prolonged exhalation needed for a normal speaking task. Take a normal breath and count slowly from one to five on one exhalation. See if the patient can do this; if he can, extend the count by one number each time, at the rate of approximately one number per half second. This activity can be continued until the patient is able to use his "best" phona-

tion during the number counts. Any sacrifice of vocal quality should be avoided, and the number count should never be extended beyond the point where good quality is lost.

4. Practice extending an even phonation, such as an /a/ or similar open vowel, for as long as possible without any noticeable phonation break or change of quality. Take a baseline measurement in the beginning, such as number of seconds the phonation can be maintained, and see whether this can be extended with practice. Avoid asking the patient to "take in a big breath"; rather, ask him to take in a normal breath of well-being, initiating a lightly phonated sigh on exhalation. See if he can extend this for five seconds. If so, progressively increase the extension, to 8, 12, 15, and finally 20 seconds. The voice patient who can hold on to an extended phonation of a vowel for 20 seconds has certainly exhibited good breath control for purposes of voice. Such a patient would not have to work on breath control per se, but he might want to combine his work on exhalation control with such approaches as hierarchy analysis (to see if he can maintain such good breath control under varying moments of stress).

5. Select from various voice and articulation books reading materials designed to help develop breath control. Give special attention to beginning phonation as soon after inhalation as possible, not wasting a lot of the outgoing air stream before phonating. Practice quick inhalations between phrases and sentences, taking care not to take "a big breath."

6. With young children who need breathing work, the clinician might begin with nonverbal exhalations. The best way to work on breathing exhalation with little children is to use a pinwheel, which lends itself naturally to the game, "How long can you keep the pinwheel spinning?" With practice, the child will be able to extend the length of his exhalations (the length of his pinwheel spinning). Another method of enhancing exhalation control is to place a piece of tissue paper against a wall, begin blowing on it to keep it in place when the fingers are removed, and keep blowing on it to see how long it can be kept in place. Both the pinwheel and tissue-paper exercises lend themselves to timing measurements; these measurements should be made and plotted graphically for the child; when a certain target length of time is reached, the activity can be stopped.

7. In those rare cases when the clinician working with a singer, actor, or lecturer decides that some formal respiration training should be given, the following steps might be taken:

   *a.* Discuss the importance of good posture, for normal posture is one of the best facilitators of normal breathing. Any real departure from good posture, such as leading forward with the head (kyphosis), may contribute to faulty breathing.

   *b.* Demonstrate abdominal-diaphragmatic breathing. First, have the subject lie supine, with his hands on his abdomen, directly under his rib cage. In this position, there will be observable distention of the abdomen upon inhalation. The downward excursion of the diaphragm, which increases the vertical dimension of the chest, cannot be viewed directly (since the diaphragm attachments are behind and inside the ribs); its effect can only be viewed by the outward displacement of the abdomen. On exhalation, as the diaphragm ascends, the abdominal distention lessens. In this form of breathing, then, the patient should try deliberately to relax the abdominal muscles during inhalation and contract them during exhalation. If he can do this successfully in the supine position, he should try to duplicate the procedure while standing with his back flat against a wall. Continuing to clasp his hands on his abdomen in the beginning will help him develop some awareness of the difference between abdominal relaxation–distention and abdominal contraction–flattening. As soon as the subject learns to breathe by this relaxation–contraction of the abdominal muscles, introduce some phonation activities to be done on exhalation. The voice patient who has been speaking "from the level of his throat," without adequate breath support, will often "feel" the difference that a bigger breath makes only when he adds phonation. The voice patient who needed respiration training in the first place needs to have respiration and phonation combined into practice activities as soon as possible.

*c.* Many books on therapeutic exercise, such as Kraus' *Principles and Practice of Therapeutic Exercises (95),* give specific exercises for patients whose voice problems may be related to such illnesses as asthma or emphysema. Respiration problems such as these may be beyond the voice clinician's area of competence, and it is advisable that he consult with respiration therapists, physical therapists, and such medical doctors as physiatrists and cardiologists.

*C. Typical case history showing utilization of approach.* J. M., a 22-year-old first grade teacher, complained of losing her voice at the end of each teaching day. While mirror laryngoscopy found her to have a normal larynx, voice testing revealed that most of the time she spoke on residual air. She seemed to take in an adequate inhalation, only to exhale a major part of it before beginning to phonate. Much of her phonation appeared to be forced, with inadequate air flow behind it. Voice therapy focused on introducing her to the necessity of "getting some air behind her voice." First the myoelastic theory of phonation was demonstrated. Then the method of abdominal-diaphragmatic breathing was demonstrated, and the patient was instructed in its use. Her roommate was also instructed in the method, so that she could help the patient during home-practice periods. Exhalation-phonation exercises were initiated, wherein the patient would practice extending both phonations and number counts on one breath. After six weeks of twice-weekly voice therapy and home practice, the patient was able to employ adequate breathing methods, and her improved breathing produced a louder voice of better quality, which did not tire with daily teaching use. Before therapy was concluded, however, the patient was in a severe automobile accident, requiring many months of hospitalization. Thus, no long-term follow-up was possible to see if her improved voice had been maintained.

*D. Evaluation of approach.* Some of the leading texts on voice disorders, such as Van Riper's and Irwin's *Voice and Articulation (162),* Murphy's

*Functional Voice Disorders (119),* and Brodnitz's *Vocal Rehabilitation (24),* present effective arguments against the need for respiration training for most voice patients. It would appear that in the average approach to vocal rehabilitation, we have swung far away from respiration as a possible factor in faulty voice production. Very few voice clinicians work with the patient in helping him improve expiratory control. But a few voice patients do exist who can profit from this kind of work. The goal in voice therapy is to help the patient produce the best phonation possible with the least amount of effort. Respiration training for the voice patient may not require anything but helping the patient learn to take an easy, normal breath—nothing more than that. There is no need for the patient to learn a certain kind of breathing, or to increase his vital capacity, etc. Rather, some practice in taking in "the breath of well-being," and in extending the phonation slightly is about all that is needed. For some patients, however, this small amount of attention to respiration is badly needed and will serve as an excellent facilitator for producing a better voice.

### XVIII. TARGET VOICE MODELS

  *A. Kinds of problems for which approach is useful.* In almost any form of voice rehabilitation, it is essential that the patient have clearly before him a target voice model. While this voice model may be the phonation of the clinician, it is more practical and useful if it is the patient's *own* "best" voice production. The search in therapy for the patient's "best" phonation requires a thorough exploration of the patient's vocal repertoire to find that *one* pitch inflection or loudness variation or head position which facilitates the optimum phonation. Any one of the twenty facilitating techniques described in this section of chapter 5 may produce the desired target voice model, either alone or in combination. Voice therapy for hyperfunctional voice problems is essentially the process of identifying and eliminating abusive vocal behaviors, replacing these faulty vocalizations with more optimum phonation *from the beginning of therapy.* In most cases, the desired target phonation does not need to be some kind of vague distant goal, but can be utilized from the start. At the time of the voice evaluation, perhaps, or during initial therapy periods, the patient may well be able to respond to the search for the "best" phonation by producing one. Using target voice models is an essential part of voice therapy for almost any kind of voice problem.

  *B. Procedural aspects of approach.*
  1. The clinician should discuss with the patient the fact that there are many different ways of producing voice, some requiring much effort and some comparatively little. The easiest kind of phonation is what we are usually seeking in voice therapy. The clinician might well use his own voice, if he can, to demon-

strate variations of pitch, loudness, and quality; this demonstration should be accompanied by ongoing comments on whatever audible effects the variations have on the sound of the voice.

2. Various phonations the patient produced at the time of the evaluation should be reviewed with regard to their good and bad effects on overall voice. There should be an ongoing search for a voice of better quality; sometimes this voice will be produced by changes of pitch, such as upward or downward pitch inflections, or perhaps by providing the patient with imagery describing the physical sensations that go with voice, or by the patient's experimenting with various head positions or body postures, or by his attempts to imitate some voice model other than his own. This search for the patient's best voice, by having him try doing different things, is a critical part of voice therapy. Too often we abandon this phonation searching prematurely. The voice clinician should stay with the search for the target voice, even if his early efforts fail. The patient will need encouragement to try different things—and so will the beginning clinician.

3. During the search for optimum phonation, the patient's efforts should be tape-recorded, so that if an optimum phonation is produced it can be captured for replay. One way of doing this is to use a loop tape recorder, setting the instrument on continuous record with no playback, but changing to continuous playback if a desired phonation is produced. Another way—and this permits saving the tape as a permanent recording—is to cut a 12- to 14-inch piece of audiotape and splice it as a tape loop; then drape the loop through the recording heads of a conventional tape recorder and record the patient's phonations; the tape loop will continually record over itself until the clinician—immediately after the desired voice is produced—stops the recording process and turns on the playback; the clinician now has a continuous recording of the optimum phonation to use as a loop playback whenever he wishes to use the patient's own best voice as the therapy model. Another method of saving a model production is to record each of the patient's trial productions on an audiotape card, such as a Language Master card. The advantage here is that the card can easily be kept in a clinical records file, at least more easily than a loop tape cartridge or an unprotected 12- to 14-inch tape loop. Whatever method is used, the patient's search for a better phonation should be recorded, so that if a target phonation is produced it may be played back as a model.

4. Have the patient listen to his own model recording and attempt to modify his voice to match that phonation. The attempt should be accompanied by some discussion of what the model phonation feels and sounds like. Once the patient can match the target phonation with a similar sounding phonation, ask him to do it again—this time without the auditory model. Vary the time delay between productions to see if he can produce the model after several minutes of not hearing it. If he can do this, his memory span and ability to re-create an inner model are sufficient to allow him to go on to some practice in using the model voice.

5. When the patient is able to produce his model voice voluntarily, or by using some facilitating technique, he is ready to practice the voice in oral reading. The

relative instability of the new voice at this time does not permit using it in real conversational situations. For this reason, early practice attempts should be confined to reading single words or short phrases aloud. The beginning attempts at oral reading should be tape-recorded for the patient's use in playback analysis. As the patient experiences the new voice in his laboratory practice, the length of the reading material should be increased to include paragraphs, poems, etc. Eventually, he will be able to use the new vocal patterns in out-of-clinic situations.

C. *Typical case history showing utilization of approach.* An eleven-year-old boy, C. R., was found to have had a persistent dysphonia for a period of three months. Laryngoscopy found "a slight cord thickening at the anterior one-third junction," and the voice evaluation found "a voice pitch level well within the adult male vocal range." In subsequent voice therapy the boy was able to use varying pitch inflections, and whenever his pitch level swept upward, his dysphonia would disappear. Loop tape recordings were made of the boy's phonation during pitch inflection and were played back to him as an example of his voice when it was free of dysphonia. The boy was soon able to match his target model without having to read with pitch inflection; practice sessions in using his voice at slightly higher pitch levels were always tape-recorded and played back for his analysis. This youngster was highly successful in using his own voice production as his therapy model. The voice therapy, which focused primarily on the target voice model approach, was terminated after twelve weeks, having produced a normal larynx and a normal voice.

D. *Evaluation of approach.* Any speech pathologist familiar with McDonald's *deep* articulation therapy approach *(104)* is aware of the search in therapy for *can do* speech behaviors. Because we have so little useful feedback information about how we phonate, and about how we speak, for that matter, it is fruitful in therapy to search for what the patient can already do in areas where he demonstrates some problem. In articulation, for example, McDonald advocates that we investigate the patient's production of a distorted phoneme to see if the presence of another phoneme before or after that one helps him produce the sound correctly; if a certain phonemic combination facilitates the correct production of the phoneme, that combination should be used in therapy. The target voice model represents basically the same *deep* approach to the problem of voice. By exploring many different kinds of voice productions with the patient, we are exploring his vocal repertoire for the good phonation that he is *already able to produce.* Once the good phonation is identified, we provide the patient with a playback of his own best production. This approach of using *can do* vocalizations gives the patient a voice model that he obviously can produce, and gives it to him early in therapy. His own best production is then shaped and extended in practice sessions, using reading materials, until he is eventually able to use it in the real world of communication. Such a gestalt approach to voice, using the patient's own best production, avoids fractionating voice production into such components as breathing, glottal attack, resonance, etc. Once a patient's voice performance is so fractionated ("you are doing this and this and this") he may be powerless to correct all the faulty components and gather them together again into some kind of beautiful voice. Starting where the patient *is,* with his own best phonation, appears to be a most viable, effective approach in most voice therapy.

## XIX. VOICE REST

A. *Kinds of problems for which approach is useful.* Voice rest is indicated only in cases of acute laryngitis or after surgery involving the larynx. Voice rest is of little benefit to the various hyperfunctional pathologies of voice, because once the patient resumes his faulty phonation patterns, his dysphonia and related pathologies return. For the patient with acute laryngitis, infectious or traumatic in etiology, voice rest does prevent further irritation of already irritated folds, and the cessation of irritation does promote healing. After a surgical procedure, such as the removal of polyps or nodules, it is essential that the irritated glottal surfaces be free of vibration, and this can only be accomplished by total cessation of voicing. The voice rest prescribed after surgery should always be as brief as possible, perhaps three to seven days in the case of the average surgery, and two weeks maximum for something like the removal of rather large polyps. The length of voice rest after surgery is the decision of the surgeon.

B. *Procedural aspects of approach.*

1. If voice rest is to be initiated, it must be complete. Explain the need for voice rest to the patient, insisting that he *not even whisper.* It is almost impossible for anyone to whisper without some glottal closure, despite evidence that the patient is producing his whisper orally or buccally. For this reason, total abstention from speech should be enforced. Communication will have to rely on gesture or writing.

2. The patient should also be counseled about no coughing, throat-clearing, or laughing. Any of these phonations will have the same deleterious effect as speech.

C. *Typical case history showing utilization of approach.* M. P., a seven-year-old girl, was successfully placed on voice rest for a period of ten days following a bilateral *cord stripping.* She complied with the no-voicing instructions to the letter and was not heard to phonate during the ten-day period. After ten days, despite the urging of her parents and the laryngologist, the child could not resume phonation. After seven more days, still with no phonation, she was referred to the speech pathologist for functional aphonia. She followed the therapeutic instructions of the speech pathologist very well, as reported by Boone (*20*), and found her voice after two days of therapy. The case illustrates how even a child can be placed on voice rest successfully, and also illustrates a complication that can develop after enforced voice rest.

D. *Evaluation of approach.* The only therapeutic value of voice rest is to promote healing during periods of laryngitis and after surgery of the larynx. Voice rest should not be used as a voice therapy device to reduce dysphonia related to hyperfunctional voice usage. Rather, the preferred treatment should be to identify and reduce, and hopefully eliminate, the vocal hyperfunction.

*XX. YAWN-SIGH APPROACH*

A. *Kinds of problems for which approach is useful.* The yawn-sigh approach is most effective with hyperfunctional problems of glottal approximation, particularly in eliminating hard glottal contacts. The approach also positively influences loudness, pitch, and quality in hyperfunctional problems without vocal fold pathology, and has proved to be an excellent facilitator of optimum voice in such disorders as contact ulcers, vocal nodules, polyps, cord thickening, and laryngitis resulting from abuse.

B. *Procedural aspects of approach.*

1. Explain very generally to the patient the physiology of a yawn, i.e., that a yawn represents a prolonged inspiration with maximum widening of the supraglottal airways (characterized by a wide, stretching, opening of the mouth). Then demonstrate a yawn and talk about what the yawn feels like.

2. After the patient has yawned, following the clinician's example, ask him to yawn again and then to exhale gently with a light phonation. In doing this, many patients are able to feel an easy phonation, often for the first time.

3. Once the yawn-phonation is easily achieved, instruct the patient to say words beginning with /h/ or with open-mouthed vowels, one word per yawn in the beginning, followed eventually by four or five words on one exhalation.

4. Demonstrate for the patient the sigh phase of the exercise, that is, the prolonged, easy, open-mouthed exhalation after the yawn. Then, omitting the yawn entirely, demonstrate a quicker, normal, open-mouthed inhalation followed by the prolonged open-mouthed sigh.

5. As soon as the patient can produce a relaxed sigh, have him say the word "hah" after beginning the sigh. Follow this with a series of words beginning with the glottal /h/. Additional words for practice after the sigh should begin with middle and low vowels. Care should be given to blending in, towards the middle of the sigh, an easy, relaxed, relatively soft phonation. This blending of the phonation into the sigh is often difficult for the patient initially, but is the most vital part of the approach for the elimination of hard glottal contacts.

6. Finally, once the yawn-sigh approach is well developed, have the patient think of the relaxed oral feeling it provides. Eventually, he will be able to maintain a relaxed phonation simply by imagining the approach.

C. *Typical case history showing utilization of approach.* J. A., a 47-year-old manufacturer's representative, had a two-year history of vocal fatigue, often losing his voice toward the end of a work day. After a two-week period of increasing dysphonia and slight pain on the left side of the neck, the man was found by a consulting laryngologist to have "slight redness and edema on both vocal processes." The subsequent voice evaluation found him to speak with pronounced hard glottal attack in an attempt to "force out his voice over his dysphonia." By using the yawn-sigh approach, the patient was able to demonstrate a clear phonation of relatively good resonance. His yawn-sigh phonations were recorded on loop tape and fed back to him as the voice model he should imitate. Because the patient reported some stress in certain work situations, the hierarchy analysis approach (facilitating technique XI) was used, isolating those situations in which he felt relaxed and those in which he experienced tension. Thereafter, whenever he was aware of tense situational cues, he employed the yawn-sigh method to maintain relaxed phonation. Combining yawn-sigh with hierarchy analysis proved to be an excellent symptomatic approach for this patient, as his voice cleared markedly and there was no recurrence of the periodic aphonia. Twice-weekly therapy was terminated after twenty-two weeks, with the patient demonstrating a normal voice and a normal laryngeal mechanism.

D. *Evaluation of approach.* The yawn-sigh is another approach which makes use of a normal, vegetative function, at which time the patient can phonate in a more natural, relaxed manner. Luchsinger and Arnold describe yawning as a "prolonged and deepened inspiration with maximal widening of the upper airways. The act of yawning is an *inborn reflex pattern. . . .*" (*101*, p. 152). The advantage of the yawn as a prelude to phonation is that during the initial stages of the yawn, the oral-pharynx is open and relaxed. With but little practice, the average patient can produce a relaxed, easy phonation if he couples the phonation with a yawn. The sigh, a relaxed and extended exhalation, provides an excellent environment for the initiation of an easy phonation. As the patient extends his sigh, he begins a soft phonation with very gentle approximation of the vocal folds. This easy phonation is often in sharp contrast to the hard, abrupt type he may regularly use. The yawn-sigh approach is an effective voice facilitator for the patient with hyperfunctional voice problems, with or without actual vocal fold pathology. We have found it to be an excellent technique for achieving some degree of vocal relaxation, particularly in situations in which the patient feels tense.

## SUMMARY

The focus of voice therapy for patients with vocal hyperfunction is the "search" for the patient's best vocal production. It is this production that should be used, whenever possible, as the patient's target model. Twenty facilitating approaches for developing the best voice in voice therapy have been described, with each approach detailed procedurally and illustrated by a typical case history.

*chapter six*

# Voice Therapy for Special Problems

*Not all voice problems are related to hyperfunctional use of the vocal mechanisms. Some particular dysphonias, such as ventricular dysphonia, require a distinctive therapeutic approach. We shall consider separately voice therapy for the deaf, and for functional aphonia, ventricular phonation, spastic dysphonia, and specific kinds of vocal cord paralysis. It will be noted that many of the voice facilitating techniques described in chapter 5 are useful with these problems as well.*

## VOICE THERAPY FOR THE DEAF

Deaf adults and children generally sound different from normal speakers. This difference has been explored in various ways, from describing the physical characteristics of the deaf voice to determining what can be done in voice therapy. Angelocci, Kopp, and Holbrook (2) have described the vowel-formant variations in the voices of deaf children as characterized usually by a depressed second formant. Zaliouk (176) has pointed out that falsetto is a frequent characteristic of the high-pitched voices of deaf children. In my own writing (19) I have mentioned several related studies (38;

156

*54; 68; 106; 158)* of cinefluorographic and spectrographic examination of what deaf children do when they speak, and have concluded that the different sound of deaf speech is related to variations from the normal in pitch, resonance, articulation, and duration. We shall consider the pitch and resonance variations of the deaf and what can be done to remedy them.

*PITCH CHANGES IN THE DEAF*

It appears that young deaf children, aged seven to eight, do not have particularly higher voices than normal-hearing children of the same age, but as deaf children become older, they do not necessarily develop the lower voice pitches of the normal post-adolescent. In a study of 17- to 18-year-old deaf boys, I reported that "deaf adolescents as a group had a mean fundamental frequency 54 cps higher than the fundamental of the normal hearing boys the same age" (*19*, p. 687). Apparently, the lowering of voice pitch as one moves from childhood through adolescence and then to adulthood requires some acoustic monitoring to match one's normal peer group. The deaf child or adult, who lacks this auditory feedback, appears to need some external guidance in using the acceptable pitch levels of his age group. What are some of the things that the teacher of the deaf or the voice clinician can do to help the deaf child develop a normally pitched voice as he gets older?

Any attempt to change the pitch level of a deaf child must begin with a discussion about the need for such a change. This discussion should center on the tested fundamental frequency of the child as compared to normative values for the child's age and sex, as presented in figure 12. The inventive clinician might prepare a chart or graph demonstrating for the child where his pitch is and where it ought to be. Since the deaf child lacks an adequate auditory model for his pitch target, he must rely on various visual devices as signals for whether his voice pitch is too high or too low. One such device is the PAD Pitch Meter *(125)*, which gives a dial reading of the subject's fundamental frequency in cycles per second. The clinician can point out the child's particular pitch value and compare it on the dial with normal target values. An excellent way of using the PAD Pitch Meter therapeutically is to ask the child to produce various vowels in isolation, prolonging them so that a pitch value reading can be made on the frequency dial. By changing the pitch of his voice, the child can attempt to match the normal value the clinician has established for him. Thin strips of plastic tape can be placed across the frequency target area, and the child can then practice phonating so that the Pitch Meter needle falls within the marked target range. This kind of practice, using target frequency zones on such a device as the PAD Pitch Meter, has been found to be a useful training approach with adolescent deaf children.

Another useful device in altering the pitch level of the deaf is to provide "cue arrows" pointing in the desired direction of pitch change. For example, for the typical deaf child attempting to lower his voice pitch, cards should be printed with an arrow pointing down. These cards should be placed wherever possible in his environment—in his wallet, on his bureau, on his desk, etc. Also, his classroom teacher and his voice clinician can give him finger cues, by pointing toward the floor. Another method for developing an altered pitch level is to have the child place his fingers lightly on his larynx and feel the downward excursion of the larynx during lower pitch productions and the upward excursion during higher ones. The ideal or optimum pitch will produce very little vertical movement. Any noticeable upward excursion of the larynx, except during swallowing, will immediately signal to the child that he may be speaking at an inappropriately high pitch level. In therapy, once an appropriate pitch level has been established, the child may be asked to read aloud for a specified time period, placing his fingers lightly on his larynx and trying to read so as not to feel any downward or upward movements.

Following any practice period using a desirable pitch level, there should be some consideration of what that new pitch level feels like. The deaf voice patient should try to analyze what he is doing when he produces a good pitch level, particularly what is happening to his breathing, what his throat feels like, what his tongue is doing, how open his mouth is, etc. The clinician should not ask such vague questions as "what does it feel like," for this can only be followed by a vague, useless response. Of more use would be: "Did you feel any difference in your throat?" "If so, can you describe it?" While the tactual, kinesthetic, and proprioceptive feedback systems give us only vague information about what we are doing when we speak, for the deaf person, who lacks adequate auditory feedback, they are vital and must be used. Any successful alteration of pitch production, therefore, must be followed by some attempt by the patient to analyze what he has produced. In the beginning, the deaf child attempting to modify his voice will need some guidance in developing these analytic abilities.

It appears that improving an inappropriate pitch level is one task that can be done well by the average deaf child or adult. When the need for changing (usually lowering) the voice pitch is pointed out to the patient, he is able to do a great deal by himself by using a pitch meter or some form of visual feedback system which can signal the inappropriateness of a pitch production. It might be added that since the average pitch level of most voices is under 250 cps, as much low frequency amplification should be provided as possible. If deaf children or adults have any residual hearing available to them, it is usually in the lower frequency range, below 250 cps, and amplification here might well permit them to achieve some auditory monitoring of their own fundamental frequency. The clinician should make use of any self-hearing available, since this will prove most helpful in the deaf individual's struggle to alter his pitch level.

Of the facilitating techniques described in chapter 5, the following may be useful in altering pitch levels of deaf children and adults: Altering tongue position (I), chewing (III), digital manipulation (IV), establishing new pitch (VIII), opening the mouth (XIII), relaxation (XVI), respiration (XVII), and yawn-sigh (XX).

## RESONANCE CHANGES IN THE DEAF

The typical voice of the deaf subject who has had no training in developing a good voice seems to be characterized by a pharyngeal focus in resonance. Typical studies of vowel resonance employing the spectrograph —Angelocci, Kopp, and Holbrook *(2)*; Ermovick *(54)*; Gruenewald *(68)*; Meckfessel *(106)*; and Thornton *(158)*—have found depressed second formants to be characteristic of the voice quality of the deaf. The second formant of the voice, when measured spectrographically, is highly influenced in its position on the acoustic spectrum by the positioning of the tongue. Poor tongue positioning, particularly the posterior retraction of the tongue, was found to be typical among forty-four deaf children, aged 7–8 and 17–18, studied by my colleagues and myself *(19)*; we concluded that deaf children often speak with a *cul de sac* resonance. This cul de sac resonance appears to be produced by the child's retracting his tongue toward the pharyngeal wall instead of placing it in a normal, more forward and higher position. Some teachers of the deaf report that any successful effort in helping the deaf child bring his tongue more forward when he speaks will result in a more normal-sounding voice.

Some of the methods described in chapter 5 under facilitating technique I, altering tongue position, are highly applicable in promoting a more forward carriage of the tongue in deaf children. The following quotation will, I think, provide the clinician with some helpful methodology for improving the resonance characteristics of a deaf speaker's voice:

Emphasis given to articulation training, particularly for tongue-alveolar sounds such as /t/, /d/, /s/, and /z/ will often promote a higher, forward carriage of the tongue. It would be particularly beneficial to require the child to whisper a rapid series of phonemes such as "ta, ta, ta, ta, ta," etc. The whispered alveolar tongue-tip sounds appear to give the deaf child a tactual feeling of "front-of-the-mouth" speech. A drill of about five minutes duration using alveolar tongue-tip sounds in a rapid series four or five times daily appears to be an effective method of developing a higher, more forward carriage of the tongue. The child follows the whispered production of these phonemes by adding voice. Usually the teacher can hear the difference in the resonance quality of the child's "ta, ta" productions as contrasted to his general conversational voice quality. Sometimes the child himself "feels" a difference when he achieves good oral resonance which then seems to give him the muscle "set" required for increased oral resonance.

It would appear that the teacher can best help the child develop oral resonance by using speech drills rather than exercises per se. It would appear that little can be achieved by giving the child such things as isolated respiration training, exercises for parts of the oral mechanism, etc. Rather, the use of speech materials appears to be most beneficial in increasing oral resonance. The following consonants would lend themselves well for front-of-mouth resonance: /w/, /wh/, /p/, /b/, /f/, /v/, /θ/, /ð/, /t/, /d/, /s/, /z/, and /l/. The following vowels have a high oral focus and might lend themselves well for practice sessions coupled with the above consonants: /i/ as in deed, /ɪ/ as in bit, /e/ as in bait, /ɛ/ as in set, /æ/ as in bat. [*19*, p. 689]

Once the deaf child is able to produce an oral-sounding voice, the clinician should help him become aware of the contrast between his oral and pharyngeal resonance. The contrasting resonances should be produced repeatedly by the patient until he develops the ability to self-monitor what he is doing when he produces good oral resonance. Through practice in producing front-of-the-mouth phonemes, he must develop an awareness of what it feels like to use the lips, the tongue against the alveolar process, and so forth. It would appear that this front tongue positioning is best encouraged by intensive *speech* drills requiring the subject to produce a rapid series of high front consonants and vowels (tongue exercises exclusive of speech practice seem to be ineffective here). The following facilitating techniques described in chapter 5 are also helpful in establishing better vocal resonance in the deaf: Altering tongue position (I); chewing (III); negative practice (XII), once good resonance has been established; open mouth (XIII); relaxation (XVI); respiration (XVII); and yawn-sigh (XX).

## VOICE THERAPY FOR FUNCTIONAL APHONIA

In aphonia, the patient has *lost* his voice completely. The terms *hysterical aphonia* and *functional aphonia* are used interchangeably to signify the loss of phonation independent of any true laryngeal disease. Thus, the patient with bilateral vocal fold paralysis who cannot phonate does *not* have functional aphonia, although he is aphonic. In the following discussion, we will be talking about the patient without voice, but with a normal larynx. We prefer the term *functional aphonia* to *hysterical aphonia*, because the latter suggests a psychiatric dimension that may not exist for the particular patient under consideration. There are different views about what the vocal management and therapy for functional aphonia should be, and these are directly related to the clinician's basic philosophy of approach.

For instance, Bangs and Freidinger (*14*) and Boone (*20*) describe a highly symptomatic approach with only minimal psychological therapy; a more psychological approach is described by Barton (*15*) and Wolski and Wiley (*172*). Both approaches report the successful reestablishment of normal voice. Most clinical reports of functional aphonia report a sudden onset of the disorder, usually precipitated by either extreme fright, major disappointment, or a temporary illness characterized by loss of voice. The patient will usually retain such non-verbal phonations as coughing or crying, but all speech attempts will be characterized by whispering with normal speaker affect (good eye contact, facial expression, etc.). The striking observation about patients with functional aphonia is how well, despite their voicelessness, they maintain their communicative contact with the people around them. It is the rare patient who allows his aphonia to isolate him from everyday speaking contacts.

As stated in chapter 3, it appears that in functional aphonia the patient is easily conditioned to continue to speak without voice. Whatever the original cause, the behavior is maintained by the reactions of the people around him. He soon develops a *no voice* set toward speaking, and a habitual response is established; he speaks this way today because he spoke this way yesterday. Most patients with functional aphonia, whether they mean it or not, express a strong desire to regain their normal voice. (But there are a few patients whose aphonia serves them well, and they will resist all therapeutic attempts at voice restoration.) The bias of this writer, developed from following aphonic patients over time, is that symptomatic voice therapy is usually effective in restoring normal voices in these patients. Once phonation is reestablished, it remains, and the patient does not develop substitute symptoms to take the place of his lost aphonia. A similar lack of symptom migration is reported by Stevens (*155*), who, in his study of three hundred patients with conversion hysteria, found that not one developed a new substitute symptom. It would appear that a trial period of voice therapy might well restore the aphonic patient's normal voice. Greene writes that "aphonic patients frequently recover their voices during the first treatment" (*67*, p. 110). We might add that most aphonic patients recover their voices with voice therapy, if not in the first session, then soon after.

Successful voice therapy for functional aphonia must begin with the clinician's explaining the problem to the patient and discussing it with him. In his physiologic description of the aphonic, the clinician must avoid implying to the patient that he could phonate normally if he wanted to. Rather, a description of what the patient is doing ("keeping the vocal cords apart") will make it clear to him that the clinician knows what the problem is. Following the physiologic description, the clinician should say something like "we will do things in therapy that will bring the cords together again to produce normal voice." The clinician should not (at the first session, at least) ask or show interest in *why* the patient is not phonating. After the explanation and discussion of the problem, the clinician should evaluate whatever nonverbal phonations the patient may have in his coughing, grunting, laughing, and crying repertoire, and then describe them to the patient as normal phonatory activities "where the vocal cords are getting together well to produce these sounds." These nonverbal phonations should then gradually be shaped into use for speech, at first confining any speech attempts to nonsense syllables, and then moving on to single words, but with no early attempts at phonating during real communication. Attempts at phonating in conversational situations (that is, in the real world of talking) should be deferred until good, consistent phonation has been reestablished under laboratory, practice conditions. This approach is illustrated in the following report of the case of a seven-year-old child with functional aphonia, reprinted from an article by Boone (*20*) by permission of the American Speech and Hearing Association:

M. P., age seven.

*Problem:* Functional aphonia

*History:* The girl had a history of hoarseness since infancy with no medical investigation of the problem until the age of seven. All other areas of growth and development were considered normal.

*Medical findings:* At age 7, the child on indirect laryngoscopic examination was found to have "bilateral vocal nodules and cord thickening at the anterior 1/3 junction." The nodules were removed with a bilateral "cord stripping" followed by a 10-day period of enforced voice rest. Following the 10-day period of voice rest, despite the laryngologist's urging, the child was unable to resume phonation. After seven additional days of complete aphonia, she was referred to the speech pathologist with this note from the laryngologist, "This child has functional aphonia with normal appearance and good motility of both vocal cords."

*Speech evaluation:* This cooperative girl answered all questions by using whispered speech, more oral in type than glottal. Articulation and language functions were found to be normal. When asked to cough, she produced a firm true-cord cough. She could cough repeatedly on instruction. Other attempts at achieving nonverbal phonations, such as yawning, gargling, and inhalation-phonation were not successful. Hearing was normal. Both the mother and the child's teacher reported that the girl faithfully followed the laryngologist's recommendation of "no talking"; no one had heard her phonate during the 10-day voice rest or in the seven additional days of continued aphonia.

*Voice therapy:* The first therapy session was scheduled for the afternoon following the initial evaluation; second and third therapy periods were scheduled for the following day. The child whispered to the speech pathologist during the first therapy period that she "wanted to talk." The speech pathologist described briefly to the girl how her vocal cords had been repaired, explaining why the physician wanted her to keep the cords apart (and not talk) until the cords had healed. It was further explained that if we keep the cords apart too long, we sometimes experience trouble getting them together to make a voice, although we can still make other sounds. This type of imagery explanation appeared comforting to the child, perhaps demonstrating to her that the "speech doctor" knew why she could not talk.

On command and in rapid response to a red signal light, the girl was asked to produce a cough. She was able to produce well a series of light coughs (phonations) and could make a soft squealing sound on inhalation. We then found she could contrast and make a similar sound on exhalation. She then practiced a rapid series of sounds on inhalation and matched these with similar-sounding noises on exhalation. Attempts at this time to extend these exhalation phonations into monosyllabic words were not successful. We then returned to the nonverbal phonations and after listening to animal noises on a phonograph recording, she voiced the "meow" of a cat.

Following the first afternoon voice-therapy session, the girl practiced at home the coughing sound, the inhalation-exhalation noises, and the "meow" sound. The mother was instructed not to ask the child to attempt to voice anything beyond these. The following morning she demonstrated to the clinician that she could produce easily the exhalation phonations, no longer requiring the inhalation-phonation as a model. After five minutes, she was able to produce good sustained phonation shaping it easily into prolonged /a/ and /o/. At this point, the clinician commented, "Your vocal cords are beginning to move well." After she produced good strong phonation on open-mouth vowels, we introduced our first actual words, requesting the child to repeat separately, "all, are, oh, oak, open, arm." On the first request to say the words, she whispered that she did not think she would be able to say them. After a few awkward attempts, she did produce the words. Her success in producing these first words again received relatively passive reinforcement by the clinician who stated, "The cords are definitely stronger now." The clinician in no way placed any of the responsibility of the aphonia on the child and frequently used the impersonal "they" or "the cords." The girl, a first-grader, was asked to repeat after the examiner a series of single words, each beginning with a peculiar phoneme, from the *Voice and Articulation Drillbook* (Fairbanks, 1960). These she repeated with surprisingly clear, strong phonation. Her pitch level, according to the mother, was slightly elevated compared with her pre-surgery voice. However, with the removal of bilateral nodules and cord-stripping, some elevation in pitch level was expected because of the reduction of cord mass.

Since the child came for her afternoon appointment with normal phonation, no formal clinic session was needed. Counseling was given to both child and parents about the need for the girl to minimize screaming and yelling to prevent recurrence of the nodules. There has been no recurrence of hoarseness or aphonia in this child during the past two years of follow-up consultation. (20, pp. 70–71)

Of the facilitating techniques described in chapter 5, the following may be used for functional aphonia: chewing (III), hierarchy analysis (XI), pushing (XV), relaxation (XVI), and respiration (XVII). If the voice clinician has any doubt about the patient's general emotional stability, as indicated perhaps by the patient's continued inability to produce some phonation, he should refer the patient for psychological or psychiatric consultation. Sometimes the aphonic patient profits most from symptomatic voice therapy concurrent with psychotherapy. If psychotherapy is needed, however, the typical case involves a fairly rapid recovery of voice in relatively brief voice therapy, with a much longer period of psychotherapy.

## VOICE THERAPY FOR VENTRICULAR PHONATION

In ventricular phonation, the patient uses the ventricular folds (false cords) as his primary source of phonation. The true vocal folds are in an open, retracted position, while the ventricular folds above are in an adducted, closed position. As the outgoing airstream passes through the approximated ventricular bands, the vibrations of the bands are heard as ventricular phonation. Ventricular phonation may develop as a purely functional disorder or it may be the substitute voice of the patient with true cord disease (such as multiple papilloma). The voice tires easily, is monotonous in its low, unvarying pitch, and serves the patient erratically and inefficiently in his daily vocal demands. Arnold and Pinto (6) describe six causes of ventricular dysphonia: habitual hyperkinetic phonation, emotional crisis, compensation after laryngeal paralysis, dysarthria, cerebellar lesion, and trauma to the true cords. Any attempt at voice therapy to reduce or eliminate ventricular phonation should be confined to cases involving the first two—continuous vocal abuse or an emotional crisis. If the ventricular voice is needed as a substitute voice because of some actual vocal cord pathology, voice therapy to eliminate ventricular phonation is contraindicated; rather, the patient might profit from some instruction in how to use ventricular phonation more efficiently.

Since the ventricular voice is usually low pitched, monotonous, and hoarse, this kind of phonation is frequently described as *ventricular dysphonia*. In the absence of true cord pathology, voice therapy is often effective in "finding" true cord phonation, which usually provides the patient with a much more satisfactory voice than the false folds can. Successful therapy for ventricular phonation, as for most other voice disorders, should begin with a frank explanation to the patient of what the problem is. Frontal tomogram sketches (as shown in figure 13) are helpful in demonstrating normal abduction-adduction of both true and false vocal folds. Even with this explanation, however, the patient may not be able to produce true cord phonation volitionally. If that is the case, the best therapy approach is to have the patient practice making prolonged inhalations with an open mouth, followed by sustained exhalations, with no attempt at phonation. This is followed by having him make an effort to phonate on inhalation. With some practice, most patients can produce some inhalation phonation. Inhalation phonation is usually true cord phonation, according to the radiographic observations of Lehmann (*99*), who found true fold adduction and marked retraction of the ventricular bands on inhalation phonation. Once inhalation phonation is achieved by the patient, efforts can be made to produce a matching exhalation phonation, usually a high-pitched squeaky sound. This is the difficult part of the therapy. Patients will be able to make the inhalation voice with relative ease, but will have a great deal of difficulty in producing the matched exhalation. It seems to be easier, however, if the patient attempts the inhalation-phonation–exhalation-phonation on the same breath cycle. Perseverance in this task will usually be the key to eliminating the ventricular dysphonia; several of our therapy failures with ventricular dysphonia seem to have been related to our not sticking with the matched inhalation-exhalation phonations long enough.

While the frontal X ray tomogram is the only sure way of confirming true cord phonation (or ventricular voice, for that matter), once the patient is able to produce an exhaled phonation, he should be asked to produce varying pitches. True cord phonation has the capability of pitch variation; false cord phonation usually does not. Once true cord phonation is established by the patient, he must abandon his inhalation-exhalation squeak and blend it down to more acceptable pitch level.

For those patients with ventricular dysphonia who cannot produce true cord voice by the inhalation-phonation–exhalation-phonation method, particular attention should be given to the overall positioning of the larynx. Characteristic of ventricular voice production is a relatively high laryngeal carriage. Van Riper and Irwin described a method of facilitating lower laryngeal positioning for this type of problem when they wrote: "We have also found that by having the case lie supine upon a cot, with his head hanging backwards and lower than his body, the abnormal raising of the larynx and hyoid can be prevented" (*162*, p. 221). External digital touch of the thyroid cartilage, as described in chapter 5 under facilitating technique IV, is a useful method for developing the patient's awareness of high laryngeal carriage.

Occasionally, a patient with laryngeal disease—e.g., extensive true cord involvement with papilloma, or unilateral adductor paralysis—will need to develop a vicarious phonatory mechanism. One such mechanism would be the ventricular folds adducting for ventricular production. It is difficult to *teach* someone to use ventricular voice. Rather, for the patient who wants to develop ventricular phonation, all we can usually do is encourage him to produce various voices, if he can. If there is no true cord adduction possible, the phonations produced after such urging will usually be ventricular in origin. If a better ventricular voice can be produced (and if the original ventricular phonation is accidental in origin, not self-induced, it will usually be possible to improve it by working on optimal control of exhalation, keeping the mandible open and relaxed, etc. Increasing both loudness and pitch variability are the usual therapy goals in improving the sound of ventricular voice, but the clinician must realize that both these goals with this problem can be only minimally achieved.

## Voice Therapy for Spastic Dysphonia

In spastic dysphonia, the patient presents a strained, choked-off type of phonation. The voice of the spastic dysphonic patient sounds similar to that of the normal speaker attempting to phonate while lifting a very heavy object. The primitive valving action of the larynx cuts in on the normal speaker when he is doing heavy lifting, and his vocal cords adduct so tightly that he can hardly speak. The same mechanism seems to operate for the patient with spastic dysphonia, except that his vocal fold overadduction occurs in the absence of any physical lifting. His tense, tight voice appears to be produced by his attempting to phonate while the vocal folds are adducted too tightly. As such, spastic dysphonia is an excellent example of a severe vocal fold approximation disorder. Why the patient speaks this way is not clearly known. Aronson and his colleagues (7) hypothesized that spastic dysphonia had a "neurologic substrate and [might] be related to the essential tremor syndrome," but in the twenty-nine patients they studied who had spastic dysphonia, none demonstrated any of the emotional problems characteristic of the syndrome. Robe, Brumlik, and Moore (137), in describing ten patients with spastic dysphonia, argue convincingly that spastic dysphonia is a symptom of central nervous system impairment. Heaver (72), on the other hand, views it as a conversion symptom of a psychiatric disturbance.

There may well be different causes for spastic dysphonia. Whatever the cause may be, however, there are almost no case study reports in the literature describing success with the problem in therapy. Luchsinger and Arnold write that "most authors who have had long experience in treating spastic dysphonia stress the generally poor prognosis of this chronic vocal disability" (101, p. 333). Regardless of the philosophy of the clinician or the approach used, spastic dysphonia appears to be most resistant to elimination. Traditionally, the most common approach has been not to work on the voice symptoms per se, but to consider the dysphonia to be but a symptom of an underlying psychoneurosis, and, therefore, to refer the patient for psychotherapy. When we add up the successes in psychotherapy, however, we find that spastic dysphonia is one neurosis (if that is what it is) that is peculiarly resistant to treatment with few, if any, patients regaining normal phonation. Recently, teaching the patient a relaxed response, such as a sigh, to use at various levels of his hierarchy of stressful-nonstressful situations, has proved to be of some help.

The patient with spastic dysphonia usually can isolate some situations in which he enjoys a normal voice. Like the stutterer and his occasions of fluency, the patient with spastic dysphonia may have a normal voice when talking to a pet animal, or to a baby, or aloud to himself. When listeners are introduced, particularly those he thinks are hypercritical, his voice will tighten and phonation will be difficult. With some self-study and inquiry from the clinician, the patient can develop for himself a hierarchy of situations, ranging from those in which his voice is normal to those few in which he can barely phonate. He must analyze his normal vocal behavior and the situations which surround it. The clinician can use the therapy periods to help the patient re-create those environments where relaxed phonation is best achieved. For example, if the patient has a normal voice when talking to his dog, efforts must be made in therapy to create a situation in which the dog seems *actually to be there*. This re-creation of optimum situations requires much practice if the patient is going to be able to employ normal phonation (as if he were actually talking to the dog). If the hierarchy analysis, as developed in chapter 5 under facilitating technique XI, is going to be effective, it is essential that a great deal of time be spent in attempting to *capture* the environmental factors which permit the patient to phonate normally. Without a normal, relaxed phonation to produce at will, the patient will not have an optimum response to use at various levels of the hierarchy.

The only success achieved by this writer with patients with spastic dysphonia has been in having the patient use an optimum, relaxed phonation at various hierarchical levels which the patient has developed for himself. Even with this approach, however, progress has been erratic and limited, with no one patient experiencing a permanent restoration of normal voice. The problem of spastic dysphonia still remains both a diagnostic and etiologic unknown, which, of course, makes the development of an effective therapeutic approach impossible.

## VOICE THERAPY FOR VOCAL CORD PARALYSIS

As indicated in chapter 3, cord paralysis may be unilateral or bilateral and of two types: adductor paralysis (inability to bring the vocal folds together) or abductor paralysis (inability to separate them). While most cord paralyses are the result of peripheral nerve lesions, about ten percent are due to central nervous system lesions caused by intracranial disease (Cunning, *40*). The symptoms and preferred therapies for each of these laryngeal disorders are highly specific and must be considered separately.

## UNILATERAL ADDUCTOR PARALYSIS

In this condition, usually caused by unilateral involvement of the recurrent laryngeal nerve, one vocal fold works normally and reaches the midline, while the involved cord remains in a fixed, retracted position. There is usually a pronounced dysphonia characterized by severe breathiness, the severity of which is dependent on the degree of glottal closure possible. As in all cases of paralytic dysphonia or aphonia, the decision regarding management belongs to the laryngologist, whose first concern is to preserve the patient's airway. In unilateral adductor paralysis, the airflow for breathing is threatened only minimally, but some attention must be given to ensuring the patient's adequacy of laryngeal valving (which, as the basic function of the larynx, protects the airway from foreign bodies). If airway patency becomes a primary problem, the laryngologist may well have to consider some surgical procedure, such as the injection of teflon into the abducted, paralyzed fold. This use of teflon increases the girth of the involved cord—sometimes permitting actual contact with the normal cord—and affords some valve closure of the airway. Of secondary importance to the laryngologist, but of prime interest to the patient and the speech pathologist, is the patient's voice. The positive effect of teflon injection on improving the voice has been reported by Kirchner and Toledo (*93*), and it does appear that a small amount of teflon injected in the paralyzed vocal fold produces better fold approximation, creating a better-sounding voice.

The preferred method of voice therapy for the problem, independent of any medical-surgical management, is the pushing approach, as described in chapter 5 under facilitating technique XV. Under conditions of pushing, the best possible adduction of the true folds occurs; if there is any flicker of adduction capability remaining in the involved cord, it will show itself under pushing conditions. Some voice texts hint that the normal cord will cross over slightly beyond the midline approximation position and make contact with the abducted cord while the patient is pushing; however, in an exhaustive review of the literature on paralytic dysphonia, Luchsinger and Arnold (*101*) report no studies which validate this assumption. In unilateral adductor paralysis, the involved cord, despite its paralysis and lack of movement to the midline, still vibrates somewhat due to the force of the passing airstream. It would appear that under conditions of pushing, the airflow rate is accelerated and thus produces a greater vibration of the involved cord, resulting in a slightly better-sounding voice. The best voice possible with unilateral adductor paralysis seems to be achieved in voice therapy which focuses on increasing breath control (facilitating technique XVII), on deliberately increasing hard glottal attack by ear training, and on practicing pushing exercises.

BILATERAL ADDUCTOR PARALYSIS

With both cords fixed in an open, abducted position, the patient will be aphonic. Bilateral adductor paralysis is more often than not the result of central brain stem impairment than of bilateral destruction of the recurrent laryngeal nerves. The patient's primary problem—more important than his aphonia—is his inability to close the airway. The aphonia resulting from bilateral cord paralysis is frequently accompanied by other symptoms of cerebral dysfunction, such as weakness or paralysis of the tongue, pharynx, or palate. Voice therapy for patients with such symptoms is probably contraindicated. Medical therapy might well include a tracheotomy to improve the efficiency of the airway as a temporary measure, since many cases of bilateral adductor paralysis eventually improve spontaneously. A permanent bilateral adductor paralysis is sometimes treated surgically, according to Sjostrom (*147*), who sections the external sternothyroid muscle so that the cricothyroid (innervated by the superior laryngeal nerve) may function as an adductor of the true folds. Such surgery can be employed only when the bilateral adductor problem is secondary to peripheral nerve damage and not the result of a central lesion. Voice therapy does very little for the patient with bilateral cord paralysis, except when the paralysis tends to diminish (if it does). Then the voice clinician can usually strengthen the whisper by employing some pushing exercises and respiration drills. Froeschels, Kastein, and Weiss (*62*), working with forty patients with bilateral adductor paralysis, reported that their voices were improved through pushing exercises. However, unless there is some spontaneous return of cord functioning, voice therapy may not be effective.

UNILATERAL ABDUCTOR PARALYSIS

In this condition, one of the vocal cords remains fixed in a central, adducted position, while the other cord functions normally. Phonation is rarely affected, since the two cords approximate one another quite well. Quiet, at-rest breathing is usually normal, and only when the patient becomes physically active is he likely to experience some shortness of breath because of the narrowing of the airway. Half of the airway is occluded by the fixed midline cord, requiring marked abduction of the normal cord to achieve an adequate glottal opening for normal breathing. The primary concern of the laryngologist is that the airway be sufficiently open to permit normal breathing; rare in these cases of unilateral abductor paralysis is surgery necessary.

While the voice may be free of dysphonia, the professional user of voice, the singer or actor, may report some loss of pitch range and some variation in register. Effective voice therapy for these patients consists of a general vocal hygiene approach, where the patient learns to use his mechanism as optimally as possible. Increasing breath control and keeping a relaxed, open vocal tract appear to be the two most useful foci in this approach.

### BILATERAL ABDUCTOR PARALYSIS

Bilateral paralysis of both vocal folds in the midline position requires immediate medical assistance to help the patient breathe. Emergency medical management of bilateral abductor paralysis includes a tracheotomy. If the symptoms of closure persist for more than a week or so, a medical decision must be made as to whether to maintain the tracheotomy longer or to construct a new airway surgically within the larynx. There are several operative procedures which may be used to create a satisfactory airway. One operation, introduced by B. T. King in 1939 and still known as the King operation, rotates the arytenoid cartilage outward, surgically fixing the cricoarytenoid joint so that the one fold is permanently fixed in an abducted, open position (*33*). Another surgical approach, known as Kelly's arytenoidectomy, relieves the closed airway by surgically removing the arytenoid and suturing its vocal cord to lateral muscle-cartilaginous structures (*34*). Woodman (*173*), reporting on 521 cases of bilateral abductor paralysis, all receiving the arytenoidectomy operation, stated that 88.3 percent of the operations were successful. "Success" in the surgical treatment of bilateral abductor paralysis means that the patient is able to breathe once again through the larynx, and not necessarily that he regains a normal voice; the dysphonia is but a small price to pay for the ability to breathe adequately again. However, voice therapy is often found useful for those patients who, after surgery, experience varying degrees of dysphonia due to the surgically produced open glottis.

Since airway patency is the primary need of these patients, voice therapy should never be started unless, in the opinion of the surgeon, the newly constructed glottal mechanism can "take it." If the surgeon feels that voice therapy is needed and that the patient can tolerate it, the approach used is very similar to that used in adductor paralysis. The patient must learn to use his voice as efficiently as possible. Pushing exercises, breathing exercises, and the trial-and-error use of various facilitating techniques may help in producing a better-sounding voice.

The reader interested especially in the aphonias and dysphonias associated with various forms of laryngeal paralyses will find Luchsinger and Arnold's comprehensive description of various aspects of paralytic dysphonia most useful (*101*, chapter 4).

## VOICE THERAPY FOR SPECIAL VOICE SYMPTOMS

*ELIMINATION OF THE FALSETTO*

In falsetto, the patient speaks with an inappropriately high, soprano-type voice. The falsetto is actually a false soprano voice and therefore does not exist in prepubescent children or in adult females, where such pitch levels are within the normal voice range. Falsetto voices, then, exist primarily in postpubertal adolescent and adult males, and the pitch level may well be around middle C (256 cps) or higher. The social penalties for a male using such an inappropriately high voice are obvious, with the individual often judged as effeminate and inadequate. In describing young men with falsetto, Arnold and Luchsinger write that "these over-protected boys show a stronger attachment to the mother than is usual" (*101*, p. 195). Whatever the psychological factors are which cause the emergence and continuation of the falsetto, the large majority of these patients can be cured of their problem permanently with but a brief exposure to voice therapy. Those few who persist in hanging on to their falsetto voices as a symptom which somehow serves them well should be referred for psychological or psychiatric therapy, particularly if they profess a desire to eliminate the falsetto voice but are unable to do so.

The laryngeal characteristics of men with falsetto voices are essentially normal, and endocrinologic factors such as the completeness of secondary sexual signs (body hair, beard, etc.) are rarely indicators of the problem. It is nearly always for some nonphysical reason that the young man continues to use his prepubertal voice, often at slightly higher pitch levels than he used as a child. Whatever the reason he began talking this way, we see evidence (primarily from his usual rapidity in acquiring a normal voice pitch in therapy) that he soon develops a set for phonating in the higher pitch, talking this way today because he did so yesterday. As in voice therapy for most other problems, the search for more optimum ways of phonating should be prefaced by a discussion and explanation of the problem.

One possible way of helping the patient produce a lower pitch level is to place your fingers externally on his thyroid cartilage and then ask him to phonate an extended *ah*. When the *ah* begins, press lightly on the thyroid cartilage (decreasing the length and increasing the mass of the vocal folds) to produce an immediate lowering of pitch; when the finger pressure is released, the pitch may revert back. Repeat the procedure and ask the patient if he can maintain the lower pitch level. This finger pressure, as mentioned under digital manipulation in chapter 5, is not always effective with falsetto voices. But it is worth trying—and if it works, use it. Most of these patients can also demonstrate normal male pitch levels when they produce such nonverbal phonations as throat-clearing, coughing, grunting, etc. If the patient can produce a normally pitched nonverbal phonation, he should then be instructed to prolong the sound, extending it as an *ah* for several seconds. His early attempts to phonate should not involve actual words, but only the nonverbal sounds. Depending on the patient's success in producing nonverbal phonation and his attitude toward doing this, move gradually into having him phonate words with the lower voice. One successful way of doing this is to blend a prolonged nonverbal phonation into the production of a word which begins with a similar-sounding vowel. Most patients will make the transition from nonverbal phonation to production of a few practice words without too much resistance. In the beginning, it is wise to stay on the practice level, using only a few words, before having the patient try to use the lower voice in conversational situations. When the patient is able to produce a few practice words with normal voice, record the new voice and let him hear it. It does very little good to record both the falsetto and normal voices, using them for contrast discrimination, since hearing his falsetto as contrasted perhaps with a normal baritone often puts the patient on the defensive. Rather, listen critically with the patient to the lower voice pitch, ignoring the falsetto when analyzing the new production. When the patient listens to his new voice, we often determine what pitch level it is and then show him how this fits into the normal adult male range. If the lower pitch level is in that normal range, we make sure the patient realizes this.

From the production of single words, proceed to phrases. At this point, the patient often profits from some practice alone, without the clinician. He can do this in a practice room with a loop tape device, saying various phrases or short sentences from a prepared list. Working alone and listening to himself in this way will enable him to become familiar with his new voice, what it sounds like and what it feels like when being produced. The typical patient will move rapidly in acquiring his new voice. Generally, two or three therapy periods (on successive days, if possible) supplemented by self-practice and listening periods are all the formal voice therapy required. The elimination of falsetto, particularly for self-referred patients who want to eliminate it, is much easier than the symptom and its psychological implications might indicate. Most clinicians report good success in permanently restoring normal voices in patients with falsetto (Luchsinger and Arnold [*101*]; Palmer [*126*]).

*ELIMINATING VOCAL PITCH BREAKS*

There is no voice symptom more annoying than to be speaking in an apparently normal voice and then suddenly experience a pitch break. The typical abnormal pitch break is a one octave break, one octave higher or one octave lower than the normal voice. We are not talking about the typical voice break experienced primarily by boys as their voices are changing; these temporary breaks usually disappear as the laryngeal mechanism matures and the youngster has had continued practice in using his new adult voice. Rather, we are considering the adult patient who complains of his voice breaking upward or downward while he speaks. He has no warning that the pitch break will occur. When it does, he often is embarrassed and sometimes will avoid speaking situations rather than face the uncertainty and tension of the pitch break. Pitch breaks are almost invariably related to the person's speaking at an inappropriate pitch level. If he is speaking at the bottom of his pitch range, his voice will break upward, about one octave. But by elevating his habitual pitch level slightly above the very bottom of his pitch range, the pitch breaks will usually "miraculously" disappear. Similarly, downward pitch breaks are usually found in persons who are speaking at too high a habitual pitch level, so that a slight lowering of pitch to a more optimum level will usually eliminate the problem. Pitch breaks tend to go in the direction of the optimum pitch level, and therapy directed toward bringing the voice nearer that level will usually markedly reduce them or eliminate them entirely.

Among the facilitating techniques in chapter 5 that have been found useful in eliminating pitch breaks are: Altering tongue position (I), chewing (III), ear training (V), eliminating hard glottal attacks (VII), open mouth (XIII), relaxation (XVI), respiration (XVII), and yawn-sigh (XX).

*ELIMINATING DIPLOPHONIA (DOUBLE VOICE)*

Normal phonation is produced by the gentle approximation of the vocal folds, tripped into vibration by the outgoing air stream. Sometimes, however, there are other free bodies besides the true folds within the vocal tract, and these of course will also vibrate in the presence of the air stream. When this occurs, the vibration of the folds coupled with that of the added body will produce double voice, or diplophonia. The second vibrating source is usually the ventricular bands, or false folds, which are not retracted enough to keep from approximating (and therefore vibrating). In some cases, the double voice is related to hypertrophy (enlargement) of the ventricular folds, which is sometimes serious enough to require surgical reduction or medical treatment. The most successful voice therapy approach to ventricular band diplophonia is the general one of having the patient learn to use his voice optimally, at optimum pitch and loudness levels, with good respiratory function, and with a relatively relaxed vocal mechanism. Diplophonia is frequently a symptom of general hyperfunctional usage of the vocal mechanism, and, except in rare cases of extreme ventricular band hypertrophy, any voice facilitating technique which reduces vocal hyperfunction may reduce diplophonia.

Van Riper and Irwin cite reports by Hayashi and Voelker on various diplophonic patients with different second vibration sources, e.g., the epiglottis vibrating against the aryepiglottic folds, or a left true cord vibrating against a right false cord (*162*, p. 221). If voice therapy is to be effective in eliminating the double voice, some identification of the second vibrating source is necessary. This can usually be done best by frontal laryngeal X ray or tomogram, which will show intralaryngeal vibrating structures with relative clarity. If, after the identification of the vibrating sites, medical-surgical treatment is indicated, this should be done before any voice therapy attempts are made. If voice therapy is indicated, after such medical investigation or treatment, the usual approach is to work toward a general reduction of vocal hyperfunction and the development of more optimum vocal behavior.

SUMMARY

The aim of most voice therapy is to help the patient achieve a normal voice. To do this, we generally attempt first to identify the things the patient may be doing wrong vocally, and then to replace the wrong vocal behavior with an easier, more optimum one. Since most voice problems are related to vocal hyperfunction, the employment of good, general voice facilitating techniques is usually indicated. But there are special voice problems that need specialized management, and it is these problems that have been considered in this chapter. We have discussed ways in which to modify the voices of deaf children and adults so that they may better approximate normal voices; we have outlined specific approaches for patients with functional aphonia and ventricular dysphonia; we have discussed the limitations of treating spastic dysphonia, describing a behavioral approach which offers some promise; and have outlined some therapeutic procedures for specific kinds of vocal cord paralysis.

*chapter seven*

# Therapy for
# Resonance Disorders

*The pharyngeal, oral, and nasal cavities are the primary sites of vocal resonance. For the voice to sound "normal," a certain amount of resonance must occur at each of these sites. Too much or too little oral-pharyngeal-nasal resonance may be the result of some structural abnormality (such as cleft palate), or faulty usage (such as posterior tongue carriage), or a combination of the two. We shall discuss several oral-pharyngeal resonance disorders from the point of view of their correction in voice therapy. Our consideration of nasal resonance disorders will include recommendations on therapy for hypernasality, denasality, nasal emission, and assimilative nasality.*

Although the human resonance system has a relatively fixed shape and size, its overall configuration changes with muscle contraction. The pharynx, for example, while relatively fixed in its vertical dimension, lengthens and shortens in relation to the positioning of the larynx: as the larynx ascends for the production of higher pitch levels, it shortens the length of the pharynx, which then provides better resonance for the higher frequencies; conversely, as the larynx descends for the production of lower pitch levels, the pharynx lengthens, thus resonating better for the lower frequencies. These vertical changes of the size and shape of the pharyngeal cavity are all produced by muscular contraction. It is this factor of muscular contraction which permits us to change the resonating characteristics of our voices. If an individual has structural adequacy of tissue and normal relationships between structures, he usually has the functional capability of producing resonance changes. Resonance therapy, therefore, basically involves learning to use muscles in such a way that faulty resonance is no longer perceived by listeners to be faulty. The individual whose resonating bodies are structurally adequate can learn to do "things" to improve the quality of his voice. We shall consider separately some of the "things" that can be done to improve oral resonance, eliminate an excessive pharyngeal focus in resonance, and minimize the effects of various problems of nasal resonance.

### THERAPY FOR ORAL-PHARYNGEAL RESONANCE PROBLEMS

Although both the oral and pharyngeal cavities are constantly changing in size and shape, the oral cavity is the most changeable of all the resonance cavities. Speech is possible only because of the capability for variation on the part of such oral structures as the lips, mandible, tongue, and velum. The most dramatic of all oral movements in speech are those of the tongue, which makes various constrictive-restrictive contacts at different sites within the oral cavity to produce consonant articulation. Vowel and diphthong production are possible only because of size-shape adjustments of the oral cavity, requiring a delicate blend of muscle adjustment of all oral muscle structures. While there are many individuals who display faulty positioning of oral structures for articulation, and thus are heard to articulate "badly," there are fewer individuals who are recognized to have problems in positioning their oral structures for resonance. Slight departures in articulatory proficiency are much more easily recognized than are minor problems in voice resonance. While an articulation error may be viewed consistently as a problem, faulty oral-pharyngeal resonance is usually accepted as "the way he talks." And nasality problems are more likely to be recognized by lay and professional listeners as requiring correction than are oral-pharyngeal resonance departures; this is particularly true of such problems as nasal emission, which is really more of an articulation problem than a resonance one. The determination of normality or abnormality vis-à-vis resonance, then, is basically a perceptual task, dependent primarily on the subjective judgments of both the speaker and his listeners. Any judgment of resonance is going to be heavily influenced by the appropriateness of pitch, the degree of glottal competence as heard in the periodic quality of phonation, and the degree of accuracy of articulation. It is these other speech-voice factors that contaminate judgments of voice quality (Sherman, *146*). Since quality of resonance, then, appears basically to be a subjective experience, the goal in resonance therapy must be to achieve whatever voice "sounds best."

The tongue occupies the greater part of the oral cavity, and, because of its relative mass within the cavity, has a primary role in shaping oral resonance. Singing teachers have long been aware of the vital role the tongue plays in influencing the quality of the voice, devoting considerable instructional and practice time to helping the singing student develop optimum carriage of the tongue. While the postures needed to produce various phonemes will attract the tongue to different anatomic sites within the oral cavity, with noticeable changes of oral resonance, more objective evidence of the role of the tongue in oral resonance may be obtained through spectrographic analysis (Hanson, *71*) and cinefluorographic analysis (Shelton, Hahn, and Morris, *144*). In the spectral analyses afforded by the spectrograph, one can study the effects of tongue positioning and the distribution of spectral formants. The second formant seems to "travel" the most, changing position up and down the spectrum for various vowel productions. The primary oral shaper for production of vowels appears to be the tongue. It should be pointed out that decisions about quality resonance (e.g., is the voice hypernasal or denasal) are almost impossible to render from the visual inspection of spectrograms. It is most difficult to quantify formant variations and relate them to variations in voice quality. In describing the difficulty of spectrographic analysis, Moll has written that "this presumably more 'objective' measure involves human judgments which probably are more difficult than those made in judging nasality from actual speech" (*111*, p. 99). Visual inspection of the spectrogram is a difficult task, particularly when one attempts to relate formant positioning to judgments of voice quality. As for the cinefluorograph, its use for studying tongue, velar, mandibular, and pharyngeal movements, when such movements apply to voice quality, becomes far more effective when a voice track is added. The addition of the speaker's voice not only enables the viewer to match the sound of the voice to the filmed analysis of the speaker's movements, but, more important, provides him with the primary vehicle for determining whether a quality problem exists; quality judgments cannot be made from the visual study of oral movements alone, but depend primarily on hearing the sound of the voice. It would appear, then, that when a speaker demonstrates a voice with less than optimum resonance, as judged either by himself or by his clinician (but, hopefully, by both), efforts might just as well be made to help the speaker develop what may be judged as a "better-sounding" voice.

REDUCING THE STRIDENT VOICE

One of the most annoying oral-pharyngeal resonance problems is the strident voice. Unfortunately, the term "stridency" carries with it many subjective interpretations; we shall use it to mean the unpleasant, shrill, metallic-sounding voice which appears to be related to hypertonicity of the pharyngeal constrictors. Fisher has described the strident voice as having "exceptional brilliance of high overtones, to the extent that the fundamental frequency is often obscured, giving the tone a brassy, tinny, blatant sound" (57, p. 119). Physiologically, stridency is produced by the elevation of the larynx and hypertonicity of the pharyngeal constrictors, resulting in a decrease of both the length and the width of the pharynx. The surface of the pharynx becomes taut because of the tight pharyngeal constriction. The smaller pharyngeal cavity, coupled with its tighter, reflective mucosal surface, produces the ideal resonating structure for accentuating high-frequency resonance. Such a voice may be developed deliberately by the carnival barker or the dimestore demonstrator for its obvious attention-getting effects; for another person, stridency may only emerge when he becomes overly tense, constricting his pharynx as part of his overall response. The person who has this sort of strident voice—and who wants to correct it—can, in voice therapy, often develop some relaxed oral-pharyngeal behaviors that will decrease pharyngeal constriction, lessening the amount of stridency. Anything that the individual can do to lower the larynx, decrease pharyngeal constriction, and promote general throat relaxation will usually result in a reduction of stridency. The reader is referred back to the twenty facilitating techniques described in chapter 5; from that list we have selected those approaches which appear to be most helpful in reducing stridency:

   1. *Approach III, Chewing.* It is almost impossible to produce strident resonance under conditions of chewing. The various steps of chewing, detailed in chapter 5, should be most helpful in reducing stridency.
   2. *Approach V, Ear Training.* Explore various vocal productions with the patient, with the goal of producing a nonstrident voice. When the patient is able to produce good oral resonance, contrast this production with recorded strident vocalizations by using loop tape feedback devices and following the various ear-training procedures.
   3. *Approach VIII, Establishing New Pitch.* The strident voice is frequently accompanied by an inappropriately high voice pitch. Efforts to lower the pitch level will often result in a voice which sounds less strident.
   4. *Approach IX, Explanation of Problem.* Although it is difficult to explain problems of resonance to someone else, sometimes such an explanation is essential if the patient is ever to develop any kind of self-awareness about the problem.
   5. *Approach XI, Hierarchy Analysis.* For the individual whose voice

becomes strident whenever he is tense, it is important to try to isolate those situations in which his nonstridency is maintained.

6. *Approach XII, Negative Practice.* Once the patient is able to produce good oral resonance voluntarily, it is sometimes therapeutically valuable to produce the strident resonance intentionally, in order to contrast the "feeling" and sound of it with the new resonance pattern.

7. *Approach XIII, Open Mouth Approach.* Since stridency is generally the product of overconstriction, developing oral openness—an excellent method of counteracting tight, constrictive tendencies—should prove to be extremely valuable.

8. *Approach XVI, Relaxation.* It is difficult to produce strident resonance under conditions of relaxation and freedom from tension. Either of the approaches—general relaxation or more focal relaxation of the vocal tract—will be helpful in reducing oral-pharyngeal constriction.

9. *Approach XX, Yawn-Sigh.* Since the yawn-sigh approach produces an openness and relaxation which is completely opposite to the tightness of pharyngeal constriction, it is perhaps the most effective approach in this list for reducing stridency.

*IMPROVING ORAL RESONANCE*

There are two problems of oral resonance related to faulty tongue position, a *thin* type of resonance produced by excessively anterior tongue carriage and a *cul de sac* type produced by backward retraction of the tongue. The thin voice lacks adequate oral resonance, making its user sound immature and unsure of himself. It is characterized by a generalized oral constriction with high, anterior carriage of the tongue and only minimal lip-mandibular opening. The user of such a voice appears to be holding back psychologically, either withdrawing from interpersonal contact by demonstrating all the symptoms of withdrawal, or retreating psychologically to a more infantile level of behavior by demonstrating a baby-like voice quality. The first type, who withdraws from interpersonal contact, employs his thin resonance situationally, particularly at times when he feels most insecure; the second type uses the thin voice, the "baby resonance," more intentionally, in situations where he or she wants to appear cute, to "get his own way," etc. The following facilitating approaches have been found useful in promoting a more natural, oral resonance:

1. *Approach I, Altering Tongue Position.* The problem of the thin voice was first discussed in chapter 5. Specific procedures are developed there to promote more posterior tongue carriage.

2. *Approach II, Change of Loudness.* When the resonance problem is part of a general picture of psychological withdrawal in particular situations, efforts at increasing voice loudness are appropriate for overall improvement of resonance.

3. *Approach III, Chewing.* Chewing promotes a more natural carriage of the tongue.

4. *Approach VIII, Establish New Pitch.* The thin voice is perceived by listeners to be drastically lacking in authority. Frequently, the pitch is too high. Efforts at lowering the voice pitch will often have a positive effect on resonance.

5. *Approach XI, Hierarchy Analysis.* Symptomatic voice therapy is based on the premise that it is often possible to isolate particular situations in which we function poorly with maladaptive behavior, and other situations in which we function comparatively well. By isolating the various situations and their modes of behavior, we can often introduce the more effective behavior into the "bad" situations, to take the place of the maladaptive kind. For those individuals who use a thin voice in specific situations, particularly during moments of tension, hierarchy analysis may be a necessary preliminary step in eliminating the aberrant vocal quality.

6. *Approach XIII, Open Mouth.* The restrictive oral tendencies of the thin-voiced speaker may be effectively reduced by developing greater oral openness.

7. *Approach XVI, Relaxation.* If the thin vocal quality is highly situational and the obvious result of tension, relaxation approaches may be helpful, particularly when used in combination with hierarchy analysis.

8. *Approach XVII, Respiration Training.* Sometimes direct work on increasing voice loudness requires some work on increasing control of the air flow during expiration.

9. *Approach XX, Yawn-Sigh.* The yawn-sigh approach is an excellent way of developing a more relaxed, posterior tongue carriage.

The cul de sac voice may be found in individuals representing various etiologic groups: the "different" sound of the voice of the patient with oral apraxia may be of this type; the cerebral palsied child, particularly the athetoid type, has a posterior focus to his resonance added to his dysarthria; some patients with bulbar or pseudo-bulbar type lesions have a pharyngeal focus to their vocal resonance; and cul de sac resonance is a typical characteristic of the deaf child. The cul de sac voice, regardless of its physical cause, is produced by the deep retraction of the tongue into the oral cavity and hypopharynx, sometimes touching the pharyngeal wall and sometimes not. The body of the tongue literally obstructs the escaping air flow and the periodic sound waves generated from the larynx below. While such a voice is often found in individuals with neural lesions who cannot control their muscles, and among deaf children and adults, it is also produced situationally by certain individuals for wholly functional reasons. Such posterior resonance is very difficult to correct in those patients who have muscle disorders related to various problems of innervation, particularly the dysarthric patient. Resonance deviations in the deaf may be changed somewhat in voice therapy as described in chapter 6. For those individuals who produce cul de sac resonance for purely functional reasons (whatever they are), the following facilitating approaches will be useful:

1. *Approach I, Altering Tongue Position.* Speech tasks designed to promote front-of-the-mouth resonance are helpful here. The reader is advised to review the section on resonance changes in the deaf in chapter 6. The approaches described there for altering tongue position in deaf children have applicability for anyone working for more forward resonance.

2. *Approach V, Ear Training.* If, in his search for a better voice, the patient is able to produce a more forward, oral-sounding one, this should be contrasted for him with his cul de sac voice.

3. *Approach XI, Hierarchy Analysis.* If cul de sac resonance occurs only in particular situations, perhaps at those times when the individual is tense and under stress, the hierarchy approach may be useful. If the individual can produce good oral resonance in low-stress situations, he should practice using the same resonance at levels of increasing stress, on up the hierarchy.

4. *Approach XII, Negative Practice.* Once the patient can produce good oral resonance volitionally, he might undertake some negative practice, deliberately producing the cul de sac voice. In negative practice, efforts must be made to contrast the feeling and the sound of the new voice with the old; indeed, the real value of the approach is in making this contrast.

5. *Approach XVI, Relaxation.* Posterior tongue retraction during moments of stress is often a learned response to tension. The patient who can learn a more relaxed positioning of the overall vocal tract may be able to reduce excessive tongue retraction.

### THERAPY FOR NASAL RESONANCE PROBLEMS

There is probably no one area of voice therapy more neglected or more confusing than therapy for nasal resonance problems. Historically, the implication in the early literature was that most problems of nasality (usually hypernasality) could be successfully treated by voice therapy, e.g., by ear training, as described by Bell (*16*) in 1890, or by blowing exercises, as advocated by Kantner (*92*) in 1947, or by the exercises for the velum suggested by Buller (*27*), or by the treatment Williamson used for seventy-two cases of hypernasality, which put some emphasis on relaxing the entire vocal tract (*167*). Most of these approaches were developed for functional hypernasality, but were later applied by various clinicians to problems of palatal insufficiency and cleft palate. For some of these structural problems, such approaches as blowing and relaxation were found to be ineffective; if the velopharyngeal mechanism was structurally unable to produce velopharyngeal closure, no amount of relaxation or exercise would have much effect in reducing excessive nasal resonance. Shelton, Hahn, and Morris have hypothesized that many individuals previously classified as having "functional nasality, that is, hypernasality which has no structural basis" actually suffer from velopharyngeal incompetence as the primary cause of their hypernasality; these authors urge thorough testing and investigation of velopharyngeal structural competence with any individual with hypernasality before initiating a voice therapy program. (*145*, p. *257*.) Moreover, the nasality exhibited by cleft palate speakers may be different from the type demonstrated by speakers without cleft palate, according to Moll, who, in summarizing many research studies, concludes that high vowels are more nasal than low vowels for cleft palate speakers with hypernasality and for normal speakers, but that the opposite (low vowels more nasal than high ones) is true for cleft palate speakers who are not hypernasal (*111*, p. 102). There is an additional inconsistency between cleft palate speakers and non-cleft palate speakers with regard to the relationship of pitch level and perceived nasality. In summarizing five separate research studies which considered the relationship of fundamental frequency to perceived nasality, Moll concluded that there was little such relationship at all. At least, he reports, there is little convincing experimental data to support the clinical view that lowering the voice pitch decreases the amount of perceived nasality; in fact, in a few studies of cleft palate speakers it was found that elevating the voice pitch diminished the perceived nasality (*ibid.*, p. 104). Any one person who demonstrates hypernasality, with or without cleft palate, must be individually evaluated with regard to his physical velopharyngeal mechanism and what he can do to produce greater oral and nasal resonance. There appear to be no summary data that can validly be generalized to any population with nasal resonance. What works for one individual in improving voice quality may not work for another, with or without the same problem.

Under the broad heading of "nasal resonance" may fall such subheadings as hypernasality, denasality, assimilative nasality, and nasal emission. No panel of sophisticated speech pathologists would be able to agree unanimously about the meanings of these terms, much less about how to remedy these problems in voice therapy. Furthermore, some critics would argue that the term nasal emission does not belong in a discussion of nasal resonance. (This author agrees with these critics and would place nasal emission under a heading of "articulation" if this book had such a section! Our discussion of nasal emission later in this chapter should help the student avoid classifying the problem as a nasal resonance disorder.) In addition, that same group of experienced speech pathologists would have real difficulty in agreeing on the classification of recorded nasal voice samples into specific nasal resonance categories. Yet such categorization is usually necessary if voice therapy for nasal resonance is to be successful. For example, the problem of hypernasality with its open velopharyngeal port demands a very different treatment from that of denasality with its closed velopharyngeal opening. Therefore, as a prelude to our discussion of the separate approaches to the four nasal disorders, let us define terms:

*Hypernasality.* Hypernasality is an excessively undesirable amount of perceived nasal cavity resonance during the phonation of vowels. Vowel production in the English language is characterized primarily by oral resonance with only slightly nasalized components. If the oral and nasal cavities are open to one another by lack of velopharyngeal closure (for whatever reason), the periodic sound waves carrying laryngeal vibration will receive heavy resonance within the nasal cavity. Only three phonemes of the English language should receive the degree of nasal prominence produced by an open velopharyngeal port: /m/, /n/, and /ŋ/.

*Denasality.* Denasality is the lack of nasal resonance for the three nasalized phonemes: /m/, /n/, and /ŋ/. In the strictest sense, therefore, denasality could be categorized as an articulatory substitution disorder. Generally, denasality also affects vowels, in that the normal speaker gives some nasal resonance to vowels. A voice with this inadequate nasal resonance sounds like the voice of the normal speaker suffering from a severe head cold.

*Assimilative Nasality.* In assimilative nasality, the speaker's vowels appear nasal when adjacent to the three nasal consonants. It would appear that the velopharyngeal port is opened too soon and remains open too long, so that vowel resonance preceding and following nasal consonant resonance is also nasalized.

*Nasal Emission.* In nasal emission, the air flow passes out of the nasal cavities, producing an aperiodic noise which is perceived by the listener as consonant distortion. This aperiodic noise is not a resonance problem per se, and, from the point of view of classification, nasal emission could be categorized as an articulatory distortion.

### THE EVALUATION OF NASAL RESONANCE DISORDERS

There are more similarities than differences between patients with resonance disorders and those with phonation disorders. For this reason, the evaluational procedures outlined in chapter 4 are equally relevant here. In addition to obtaining the necessary medical data, the clinician must pursue case history information (description of the problem and its cause, description of daily voice use, variations of the problem, onset and duration of the problem, etc.). The clinician must observe closely how well the patient seems to function as a person in the clinic and in out-of-clinic situations. Considering how subjective our judgments of resonance disorders are, it is crucial that the clinician know how the patient perceives his own voice. A mild resonance problem, for example, can be perceived by the patient and/or others as a severe problem, while a severe resonance problem may be virtually ignored by the patient and/or the people about him.

*Analysis of Voice in Speech.* An obvious way to begin the evaluation of a person with a nasal resonance disorder is to listen carefully to his voice during spontaneous conversation. This can provide the clinician with a gross indication of what the problem may be (assimilative nasality, hypernasality, etc.). It should be recognized that it is extremely difficult to make a clinical judgment about nasality by listening to someone as he speaks; in fact, such a judgment is very likely to be wrong. For example, Bradford, Brooks, and Shelton (23) found that neither a group of four experienced judges nor one of four inexperienced judges could reliably judge the recorded voice samples of children producing /a/ and /i/ with nares open and closed (by digital pressure). The judges were similarly unreliable when judging nasality from conversational speech samples. While the judgment that "there is something nasal about the speech" is usually correct, there are few examiners who can quickly and reliably differentiate the type of nasality (hypernasality, assimilative nasality, denasality) from such a conversational sample. It would appear that voice quality judgments are more accurate if made on the basis of a tape-recorded sample of the patient's conversational speech, his vowels in isolation, and his sentences (some with only oral phonemes and some loaded with nasal phonemes). The taped sample allows the clinician repeated playback, permitting him, if he likes, to focus on a specific parameter (loudness, pitch, quality) on each playback, which may increase his objectivity. To counter the "halo" effect, the influence of a speaker's articulation on the judgment of his nasality, Sherman (146) developed a procedure of playing the connected speech sample backward on the tape recorder, thus precluding the identification of any articulation errors. Reverse playback is most helpful in differentiating between hypernasality and denasality. Spriestersbach (152) found that that reverse playback of speech samples of cleft palate subjects reduced the correlations between articulation proficiency/pitch level and judgments of nasality. Until standardized approaches are developed for assessing the nasality of speakers, the best thing the clinician can do is develop materials and speaking tasks which elicit representative samples of the patient's speech, and use these samples for the various listener judgments that must be made. He should then supplement his judgments with some stimulability testing and other testing techniques.

*Stimulability testing.* The basic purpose of stimulability testing, as described by Milisen (107), is to see how well the patient can produce an errored sound when he is repeatedly presented with the correct sound through both auditory and visual stimuli. One way of distinguishing between true problems of velopharyngeal structure (where the mechanism is wholly incapable of adequate closure) and functional velopharyngeal inadequacy (where the mechanism has the capability of closure) is to see if the patient can produce oral resonance under stimulability conditions (Morris and Smith,

*115*). Obviously, the patient's success in producing oral resonance would be a strong indication that velopharyngeal closure is possible. Shelton, Hahn, and Morris write:

> If repeated stimulation consistently results in consonant productions which are distorted by nasal emission and vowels which are unpleasantly nasal, the inference can be drawn, at least tentatively, that the individual is not able to change his speaking behavior because of velopharyngeal incompetence (*145*, p. 236)

Success in producing oral resonance under conditions of stimulability would be a good indicator for voice therapy and, also, a favorable prognostic sign.

*Articulation testing.* Articulatory proficiency can provide a good index of a patient's velopharyngeal closure. Nasal emission, the aperiodic escape of noise through the nose, is a most common articulation error on plosive and fricative phonemes among subjects with inadequate velopharyngeal closure. Even though the patient may have his articulators in the correct position, vis-à-vis their lingual-alveolar-labial contacts, the error is produced because increased oral pressure escapes nasally through the incomplete posterior palatal closure. The presence or absence of nasal emission, therefore, is a most important diagnostic sign with regard to velopharyngeal adequacy. It is important in articulation testing to distinguish between errors which are the result of faulty articulatory positioning and errors related to inadequacy of the velopharyngeal structure.

Denasality in its purest and most overt form would be exhibited on an articulation test with these substitutions for the nasal phonemes: b/m; d/n; g/ŋ. Assimilative nasality would be observable only for vowels in words containing a nasal phoneme. Nasal emission would be most commonly observed in patients with palatal insufficiency in affricates (such as tʃ), fricatives (such as s), and plosives (such as p). Hypernasality *per se* would not be isolated on an articulation test. The clinician should be alert to the relatively high number of articulation errors often present in the speech of patients with cleft palate. In fact, from a speech therapy point of view, there is often more merit in focusing on articulation errors in cases of cleft palate than on resonance per se; as speech intelligibility improves, the hypernasality of these patients interferes less and less with effective communication. The type of articulation test or tasks used to assess articulatory proficiency is a matter of clinical choice. With the increasing availability of diagnostic aids for determining adequacy of velopharyngeal closure, the clinician must not abandon his articulation assessment, which may well be one of his most valid tools for diagnosing nasal resonance.

*The Peripheral Oral Examination.* By direct visual examination, the clinician can make a gross observation of the relationship of the velum to the pharynx, note the relative size of tongue, make a judgment of maxillary-mandibular occlusion, view the height of the palatal arch, survey the general condition of dentition, and determine if there are any clefts or open fistulas in the palate. It should be remembered that direct visualization of palatal length and movement provides only a gross indication of velopharyngeal closure, since the anatomic point of closure is superior by some distance to the lower border of the velum. That is, a lack of velar contact with the pharynx at the uvular tip end of the velum is not an indication of lack of closure further up where closure usually occurs. A markedly short palate or a palate with obvious pharyngeal contact can be noted on direct inspection of the oral cavity, and such a notation would be diagnostically important. The less obvious problems of borderline closure cannot be determined by direct inspection and probably require cinefluorographic confirmation.

The degree of velar movement can be determined with some validity by directly viewing the soft palate, and is extremely important to know when crucial management decisions are being made, i.e., when it is being decided whether a child should have a pharyngeal flap or an appliance, or speech therapy (to be discussed in our section on the treatment of hypernasality). Velar movement is sometimes impaired in what might appear to be a normally symmetrical palate; here, the patient has a sluggish palate, sometimes as a symptom following a severe infectious disease (influenza, encephalitis, etc.). Pharyngeal movement is almost impossible to determine by direct oral examination; it is best seen by lateral-view cinefluorographic film. In some problems of nasality, particularly those not associated with palatal insufficiency, the relative size and carriage of the tongue may have some diagnostic relevance: For example, some problems of "functional" nasality may be related to inappropriate size of tongue for the size of the oral cavity, or to innervation problems of the tongue.

The clinician should make a thorough search for any openings of the hard or soft palate which might contribute to an articulation distortion or to some problem of nasal resonance. Some patients will have a small opening (fistula) or lack of fusion around the border of the premaxilla, particularly in the area of the alveolar ridge; in some individuals such a fistula may produce air-stream noises, creating articulatory distortion, but almost never will such an isolated opening this far forward on the maxilla produce nasal resonance. The absence or presence of soft-palate and hard-palate clefts should be noted; if such clefts have been previously corrected surgically, the degree of closure should be noted. In the case of a bony-palate defect, for example, sometimes the bony opening has been covered by a thin layer of mucosal tissue, not thick enough to prevent oral cavity sound waves from traveling into the nasal cavity. This same observation applies to the occasional sub-mucosal cleft seen usually at the midline of the junction of the hard and soft palates. Any other structural deviations—of dentition, occlusion, labial competence, etc.—should be noted and considered with regard to their possible effects on speech production and nasal resonance.

*Other Measures of Nasality.* Attempts have been made in recent years to relate listener judgments of nasality to various physical measurements in an attempt to objectify clinical evaluations of nasality. Moll presents an effective discussion of the relative merits of subjective listener judgments of nasality as compared to "objective" measures using instrumentation, concluding that a valid measure of nasality "must be related closely to listener perceptions" (*111,* p. 100). Like most other clinical evaluations, the judgment of nasality should not be a dichotomous choice between listener judgment and instrument data, but rather a judicious combination of both. The clinician assessing nasality in any one particular patient might well add to his clinical judgment data from any or all of these sources:

1. *Cinefluorography.* Lateral X ray films, using cinefluorography, have been found most useful in determining the adequacy of velopharyngeal closure in procedures developed by Moll (*111*) and Shelton, Hahn, and Morris (*144*). The cinefluorograph will show clearly the degree of midline closure between the velum and the pharynx. However, movement of the lateral pharyngeal wall, which may also contribute to closure, will not show clearly on lateral films, and attempts at frontal filming showing a frontal, coronal view of the area have not been found helpful (*144*). By working closely with the radiologist, the speech pathologist can learn to "read" cinefluorographic films in such a way that his evaluations of the adequacy of palatal movement and velopharyngeal closure will be greatly enhanced. Such lateral films should be used whenever judgments about velopharyngeal adequacy are difficult to make.

2. *Manometric measurement.* There are two types of manometers used clinically, the water-filled U-tube and the mechanical pressure gauge. Both of these are basically devices which measure the amount of pressure of the emitted air stream. Both measure air flow pressure, and not nasality; however, in comparing oral with nasal readings, some indication of velopharyngeal competence is given, which may, of course, have some relevance to the judgment of nasality. The water-filled U-tube works in this way: a glass U-tube is partially filled with a colored liquid, and one end of the tube is fitted onto a rubber hose. The free end of the hose is fitted with a nasal olive. The olive is emplaced nasally, and any utterance of the patient that is characterized by nasal emission will displace the liquid, providing the patient and clinician with some visual evidence of nasal emission.

The second type of manometer is available commercially as the Hunter Oral Manometer.[1] This small instrument has three pressure dials which can provide pressure readings for the patient under two conditions, nares open and nares pinched closed. It is used in this way: with nares open, the patient blows into the mouthpiece, which produces a pressure peak value; the patient is then asked to pinch his nostrils and blow again through the mouthpiece; if he has some velopharyngeal inadequacy, the pressure value will be higher under the condition of nostril pinching, which in effect impedes the flow of air through the nasal cavity, producing an increased oral pressure value. In a subject with a normal velopharyngeal mechanism, the nares-open–nares-closed ratio would be 1.00; if dividing the nares-closed reading into the nares-open reading produces a value of less than 1.00, the indication is that there is some nasal escape of air under the nares-open condition. Such information would be added to other clinical knowledge about the patient, since manometric pressure ratios alone, with no other clinical testing data, do not tell us very much.

  3. *Spectrographic analysis of voice samples.* The spectrograph appears to be coming into increasing use as a clinical tool in analyzing voice patterns, and recently it has been applied in finding spectral characteristics that will identify nasal speakers (Dickson, *47*; Hanson, *71*). It is doubtful that the visual write-out provided by the spectrograph can provide the clinician with any more information about the type of nasality he hears than he would obtain from listening carefully to the same samples. The spectrograph is helpful in identifying the aperiodic noise of nasal emission, but beyond this it is most difficult to differentiate between spectrograms of speakers with hypernasality and of those with denasality or assimilative nasality. As clinicians learn to use what spectral analyses the spectrograph can provide, however, the instrument may well become a most useful tool for studying various parameters of nasality.

*TREATMENT OF HYPERNASALITY*

The presence of excessive nasal resonance (hypernasality) is relatively dependent upon the judgment of the listener. That is, some languages and regional dialects require heavy nasal resonance and therefore consider pronounced nasalization of vowels to be normal. Others, however, such as general American English, tolerate little nasal resonance beyond the three nasal consonants. Thus, the native New Englander with his nasal "twang" exhibits normal voice resonance in Boston, but when he travels to Cleveland the people there perceive his voice as excessively nasal. There will be variations in the degree of nasality among the voices of the people in Cleveland, of course, but a certain amount of resonance variability can exist among any particular population without anyone being bothered by it. If, however, a particular voice in Cleveland (or any other place) stands out as "excessively nasal," then that voice will be considered as having a resonance disorder.

[1] Hunter Oral Manometer, Hunter Manufacturing Company, Iowa City, Iowa.

The judgment of hypernasality, then, is as dependent upon the speech/ language milieu of the speaker and his listeners as it is upon the actual performance of the speaker.

The speaker who is judged to be hypernasal increases the nasalization of his vowels by failing to close his velopharyngeal port. This failure to close the velopharyngeal opening may be related to structural-organic defects or it may have a functional etiology. Hypernasality, known unfortunately in some circles as hyperrhinolalia, frequently accompanies cleft palate or a short palate. Among other organic causes of the disorder are surgical trauma, accidental injury to the soft palate, and impaired innervation of the soft palate as a result of poliomyelitis or some other form of bulbar disease. Sometimes temporary hypernasality may follow tonsillectomy as the child attempts to minimize the pain by not moving his velopharyngeal mechanism (Hanley and Manning, *70*). There are some people who speak with hyper-nasal resonance for purely functional reasons, perhaps maintaining a linger-ing internal model of a previously acceptable form of resonance, or perhaps imitating the voice of someone they consider particularly attractive (such as a famous political figure). While it is possible that the majority of persons with hypernasal voices have some structural basis for their lack of velo-pharyngeal competence, the ease of imitating a hypernasal voice tells us that it could be relatively easy to become hypernasal with perfectly adequate and normal velopharyngeal equipment. Hypernasality is one voice problem where the distinction must be made between organic and functional causes, as the treatment recommended will be quite specific to the diagnosis. Con-sistency of nasal resonance under conditions of stimulability will provide important diagnostic information as to whether the cause is organic or functional, and additional data can perhaps be obtained through lateral view cinefluorography and manometric measurements. Organicity (palatal in-sufficiency) would be indicated by continued hypernasality even with stimu-lability, by cinefluorographic evidence of lack of velar and pharyngeal contact, and by open-nares–closed-nares manometric ratios under 1.00. Hypernasality related to functional causes would more likely be character-ized by inconsistency of nasal resonance, with some good oral productions displayed, under conditions of stimulability; by cinefluorographic evidence of normal velopharyngeal contact, particularly during such vegetative acts as swallowing; and by normal manometric ratios of 1.00.

If there are any indications of physical inadequacy of velopharyngeal closure, the primary role of the speech pathologist would be to refer the patient to a specialist who could provide the needed physical correction—a plastic surgeon, say, or a prosthodontist. There is very little evidence that voice therapy to improve resonance will have any positive effect in the presence of physical inadequacy. In fact, there is some indication that voice therapy to improve the oral resonance of patients with palatal insufficiency (those who lack the physical equipment to produce closure) will usually not only fail, but that this failure will be seen by the patient as his own fault—as a defeat indicating his low personal worth—and thus will take an obvious toll on his self-image. An example of the uselessness of speech therapy in the presence of a severe inadequacy of velopharyngeal closure is provided by this case of a teenaged girl who had received speech therapy for both articulation and resonance for a period of seven years:

B. B., aged fourteen, had received seven years of group and individual speech therapy in the public schools and in a community speech and hearing clinic for "a severe articulation defect characterized by sibilant distortion, and for a severely nasal voice." The mother became upset because of the girl's continued lack of progress and her tendency to withdraw from social contact with her peers, which, the mother felt, was related to her embarassment over her continued poor speech. The child was evaluated by a comprehensive cleft palate team, which, after reviewing her history, found that her nasality could be dated from a severe bout of influenza when she was six years old. The influenza had been followed immediately by a deterioration of speech. Subsequent speech therapy records were incomplete, although the mother reported that the therapy had included extensive blowing drills, tongue-palate exercises, and articulation work. Physical examination of the velar mechanism found the child to have good tongue and pharyngeal movements, but bilateral paralysis of the soft palate; even on gag reflex stimulation, there was only a "flicker" of palatal movement observed. Lateral cinefluorographic films confirmed the relatively complete absence of velar movement. The examining speech pathologist found the girl to have normal articulation placement of the tongue for all speech sounds, despite severe nasal emission of air flow for fricative and affricate phonemes. Low back vowels were relatively oral in resonance, while middle and high vowels became increasingly nasal. It was the consensus of the evaluation team that, with her structural inadequacy, this child was (and had been) a poor candidate for speech therapy. It was recommended that she receive a pharyngeal flap and be evaluated again several weeks after the operation. The surgery was successful and had an amazingly positive effect on the child's speech. While hypernasality disappeared, some slight nasal emission remained. The girl was subsequently enrolled in individual speech therapy, where she experienced total success in developing normal fricative-affricate production.

Such a case dramatically shows the futility of continued speech therapy when real structural inadequacy exists. Indeed, whenever I wish to give students a vivid illustration of the point, I play recordings of this young lady's voice made before and after her operation. Without that operation, she could have received speech therapy for the rest of her life, with no effect whatsoever on her speech. If velopharyngeal insufficiency is found, there appear to be two primary alternatives for treatment, surgical or dental.

*Surgical treatment of hypernasality.* The evaluation may reveal the existence of such structural inadequacies as open fistulas, open bony and soft tissue clefts, submucous clefts, and short or relatively immobile soft palates. The plastic surgeon is usually the medical specialist most experienced in making decisions about the time of surgical closure of palatal openings and about the type of surgery required. Besides actually closing the openings of fistulas and clefts, a common surgical procedure for palatal insufficiency (of both length and movement) is to create a pharyngeal flap. Here, the surgeon takes a small piece of mucosal tissue from the pharynx and uses it to bridge the excessive velopharyngeal opening, attaching the tissue to the soft palate. This tissue appears to act as an excellent diverting structure, deflecting both air flow and sound waves into the oral cavity. Bzoch (*28*), discussing the physiological and speech results for forty patients who had received pharyngeal flap surgery, reported that the procedure was most effective in reducing both hypernasality and nasal emission (if present) in most of the subjects. While pharyngeal flap surgery, or any other form of palatal surgery, must not be thought of as a panacea for all resonance problems, it will often help align oral-nasal structures in such a way that, for the first time, speech and voice therapy can be effective. If diagnostic procedures have established that velopharyngeal inadequacy contributes to a problem of hypernasality, a surgeon should certainly be consulted about the feasibility of surgical correction of the observed structural inadequacies.

*Dental treatment of hypernasality.* Both the orthodontist and the prosthodontist may play important roles in the treatment of individuals with hypernasality, particularly those with a problem of cleft palate. The orthodontist may face the problem of expanding the dental arches so that the patient can experience "maximum alveolar growth" (Rosenstein, *139*). The prosthodontist, by constructing various prosthetic speech appliances (obturators), may be able to help the patient preserve his facial contour, filling in various maxillary defects with prostheses to cover open palatal defects such as fistulas and clefts, and may also be able to build speech training appliances to provide posterior velopharyngeal closure (Rosen, *138*). In evaluating twenty-one adults with acquired or congenital palate problems, Arndt, Shelton, and Bradford (*3*) found that both groups made significant "articulation and voice gains with obturation." Many cleft palate subjects are fitted by the prosothodontist with acrylic bulbs at the end of their appliance; if the bulb is well positioned against the posterior and lateral pharyngeal walls, there will often be a noticeable reduction of both nasality and air escape. The occasional patient whose soft palate is relatively immobile might well profit from consultation with the prosthodontist about the possibility of being fitted with a lift appliance to hold the immobile palate in a higher position so that some pharyngeal contact will be possible. For nasality problems related to velopharyngeal inadequacy, the speech pathologist should freely consult both the orthodontist and the prosthodontist for their ideas on how to achieve adequate functioning of the oral structures.

*Voice therapy for hypernasality.* Any attempts at voice therapy for hypernasality should be deferred until both the evaluation of the problem and attempts at physical correction have been completed. The primary requirement for developing good oral voice quality is the structural adequacy of the velopharyngeal closing mechanism. Without adequate closure, voice therapy will be futile. However, there are individuals who, for functional reasons, speak with hypernasality, and for these people voice therapy can be helpful in developing more oral resonance. Added to this group are occasional patients who have had surgical or dental treatment which has left them with only a marginal velopharyngeal closing mechanism; in voice therapy, this mechanism may be trained to work more optimally. If voice therapy is indicated for improving orality of resonance, the following facilitating approaches should be used:

1. *Approach I, Altering Tongue Position.* A high, forward carriage of the tongue sometimes contributes to nasal resonance. Efforts in developing a lower, more posterior carriage may have some effect in decreasing the perceived nasality.

2. *Approach II, Change of Loudness.* A voice that has been perceived as hypernasal will sometimes be perceived as more normal if some other change in vocalization is made. One change that often accomplishes this is an increase in loudness; by speaking in a louder voice, the patient will frequently sound less hypernasal.

3. *Approach V, Ear Training.* If the patient is motivated to reduce his hypernasality, a great deal of time should be spent in therapy in helping him learn to hear the differences between his nasal and oral resonances.

4. *Approach VIII, Establishing New Pitch.* Some patients with hypernasality speak at inappropriately high pitch levels, which contributes to the listener's perception of nasality. Speaking at the lower end of one's pitch range seems to contribute to greater oral resonance.

5. *Approach IX, Explanation of Problem.* No voice therapy should ever be started without first explaining to the patient what the problem seems to be.

6. *Approach X, Feedback.* Developing an aural awareness of hypernasality and some oral-pharyngeal awareness of what hypernasality "feels" like is a most helpful therapeutic device.

7. *Approach XIII, Open Mouth.* Hypernasality is sometimes produced by an overall restriction of the oral opening. In such cases, efforts at developing greater oral openness may have some effect in reducing the listener's perception of excessive nasality.

8. *Approach XVII, Respiration.* Increased loudness is often achieved by respiration training.

9. *Approach XVIII, Target Voice Models.* In therapy for hypernasality, it is important to "capture" on tape any good oral resonance the patient may produce and play it back to him as his own oral model .The target for oral resonance is the patient's own oral production.

## TREATMENT FOR DENASALITY

Beyond the nasal resonance required for /m/, /n/, and /ŋ/, vowels in American English require a slight nasal resonance. Lack of nasal resonance in severe cases produces actual articulatory substitutions for the three nasal phonemes as well as slight alterations for vowels. Denasality (hyponasality) is characterized by the diversion of sound waves and air flow out through the oral cavity, permitting little or no nasal resonance. More often than not, this problem appears to be related to some kind of nasopharyngeal obstruction, such as excessive adenoidal growth, severe nasopharyngeal infection as in head colds, large polyps in the nasal cavity, etc. Some patients who are hypernasal before surgical or dental treatment emerge from such treatment with complete or highly excessive velopharyngeal obstruction; perhaps the pharyngeal flap is too broad, permitting little or no ventilation of the nasopharynx, or an obturator bulb may fit too tightly, resulting in no nasal air flow or nasal resonance. Such obstruction is the usual reason for a denasality problem, and the search for it must precede any attempt at voice therapy.

The first obstruction to nasal air flow can be made simply as part of the overall resonance evaluation: ask the patient to take a big breath, close his mouth, exhale through his nose. Then test the air flow through each nostril separately, compressing one nostril at a time by compressing the nares with a finger. If there is any observable decrement in air flow, the nasal passages should be investigated medically. Appropriate medical therapy should precede any voice therapy.

Only rarely will patients have markedly denasal voices for wholly functional reasons. While their denasal resonance in the beginning may have had a physical cause, that cause is no longer present, and the denasality remains as a habit, a "set." Occasionally a patient has chosen a denasal voice as a model, for whatever reason, and has learned to match its denasality with some consistency. Voice therapy for increasing nasal resonance might include:

1. *Approach V, Ear Training.* Considerable effort must be expended in contrasting for the patient the difference between the nasal and oral productions of /m/,/n/, and /ŋ/. Oral and nasal resonance of vowels can also be presented for listening contrast.

2. *Approach IX, Explanation of Problem.* The resonance requirements for normal English must be explained to the patient, and his own lack of nasal resonance, particularly for /m/,/n/, and /ŋ/, pointed out. If the patient's problem is wholly functional, this explanation is of primary importance.

3. *Approach X, Feedback.* Emphasis must be given to contrasting what it sounds like and "feels" like to produce oral and nasal resonance. The patient should be encouraged to make exaggerated humming sounds both orally and nasally, concentrating on the "feel" of the two types of productions.

4. *Approach XVIII, Target Voice Models.* Following the procedures for this approach in chapter 5, search with the patient for his own best production of nasal resonance for the nasal phonemes, with a slight increase of nasality for vowel productions. Combining this and the feedback approach may help the patient develop a greater awareness of nasality as he attempts to match his good production by both feeling and sound.

Practice materials for increasing nasal resonance have been set down by a number of voice and articulation authorities, among them Akin (*1*), Eisenson (*53*), Fairbanks (*55*), and Fisher (*57*).

### TREATMENT FOR ASSIMILATIVE NASALITY

The nasalization of vowels immediately before and after nasal consonants is known as assimilative nasality. Performance on stimulability testing will provide a good clue as to whether such nasal resonance is related to poor velar functioning or is functionally induced. There are a few neurological disorders, such as bulbar palsy or multiple sclerosis, in which the patient is unable to move his velum quickly enough to facilitate the movements required for normal resonance. His velar openings begin too soon and are maintained too long, lagging behind the rapid requirements of normal speech and producing nasalization of vowels which occur next to nasal phonemes. Most cases of assimilative nasality, however, are of functional origin, with the patient showing good oral resonance under special conditions of stimulability.

It is important to remember here that in connected speech, all sounds are interdependent; as one sound is being produced, articulators are positioning for the next sound. This phonemic interdependence allows for a certain amount of assimilation, even in normal speech. In assimilative nasality, therefore, we are dealing once again with a perceptual problem; that is, whether the speaker's nasalization of vowels adjacent to nasal phonemes is excessive or not depends on the perception of the listener. The perception of assimilative nasality is of course related to the perception of excessive nasality; a normal, minor amount of nasality in the vowels following nasal phonemes would not be perceived, and increased amounts of nasal resonance would be judged quite differently by different listeners according to their individual standards and experience. Therapy for assimilative nasality is likewise highly variable, being related largely to the locale (in some areas such resonance is a normal voice pattern), the standards of the speaker or his clinician, their motivations, etc. Voice therapy for assimilative nasality is best attempted only by those patients who have strong motivations to develop more oral resonance. These approaches might be used:

1. *Approach V, Ear Training.* Ear training should help the patient discriminate between his nasalized vowels and his oral vowels. He might profit from listening to recordings of his own oral-consonant/vowel/oral-consonant words as contrasted with his nasal-consonant/vowel/nasal-consonant words, such as these pairs: bad–man, bed–men, bead–mean, bub–mum, etc. Voice and diction books often contain certain word pairs matching monosyllabic words using /b/, /d/, and /g/ with those using /m/, /n/, and /ŋ/. Once the patient can hear the differences between oral and nasal cognates, see if he can produce them.

2. *Approach IX, Explanation of Problem.* Since nasal assimilations are difficult to explain verbally, any attempt at explanation should be accompanied by demonstration. The best demonstration appears to be in presenting the contrast between oral and nasal resonance of vowels which follow or precede the three nasal phonemes.

3. *Approach X, Feedback.* While feedback can certainly be attempted with the problem of assimilative nasality, experience has found that few patients can monitor well what they are doing during conditions of ongoing feedback. Learning to listen to oneself critically with delayed feedback provided by some kind of auditory loop tape device has been found to be helpful.

*TREATMENT FOR NASAL EMISSION*

While nasal emission is not a nasal resonance problem, it frequently accompanies hypernasality as a symptom of palatal insufficiency. Whenever high intraoral pressure fricatives or affricates are produced, they are attended by a great deal of nasal noise. This nasal escape of the air stream is invariably the result of incomplete velopharyngeal closure. Sometimes the incomplete closure is related to a palate which is slightly too short to effect good contact with the pharynx. Or it may be related to inadequate movement of both the velum and the pharynx. A weakened velum or a velar mechanism which operates ineffectively when the individual is fatigued or nervous may result in nasal emissions which are heard only during these moments of fatigue or stress. In any case, nasal emission is virtually a sure sign of velopharyngeal inadequacy: it almost never exists for purely functional reasons. The articulation distortion created by nasal emission is treated effectively by either surgical or prosthodontic treatment. Speech therapy by itself will seldom have appreciable effect in reducing nasal emission.

SUMMARY

Oral, pharyngeal, and nasal resonance are important components of the voice. Too little or too much resonance of a particular type may be perceived by listeners as a problem in resonance. In this chapter, the problems of stridency and other oral-pharyngeal resonance deviations were presented, and recommendations were made for specific therapeutic approaches that have been helpful in improving oral resonance. Nasal resonance problems were specified as hypernasality, denasality, assimilative nasality, and nasal emission (which was discussed as an articulation, rather than a resonance, problem). The focus in the evaluation of nasal resonance disorders was on determining whether the patient had the normal velopharyngeal mechanisms required for normal-sounding oral and nasal resonance. It was stressed that considerable attention should be given to the possibility of developing such structural adequacy, if lacking, by the evaluation team, the plastic surgeon, the prosthodontist, the orthodontist, and the speech pathologist. For voice therapy indicated for functional resonance variations, specific facilitating approaches were outlined.

# chapter eight

# Voice Therapy
# for the
# Laryngectomy Patient

*The surgical removal of a cancer of the larynx generally involves the total removal of the larynx, a laryngectomy. Patients who have undergone this procedure are called laryngectomees. The laryngectomee's most obvious problem after his operation is loss of voice, which frequently brings him to the speech pathologist for voice rehabilitation. Often competing with voice training in the beginning are the physical and emotional problems experienced by the patient. We shall consider various voice rehabilitation procedures, including the use of the artificial larynx and esophageal speech.*

Rehabilitation of the laryngectomy patient probably begins on the day the surgeon tells the patient that he has cancer which will require surgical removal of the larynx. While a diagnosis of cancer is always difficult for the physician to transmit to the patient, it is even more difficult when a laryngectomy and its resulting loss of voice are involved. After the operation, the patient will *not be able to speak*. The patient fears, quite legitimately, that he will never be able to talk again, and it is the economic and social implications of this that most bother him. Up until this time, the patient has probably never given any thought to the vital importance of voice, or to how the larynx serves as protector to the airway, or to what a laryngectomy entails. Many surgeons prefer to answer the patient's questions preoperatively, perhaps referring the patient to a speech pathologist or to a lay laryngectomee for some demonstration of postoperative voice training procedures. A visit with a laryngectomee will also provide the patient with positive proof of another person's successful accommodation to the same kind of surgical procedure and to the resulting problems that may ensue.

With improved surgical techniques and medical management of the laryngectomee, most of these patients survive the operation and experience good results. Gardner (*63*) reports that some 4,000 persons are laryngectomized every year in the United States, and that over 8,000 laryngectomees belong to the International Association of Laryngectomees (IAL, 219 East Forty-second Street, New York, New York, 10019). Fortunately, cancer of the larynx, which comprises from three to five percent of all human cancer, is one of the most curable malignancies (Holinger, Johnston, and Mansueto, *75*). It may strike at any age, although it occurs most often in the fifties and sixties, and is about ten times more frequent in men than in women. Most laryngeal cancer is accompanied by persistent hoarseness, and this hoarseness must be considered as a prominent, early warning sign. The earlier the cancer can be detected, the better the chances of its successful elimination. Later symptoms of laryngeal cancer are pain (rarely severe), shortness of breath (dyspnea), difficulty in swallowing (dysphagia), and the presence of small nodal masses in the neck (*ibid.*).

While the surgeon is concerned primarily with the elimination of the cancer, those involved in the total rehabilitation of the laryngectomee are concerned with teaching him a new and satisfactory voice and helping him overcome any psychosocial problems from his loss of voice. We shall consider the total rehabilitation of the laryngectomee from these points of view: the preoperative visit, postoperative medical care, the postoperative visit, physical problems after laryngectomy, voice training, and psychosocial adjustment.

## THE PREOPERATIVE VISIT

There is by no means any unanimity among surgeons about the advisability of having preoperative visits for the patient about to have a laryngectomy. The decision for a preoperative visit by a speech pathologist or by a laryngectomee who demonstrates a well-adjusted, functioning personality must belong to the surgeon. There may well be some patients who, because of too much tissue removal or because of intellectual or personality problems, will never learn to use esophageal speech. To expose such a patient before surgery to a good esophageal speaker is in fact implying to the patient that he, too, will be able to speak again with a little training. After the operation, he may interpret his own faulty voice, as compared to the excellent voice of the speaker who came to visit him, as a sign of personal failure. As Diedrich and Youngstrom have written, "When a successfully speaking laryngectomee pre- or postoperatively visits a patient there is the implication that the patient will learn to speak as the visitor does. Obviously, this is not true." (*49*, p. 138.) It might be better at the time of the preoperative visit, if such a visit is requested, to include both a speech pathologist and a laryngectomee, the latter coming along to demonstrate overall successful adjustment (he is back in the community at his former job), rather than good speech per se.

In 1962, in Cleveland, Ohio, this writer joined other concerned persons (surgeons, speech pathologists, and laryngectomees) in developing a comprehensive plan to be used in Cleveland for rehabilitating the laryngectomee. The plan was published and distributed by the Cleveland Hearing and Speech Center, the Cleveland Lost Chord Club, and the local chapter of the American Cancer Society. Three separate brochures were developed: *A Plan for Rehabilitating the Laryngectomee, A Suggested Plan for Surgeons (133)*; *Cleveland Lost Chord Club, Instructions for Visitants (36)*; and *Cleveland Lost Chord Club (35)*. Part of the plan included specific suggestions for preoperative visits. One was that the request for a preoperative visit be initiated by the surgeon, who would call the local laryngectomee club, in this case the Cleveland Lost Chord Club. The Club had selected from its membership a group of laryngectomees to function as visitants, their primary task being to visit new patients preoperatively and postoperatively. The criteria used for selecting these visitants included:

a. Intelligible, fluent, and well-phrased esophageal speech.
b. Successful adjustment to the problem of communication.
c. Successful emotional adjustment.
d. A pleasant personality free from secondary undesirable speech habits.

At the request of the surgeon, the visitant would call on the patient in the hospital, giving him pamphlets and written material provided by the American Cancer Society. Although the visitant demonstrated his speech simply by being there, his primary role was changed from that of a model speaker to that of a new, understanding friend. The preoperative visit would be brief, never exceeding 15 minutes, and would conclude with the visitant saying that he would be back to see the patient a few days after the operation. This implication of some continuity, of someone caring that the patient got back into the world as a speaking person, probably provided both the patient and his family with some needed reassurance.

A brief preoperative visit by the speech pathologist and a laryngectomee of his choice is perhaps the best way to provide the most relevant information about the patient and also give the patient some psychological support. It is important for the speech pathologist to assess how the patient speaks before the operation. Through conversation, he should roughly evaluate the patient's articulatory proficiency and overall speech intelligibility, and, since the long-term goal will be to help the patient achieve intelligible speech, he should evaluate the patient's performance (independent of his obvious voicing problems) in terms of speed of speech, dialect or accent, articulation errors, degree of mouth opening when speaking, eye contact, etc. In the brief preoperative contact with the patient and his family, it is important that the "speech doctor" convey to them his confidence that the "patient will talk again." In assuring the patient that a method will be found that he will be able to use, the speech pathologist should describe several methods of therapy and give a brief demonstration of the artificial larynx. He might tell the patient that as soon as his surgeon gives the "go ahead," he will be provided temporarily with an artificial larynx, so that he will be able to talk to people instead of writing out his messages (as so many laryngectomees have been instructed to do, as if using the artificial larynx would contaminate their chances of learning esophageal speech).

The speech pathologist should then introduce his laryngectomee companion, stressing in the introduction the laryngectomee's employment, social milieu, etc. The laryngectomee should then discuss how his life after the operation has closely paralleled his life before it (hopefully, this will be the case). He may answer a few of the patient's questions about learning to speak again, or about the local laryngectomee club, etc. The laryngectomee should make it clear to the patient that after the operation he will come back and visit a bit longer. The speech pathologist should conclude the preoperative visit by saying that speech instruction will be started as soon as the surgeon gives the word, and that until that time, after the operation, it will probably do little good to carry out any kind of speech practice. (There are differences of professional opinion, however, on preoperative speech practice; for example, Gardner and Harris [64] recommend several days of practice before surgery, while Diedrich and Youngstrom [49] regard preoperative practice much more cautiously.)

It would appear that the speech pathologist, in whatever locale he finds himself, should take an active part in developing and maintaining a workable plan for the rehabilitation of the laryngectomee. Part of such a plan must include some procedures regarding the preoperative visit, if such visits are regularly requested by surgeons in that locale. The International Association of Laryngectomees and the American Cancer Society provide guidelines for local laryngectomee programs, although there appears to be little consistency of approach to the problems of preoperative visits. Such visits seem to be highly dependent on the personalities and philosophies of the people involved. This writer favors the preoperative visit of the speech pathologist and laryngectomee together. There are rather impressive data available supporting the benefit of preoperative visits. Horn (82), polling IAL members by questionnaire on the subject of preoperative visits, found that only three percent of the patients responding disapproved of such visits, while only one-half of one percent reported that their physicians did. It would appear that the majority of laryngectomees benefit from the preoperative visit, probably more from a psychological point of view than anything else.

### POSTOPERATIVE MEDICAL CARE OF THE LARYNGECTOMEE

It would be beyond the scope of this book to describe in any detail the surgical and medical problems surrounding the problem of laryngectomy. It is important, however, that the speech pathologist in his initial contacts with the laryngectomee appreciate the postoperative medical problems the patient may be facing. As important as voice restoration may be, and as important as the speech pathologist's role may become, the primary consideration during and immediately after surgery is the preservation of life. Control of bleeding, preservation of the airway, prevention of infection, and nourishing the patient are of primary concern to the medical team caring for the patient. In the typical laryngectomy, the entire laryngeal mechanism is removed, including the hyoid bone (see Figure 25). The hypopharyngeal opening into the esophagus and the esophagus itself are usually well preserved, although some of their sphincteral functions may be somewhat diminished by the removal of their attachments (hyoid bone, thyroid and cricoid cartilages). The trachea, which loses its connection with the pharynx and mouth, is brought to the skin surface and attached directly superior to the suprasternal notch; at this level, a permanent opening (tracheotomy) is constructed, through which the patient will forever breathe. If there were known or suspected cancerous nodes in the neck, the patient may have had, in addition to his laryngectomy a radical neck dissection. This procedure involves the removal of the cervical lymph nodes as well as many of the normal-appearing nodes adjacent to the suspected cancer site. The dissection is usually done initially on one side only, sometimes followed later by the same procedure on the other side. Radical neck dissection greatly increases the site of surgical alteration, and the postsurgical medical and nursing care required is usually more intensive.

[ The new laryngectomee usually requires a day or two of absolute bedrest following surgery. The head of the bed should be slightly elevated so that the patient's head will be slightly flexed toward the chest, thus avoiding any tension on the sutures (Holinger, Johnston, and Mansueto, 75). Ambulation is started as soon as the patient's condition permits, frequently on the second or third day. The patient's fluid and caloric intake require constant

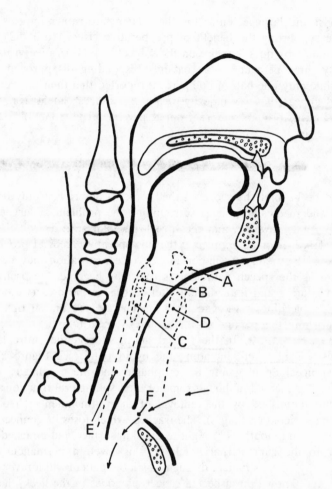

Fig. 25. The laryngectomee, before and after surgery. The broken line designates normal structures present before the surgical operation. The patient has had removed (A) the hyoid bone; (B) the arytenoid cartilages; (C) the cricoid cartilage; (D) the thyroid cartilage. Note (E), the posterior tracheal-anterior esophageal wall. After the operation, the residual neck and head structures of the laryngectomee are shown in the solid lines; the new tracheal opening, the tracheotomy, is seen at (F).

monitoring, and attention must be given to his vital cardiac, pulmonary, and urinary functions. The patient will receive various antibiotics and analgesics (pain killers) as required. Of frequent postoperative concern is the maintenance of an open airway. The patient is fitted with a tracheotomy tube (cannula), which fits through the open stoma and extends down into the trachea. It is important in the beginning that this tube be cleaned every one to two hours to keep excessive secretions and crusting from obstructing the flow of air (Jimison, 88). To prevent the patient from swallowing, and thus give the pharyngeal and esophageal structures time to heal, the patient is fitted with a feeding tube inserted through his nose and going directly through the pharynx into the esophagus and hence into the stomach. The feeding tube is usually removed on the eighth to the tenth postoperative day, if there is no unhealed fistula (small opening) between the pharynx and the skin (Holinger, Johnston, and Mansueto, 75).

It is at about this time, when the fistulas are healed, that the surgeon gives his approval for the beginning of speech instruction, which may mean the introduction of the artificial larynx, permitting the patient to talk to other people. (Sometimes the artificial larynx is introduced earlier than this.) The referral to the speech pathologist and the beginning of voice instruction should be started, if possible, before the patient leaves the hospital. Before the patient is discharged, also, he usually will have received detailed nursing instructions on the care of his excision sites, maintenance of the airway, how to keep the cannula clean, etc.

## THE POSTOPERATIVE VISIT

The surgeon usually requests the postoperative visit six or seven days after surgery. It is at this time that the speech pathologist and/or the laryngectomee visitant often realize that their role in the rehabilitation of the patient is far more than teaching him to use a new voice. It is not until after the operation, when the patient actually begins to experience its many overwhelming effects, that he may be frightened and depressed, requiring realistic and straightforward answers to the questions he poses to his visitors. Diedrich and Youngstrom vividly describe the laryngectomee's new problems:

Laryngeal amputation is much more subtle than losing an arm or leg. In fact, just to say the word amputation gives one a different feeling about what is lost than to say the word laryngectomy. The full impact of amputation of the larynx is not ordinarily apparent. A fully clothed laryngectomee walking down the hall does not look much different from anyone else. It is not until he is asked to speak, cough, breathe, eat, smell, bathe, lift, cry, or laugh that his differences become apparent. In other words, little is left unaffected in the laryngectomee's physical, psychological, and social behavior. [49, p. 66]

The first postoperative visit, therefore, should have a certain amount of flexibility to it, so that the visitors can respond to whatever questions the patient may have about these physical and psychological changes, and perhaps alleviate some of his concerns about talking again. There is some advantage to bringing some printed material, such as a few of the pamphlets on laryngectomy problems provided by the American Cancer Society or by local IAL clubs. These materials offer the patient and his family answers to many problems they may be facing. Selected laryngectomees from local

IAL clubs are often effective at the time of the postoperative visit in relating their first-hand experiences in meeting some of the postoperative problems the patient may have; for example, the physical problem of mucus in the stoma is often an early complaint, and it should be pointed out to the patient that successful control of excessive mucus at the stoma site is usually developed early. Just as with the preoperative visit, the combination team of the speech pathologist and the laryngectomee visitant appears to be most appropriate for the first visit after surgery.

Gardner (63) recommends that whenever possible, either before surgery or shortly after, the patient should view a film such as *You Can Talk Again* (175), which portrays a patient's recovery after surgery, his learning to speak again, and his return to business. After showing the film, the speech pathologist should have a frank discussion with the patient, making it clear that most laryngectomees learn to use satisfactory speech again and that for most patients successful rehabilitation means going back to the same psychosocial status they enjoyed before the operation. It seems to be tremendously important for the speech-voice learning sequence which follows that the patient *believe* in his teacher, and this means that the speech pathologist must convey to the patient that he understands what the problems are and what must be done to overcome them.

Before his first visit to the new laryngectomee, the speech pathologist should ask the surgeon when the patient will be able to begin his speech-voice training and when he will be able to use the artificial larynx. The decision as to when to begin either speech training or artificial larynx usage is dependent on the overall surgical healing of the patient. Sometimes difficulty in healing or the development of fistulas will be aggravated by speech practice or by using the artificial larynx. Training should begin, whenever possible, as soon as the patient's physical condition permits. Several studies by questionnaire (Horn, 82; Diedrich and Youngstrom, 49) have found that the average time lapse between the operation and the beginning of speech training is from two to four months. In this interim, the average patient relies primarily on writing as his method of communication. Horn further reports that adequate speech proficiency is not acquired until seven months after surgery, while Diedrich and Youngstrom place the time at up to one year. During this protracted time of acquiring adequate speech, usually of the esophageal type, the typical patient relies on writing as an auxiliary aid to communication. Diedrich and Youngstrom make a strong argument for utilizing the artificial larynx as a regular training device before the patient learns esophageal speech, a view previously espoused by Martin (103) and Miller (110), but somewhat lost in the literature. Why have the patient write his communications before or during the early learning stages of esophageal speech when the artificial larynx can provide actual speech practice and oral communication right from the beginning? It would appear that the artificial larynx helps the patient develop an early awareness of the relative independence of voice from articulation (he can still articulate), appreciate the need for phrasing, and develop articulatory skill post-operatively (the reduction in articulation proficiency that some patients experience after surgery responds well to practice). The clinician should demonstrate for the patient the use of an electronic larynx, such as the

Fig. 26. Two artificial larynges. The Western Electric artificial larynx is shown in the top photograph. It is held in the hand and the vibrating head is placed firmly against the neck, permitting its sound vibrations to be introduced through the skin into the patient's hypopharynx. The Cooper-Rand artificial larynx, shown in the bottom photograph, is carried in the pocket with a connecting wire attached to the vibrating oscillator; the oscillator is held in the hand and is attached to a small metal rod which introduces the voice sound directly into the patient's mouth.

Western Electric Artificial Larynx[1] or the Cooper-Rand Artificial Larynx[2] (both shown in figure 26), which most patients can learn to use with relative ease. However, *learning* to use an instrument is required, since few patients are able to use it well without some formal instruction. We shall discuss artificial larynx instruction under the heading of Voice Training in the next section of this chapter.

While a portion of the first visit may be devoted to providing some instruction in using the artificial larynx, this is also when the first discussion and demonstration of esophageal speech begins. The patient can be told that the odds are heavy on his side that he will learn to speak again with a satisfactory voice. He can also be told that we are not restricted to any one way of teaching him in the beginning. What works best for him will be the initial method of instruction used. However, the patient need *not* be told on this first visit that the odds are good that even after developing esophageal speech, he may not be pleased with his new voice: of the eighty-seven laryngectomee respondents in the study that Diedrich and Youngstrom conducted by questionnaire (*49*), 56 percent of the esophageal speakers rated their speech as good or very good, 23 percent as average, 11 percent as fair, and 10 percent as poor; in the self-evaluations made by the fourteen artificial larynx users, 67 percent rated themselves as good or very good, 17 percent as average, 5 percent as fair, and 11 percent as poor. These data offer strong support for taking a more eclectic approach to speech teaching with the new laryngectomee. Some patients may be better off using the artificial larynx exclusively, or only at the beginning of their training, or as a supplementary speaking device whenever they feel the need for it. It would also appear that the method of esophageal teaching should be tailored to fit the capabilities of the specific patient. Attempting to teach everyone by the same approach seems to be a sure way of guaranteeing failure for some patients. The clinician should remember that his basic task is to help the patient achieve a new voice by whatever method best serves that patient. Because one laryngectomee learns in one way does not mean that the next patient can learn only in that way too. While we must not convey to the patient any of the controversy that may surround the method of instruction, we should make him aware that there are indeed different methods of approach.

There are three approaches to teaching esophageal speech, and it has been found useful to describe and demonstrate them briefly at the first visit. If it appears appropriate, the patient might be asked to imitate the demonstration by the speech pathologist or laryngectomee visitant. The primary problem in teaching esophageal speech is to discover with the patient the

[1]The Western Electric Artificial Larynx is distributed through any local Bell Telephone office.

[2]The Cooper-Rand Artificial Larynx is distributed through the Rand Development Corporation, 13600 Deise Avenue, Cleveland, Ohio 44110.

best method for him of achieving air intake. In some manner, the patient must get air into his esophagus, releasing it when he wants to voice. It is the release of the air trapped in the esophagus which sets up the airflow that will vibrate the superior esophageal and lower pharyngeal mucosal lining, producing the pseudo voice. The three methods of achieving air intake for esophageal speech are:

1. *The swallow method.* In the swallow method, as advocated by Doehler (*50*), the patient opens his mouth, then closes his mouth, then swallows air with his lips closed, and then quickly opens his mouth again. One way of helping the patient achieve the swallow is to ask him to do it by imagining that he is swallowing a small amount of water. This dry swallow seems to open the esophagus, permitting the injection of air, which is accomplished by the tongue and pharyngeal muscles squeezing the air in the natural swallowing motion. In our actual esophageal speech training, we use the swallow approach only when our other two approaches fail.

2. *The inhalation method.* In the inhalation method, the patient is able to introduce air directly into the esophagus when he takes in a normal pulmonary inhalation (Froeschels, *61*). The inhalation method is regarded as the *natural method,* since it does not require the patient to relinquish the tendency to breathe out when voicing; that is, he takes in the esophageal air on inhalation and expels it for phonation during his normal exhalation (Gardner, *63*). The patient is asked to take in a breath with his mouth open (the palate is usually closed), and reminded that the main inhalation *to his lungs* is achieved through his tracheal stoma. Any air in his mouth might well flow into his esophagus. If it does, he will produce an esophageal voice (sounding, perhaps, like a burp or a belch) on exhalation. It is the rare patient, however, who is able to take air into the esophagus in this way on the first attempt.

3. *The injection method.* The injection method is used by the largest number of esophageal speakers, although most laryngectomees who use it may be unaware that they are doing so. This is the method commonly used by those laryngectomees who, when queried, reply, "I have no idea what I do when I talk." The method is achieved by trapping or squeezing air between the tongue and the hard and soft palate and pharynx, forcing the compressed air mass backward into the hypopharynx. If the esophagus is open at this time, the air will rush into the esophagus and be entrapped there for phonation. It would appear that the voiceless plosive consonants, /p/, /t/, and /k/, serve as excellent facilitators for trapping or squeezing the air back into the esophagus. Frequently, the repetition of the /t/ results in trapped esophageal air and its immediate voice production, "taw." Diedrich and Youngstrom (*49*) present numerous tracings of cinefluorograms which show actual tongue, palatal, and pharyngeal movements in both the inhalation and injection methods, and which also clearly show that the typical vibrating part (P-E segment, pharyngeal-esophageal segment) includes more muscle fibers than just the cricopharyngeus. The ease with which many patients are able to employ the injection method makes it the most frequent demonstration method at the time of the first postoperative visit.

## PHYSICAL PROBLEMS OF THE LARYNGECTOMEE

Some laryngectomees are more concerned about their physical changes following laryngectomy than they are about their inability to speak. While the Horn study (*82*) found that laryngectomees in general report that their present health is about the same as it was before the operation, there are some physical problems peculiar to this group. Those most typically reported appear to be air-intake problems, digestive difficulties, diminished taste and smell, smoking-habit changes, and difficulty in lifting weight.

*Air intake problems.* Many new laryngectomees are bothered a great deal by the natural increase of mucus in the trachea and at the stoma site. It is physiologically desirable for pulmonary air to be relatively warm and moist, which is the basic reason for the increase of tracheal mucus in the laryngectomee. In cold, dry surroundings there is often tracheal irritation, which causes increased mucus and coughing; this problem can be reduced somewhat by moistening the air in the home with a humidifier or steam inhalation device. Coughing is a frequent problem for the laryngectomee. His cough is more of an aspirate wheeze, to which other people often react negatively. Most laryngectomees report that they try to avoid coughing in public, excusing themselves, if necessary, to cough and clean their stomas of excessive mucus in private. The collection of mucus in the stoma area presents a situation which requires systematic care by the laryngectomee. He is instructed always to wear some protective covering over the stoma, such as a crocheted bib, a gauze bib, or a metal or plastic screen guard; this covering protects the airway from irritants and also provides a site where moisture (mucus, airstream) can collect to help moisten stoma inhalations. The patient develops a regular schedule for cleaning the stoma covering and removing excessive mucus, using a gauze pad or handkerchief (he should avoid using a lint-type paper tissue). Gardner (*63*) reports that laryngectomees do very well in various dusty, fume-laden industries, so long as they employ protective masks over the stoma. Most laryngectomees soon discover that in bathing and showering they must take special care to protect the stoma from water; the relative ease with which water can enter the neck stoma makes such activities as swimming, boating, and stream fishing extremely hazardous. For more detailed descriptions of stoma care, such as cleaning the cannula, the reader should refer to Jimison (*88*) or to materials provided by the American Cancer Society, such as articles on the subject in the *IAL News* (published by the International Association of Laryngectomees). Some of the breathing problems and special needs of the laryngectomee are outlined in *First Aid for Laryngectomees* (*56*); for example, if artificial respiration is ever necessary for the laryngectomee, these warnings are given: keep the neck opening clear, avoid twisting the head to one side, apply oxygen only to the stoma, avoid throwing water on the head, and use mouth-to-stoma breathing.

*Digestive difficulties.* The trapping of air in the esophagus for esophageal speech carries with it the possibility that some esophageal air will move down into the stomach and into the intestinal tract. Gardner (*63*) reports that among fifty-four laryngectomees with no gastrointestinal symptoms before surgery, forty-one (76 percent) acquired such symptoms chronically after surgery. Gardner believes that one of the negative features of the swallow method is its high frequency of gastric complaint. The patient swallows his air into the stomach, experiencing the subsequent symptoms of bloating, pain, and flatulence. Diedrich and Youngstrom found that 71 percent of their questionnaire respondents reported an increase of gastrointestinal symptoms, often trapping "more air than they utilize in the phonation of phrases and short sentences" (*49*, p. 122). Other findings vis-à-vis digestive problems in the same questionnaire were that about one-third of the respondents had difficulty in swallowing and sucking, about half had difficulty in drinking from a fountain or drinking soup with a spoon, over one-third permanently took longer to eat, and the majority reported an increase of heartburn. Another feeding problem to which the laryngectomee must learn to accommodate is that simultaneous eating and talking (difficult and undesirable in normal people) is almost impossible for the esophageal speaker.

*Diminished taste and smell.* Related to the problem of feeding is the possibility that after surgery the patient will experience diminished taste. Forty-one percent of the laryngectomees in the Horn report (*82*) and 31 percent of those in the Diedrich and Youngstrom sample (*49*), indicated that their taste was less accurate after surgery. In elaborating on the taste problem, Diedrich and Youngstrom write that only 4 percent of their group had no sense of taste and that for many patients only strong sweet or acid tastes could be detected. The sense of smell, however, is usually diminished or wholly absent; the inability to smell normally was reported by 79 percent of Horn's respondents and 95 percent of Diedrich's and Youngstrom's. Over time, however, some laryngectomees do report a gradual increase in their ability to smell, although for the majority of patients the sense of smell remains permanently impaired. Such warning smells as rubber or wood burning, escaping gas, or an approaching skunk may go wholly undetected by the laryngectomee.

*Smoking habit changes.* Most of the laryngectomees in the reports we are drawing on had been relatively heavy smokers before their operations. Ninety-three percent of the Diedrich and Youngstrom respondents had been smokers with over 70 percent smoking more than one pack a day (*49*, p. 74). Horn (*82*) reported that of the 80 percent of the laryngectomees in his survey who had smoked cigarettes before their operations, 23 percent were still smoking after their operations. Despite the increasing evidence being published on the close relationship between heavy smoking and laryngeal cancer, only 44 percent of the laryngectomees polled by Horn felt that their smoking had anything to do with the development of their laryngeal cancer. About one out of four laryngectomees continue to smoke after their operations, despite the mechanical-physical difficulty in doing so. The laryngectomee emplaces his cigarette orally, and then, by the same method he employs for esophageal speech air-intake, brings the smoke out through his nose or into the esophagus. The smoke in the esophagus will remain there until the patient belches it out. One laryngectomee, who happens to be a head waiter in a fashionable restaurant in Cleveland, tells a story about the time he was smoking a cigarette in the lavatory during a work break: Before returning to his head-waiter post, he forgot to check to make sure that all the smoke had been expelled from his esophagus; in came four customers who were rather startled at his esophageal speech punctuated by blue puffs of smoke coming out of his mouth with each word he spoke. It would appear that the mechanical-physical difficulty of smoking, coupled with a possible decrease in both taste and smell, contributes to the sharp reduction of smoking after laryngectomy.

*Difficulty in lifting weight.* One of the primary functions of the larynx is its valving capability; that is, under moments of heavy physical stress, such as heavy lifting, the laryngeal folds shut tightly, producing in effect a fixed thorax. Anyone attempting to talk while trying to lift something like a heavy appliance is familiar with this laryngeal sphincteric action. It has been postulated and occasionally observed in laryngectomees that because of their lack of a laryngeal valving mechanism they are unable to do heavy lifting. Diedrich and Youngstrom addressed themselves to this question, finding that 45 percent of their population had no lifting difficulty, 42 percent some difficulty, and 13 percent great difficulty. Commenting on this problem, they write:

Although not asked in this questionnaire, it has been our impression that in general, patients who have led active physical lives (farmer) suffer less of an impairment in weight lifting than those who have a sedentary occupation (office clerk). [*49*, p. 74]

It would appear that for the overall population of laryngectomees, weight lifting is not seriously impaired. For the particular patient, however, the inability to lift large weights after the operation may necessitate a change of occupation.

### VOICE TRAINING OF THE LARYNGECTOMEE

The primary goal of the speech pathologist working with a laryngectomee is to help the patient develop functional speech. The term *alaryngeal speech,* first introduced by Kallen (*91*) and more recently popularized by Diedrich and Youngstrom (*49*), refers to any kind of nonlaryngeal phonation, whether it be esophageal, buccal, via an electronic larynx, or whatever. The focus of early voice therapy is to help the patient develop a phonation source, and the most difficult task in therapy is usually to teach the patient to make the first satisfactory sound. Once the patient is able to achieve some form of phonation, using some type of alaryngeal mechanism, subsequent therapy consists of refining the method employed. In esophageal speech, for example, the most difficult task in therapy is to get the patient to take in air esophageally and then be able to release it for phonation.

Voice training of the laryngectomee will usually begin at the time of the first postoperative visit. Before the actual initiation of voice training, it may be helpful to determine the adequacy of the patient's hearing. If some hearing loss is found, particularly the high frequency loss found in older persons, some use of amplification may be helpful in therapy.

We shall first consider the specific steps involved in training the patient to use an artificial larynx. Procedures for teaching each of the three methods of esophageal speech (swallow, inhalation, and injection) will then be developed separately.

*USING THE ARTIFICIAL LARYNX*

There is an artificial larynx of the pneumatic type, which requires the passage of air from the stoma through the vibrating body of the instrument and on into the oral cavity opening. With the more recent development of a relatively low-cost, electronic, artificial larynx, there is far less use today of the pneumatic type. For this reason, we shall restrict our discussion to the electronic type of artificial larynx, of which two models are shown in figure 26. The electronic larynx is battery-powered, transistorized with its vibrator activated by a button switch. Its vibration usually makes a continuous buzzing sound, not too unlike the sound of an electric razor. Some models have the capability of pitch variation, which is controlled by the amount of finger pressure applied to the activating switch. The electronic larynx has a vibrator at one end, which must be placed snugly against the skin of the neck at a particular anatomic site; the site will vary for each individual. After some demonstration and practice, the typical laryngectomee can effectively master the artificial larynx.

The biggest problem in using the artificial larynx is the resistance that many laryngectomees, physicians, and speech pathologists offer to the patient who wants to use one. It is frequently stated that if the new laryngectomee uses an artificial larynx before learning esophageal speech, he will never develop good esophageal speech. Furthermore, the argument may proceed, not learning esophageal speech is tantamount to a personal defeat. Witness, for example, what Greene has written: "One thing, however, is certain:

that any individual who decides to use an artificial larynx thereby tacitly acknowledges defeat and ceases all further attempts to produce pseudo-voice" (*67*, p. 211). On the other hand, Diedrich (*49*) presents the view that the issue need not be one of dichotomous alternatives—using the artificial larynx or using esophageal speech—but rather of using *both* approaches in such a way that they complement one another. The fact is that using the artificial larynx as an *aid* to learning good esophageal speech is a clinical reality with many patients. Rarely has this clinician found new laryngectomees becoming dependent on the artificial larynx when it is presented to them as part of their total speech training program. Some may well continue to use the electronic larynx for part of every speaking day, particularly when they do not feel well or are fatigued. An occasional patient may even prefer to use the artificial larynx exclusively. So be it. Most laryngectomees prefer to use esophageal speech, particularly after they have developed some proficiency at it. There is growing support among voice rehabilitationists (Diedrich and Youngstrom, *49*; Heaver and Arnold, *73*; and Martin, *103*) that the artificial larynx should be introduced early to the new laryngectomee who is learning esophageal speech.

The speech pathologist might introduce the artificial larynx to the new laryngectomee by following these steps:

1. In telling the patient that efforts will now begin to help him learn to talk again, point out to him that he faces two problems—first, learning to articulate (pronounce) his words again, and second, finding a new source of voice—and that at this time it is the articulation that will be tackled. Next, demonstrate to the patient that he has basically the same capability of articulation that he had before his operation, but that he may have to make some of his sounds a bit differently, employing intraoral pressure for some plosive and sibilant sounds instead of the usual pulmonary airstream. If possible, demonstrate the intraoral whisper for him, articulating to produce a "sound" with no pulmonary airstream. Then ask him to imitate these intraoral productions (which are, in fact, easier for the laryngectomee to produce than for the normal person with a larynx). Warn him not to try to push the sounds out by using pulmonary air (the use of pulmonary air will be indicated by excessive stoma noises). The level of complexity of the discussion and the amount of positive reinforcement provided the patient for his correct productions are individual matters which must be decided upon by the clinician. It would appear, however, that the simpler the explanation and the more focus given to the actual demonstration, the easier the learning task will be.

2. When the patient is able to produce an intraoral whisper, introduce him to an orderly presentation of consonants, perhaps having him whisper each one five to ten times. The best presentation seems to be along the general order of acquisition of consonants (/m/, /p/, /b/, etc.), first practicing the phonemes that are easiest to produce, and then going on to more difficult ones. The patient should work for clarity of articulation. Point out to the patient his relative lip, tongue, and palatal competencies, as demonstrated by his accurate whispering

of the consonants. Then go back to the first point made in the therapy, that learning to talk again is a twofold process: articulation and voice. Tell the patient that his success in practicing the whispered productions means that he is doing very well in the first area. The whispering practice will vary in length, depending on the intelligibility and motivation of the patient.

3. Now is the time to demonstrate the artificial larynx. After showing and explaining its mechanical features, and then demonstrating its operating procedures, the clinician should place the vibrating surface of the instrument tightly on his own neck, at a site where he has previously determined his best voice to be. He might well repeat some monosyllabic words that include some of the phonemes the patient has just finished using in articulation practice. To these articulations, the clinician should explain, the artificial larynx will introduce the second phase of speech, voicing. The clinician might also use the artificial larynx to demonstrate some connected speech.

4. Next, in offering the instrument to the patient, a great deal of care must be taken to achieve a good *seal* between the neck skin of the patient and the surface of the vibrator. The vibrator head must be firmly buried against the neck, or the sound source will escape free-field and not be directed into the oral cavity. This optimum site of contact, such as just above the site of the laryngeal excision in the midline, will be found best by trial and error. The patient should say the same monosyllabic word repeatedly as he searches for the site of contact where the intraoral speech/voice sounds best. Much time should be given to achieving this optimum contact of vibrator and neck, for a great deal of early disillusion with the artificial larynx can come from improper positioning of the instrument. Patients with extensive scarring, such as those who have had radical neck dissections, may experience real difficulties at first in finding the optimum site of contact. No practice in using the instrument should begin, however, until this critical contact point has been found. Also, once a good sound has been established, the patient will require some practice in working the on-off switch to match his articulations. Most patients can learn to do this rather quickly.

5. The patient should then practice saying single monosyllabic words in a series, and after that go on to phrases and short sentences. At this point, the clinician should remind the patient that he is now practicing speech. The sharper and clearer he can make his articulation, the more intelligible his speech will be. The patient should be instructed to discard his writing pad and begin talking to everyone. The tremendous advantage afforded by the artificial larynx is that it permits the patient to talk shortly after the operation, providing him with valuable articulation practice. The more he talks using the artificial larynx, the better his speech will usually become. Point out to the patient that the artificial larynx is providing him with a voice source while he practices improving his articulation. After a few days of practice using the instrument, he will start learning how to supply his own voice by using some form of esophageal voice. Make it very clear to the patient that the artificial larynx and esophageal speech are not competitive forms of voice, but that he will find them compatible with one another in helping him achieve good functional speech *whenever he needs to talk.*

For an excellent review of the controversy over the artificial larynx and the methods of using it, the reader is referred to pages 138–48 in Diedrich's and Youngstrom's *Alaryngeal Speech* (*49*).

Three methods of teaching esophageal speech may be employed: swallow, inhalation, and injection. Whichever method works best with the individual patient appears to be the method of choice, although the injection method (which requires articulation practice) appears most compatible to use with the early exposure to the artificial larynx.

### THE SWALLOW METHOD OF ESOPHAGEAL SPEECH

The critical task in learning esophageal speech is to get enough air into the esophagus to ensure its functional availability for pseudoglottal phonation. The better esophageal speakers appear to be those with a bigger esophageal air reservoir and a faster rate of airflow, according to Snidecor and Isshiki (*149*), who have studied various physiologic aspects of the esophagus in esophageal speech. The swallow method of air intake, while taught far less today than previously, utilizes the esophageal relaxation of the cricopharyngeus as experienced during normal swallowing to permit the entry of air into the esophagus (Morrison, *116*). The patient is taught literally to swallow air. Carbonated beverages may be used to facilitate the forming of a pocket of air within the esophagus. In bringing up the air pocket, the patient belches, adding to the emitted air the articulation of the desired word. The primary method of teaching esophageal speech in the early 1950s was the swallow method, as outlined and discussed in some detail at the First Institute on Voice Pathology held in Cleveland in 1952, the Proceedings of which (*134*) include some of the controversy on teaching methods as presented by laryngologists, speech pathologists, and lay laryngectomee teachers. In teaching the swallow method of air intake, the following steps might be taken:

1. Provide the patient with some explanation and demonstration of the swallow method. The basic purpose of swallowing is to trap air within the esophagus to make it available for the new voice. After demonstrating the swallow method of air intake, follow immediately with the production of a word. This demonstration is best performed by the teacher, either a speech pathologist or a laryngectomee.

2. Ask the patient if he ever belched or burped before the operation. If he can remember belching or burping, some time should be spent on trying to re-create what it felt like to do so. Can the patient remember how it felt to belch? Can he belch voluntarily? With the occasional patient who can belch voluntarily, one can short-cut the teaching of the first sound considerably: it is not difficult to skip ahead and add speech articulation *on top* of the belch to produce some monosyllabic words. If, after considerable exploration, the patient relates no history of belching or is unable to produce a belch voluntarily, the clinician should go on to the next step.

3. Ask the patient to open his mouth, close his mouth, deliberately swallow (air), and open his mouth and say, "taw." Monosyllabic words beginning with /t/, /d/, /k/, and /g/ seem particularly effective to start with, perhaps because they aid in the injection of air into the esophagus as effectively (or more so) than the swallow method. The open-mouth–close-mouth–swallow procedure should be repeated several times in rapid sequence; the steps are almost over-lapping. If, after the swallow, the patient is unable to produce the "taw," the clinician might introduce other phonemically similar combinations. The proce-dure may have to be repeated several times before the patient achieves a sound. If the method is still unsuccessful, ask the patient to take a small swallow of ginger ale or water, and then, immediately after swallowing it, to say the word. If, with the additional help of a swallowed beverage (which aids in opening the esophagus), the patient is still unable to produce sound, it would probably serve his best interests to abandon the swallow method and try the inhalation or injection method instead.

4. The patient who is successful in producing "taw" should continue saying the word in a series of productions, each requiring its own swallow sequence. The "taw" sequence should be followed by practice with other monosyllabic words beginning with /t/. Words beginning with /d/, /k/, and /g/ can be used if the patient can successfully say them. At this stage of training the clinician should avoid any phoneme sequence which the patient cannot produce easily. Emphasis should be given to saying one monosyllabic word at a time, one word per swallow, until the patient achieves relative success on each attempt.

5. The typical laryngectomee who is learning esophageal speech wants to use his newly acquired skill as soon as possible. Once the patient is successful at the single-word level, he may attempt to speak in phrases and sentences, usually with only minimal and erratic success. He should be cautioned to stay on the single-word level until he enjoys consistent voicing success. At this point, he should attempt to say the same words he has been saying, but without the deliberate swallow effort. In effect, he will then be using the injection method, renewing his esophageal air supply as he speaks.

6. Review the swallow process with the patient. It is a method he will be able to use in the future whenever he experiences some difficulty in getting started on air intake. For example, some good esophageal speakers complain that at specific times (such as when they are fatigued, or early in the morning, or whenever) they have difficulty in achieving good voice. Going back to the deliberate swallow is often an effective way of achieving good air intake and, therefore, good voice. Beyond this point, the patient will find helpful the practice materials included in such esophageal speech manuals as Doehler's *Esophageal Speech, A Manual for Teachers* (50) and Hyman's and Keller's *How to Speak Again* (84), or in the lists of words grouped together by the desired phoneme that are included in most voice and articulation textbooks.

## THE INHALATION METHOD OF ESOPHAGEAL SPEECH

The flow of air in normal respiration is achieved by the transfer of air from one source to another because of the relative disparity of air pressure between the two sources. For example, when the thorax enlarges because of muscle movement, the air reservoir within the lung increases in size, rarifying (decreasing) the air pressure within the lung. Since the outside atmospheric air pressure is now greater, the air rushes in until the pressure within equals the pressure without. The flow of air is always from the more dense to the less dense air body, and the flow continues until the two bodies are equal in pressure. It is by this same airflow mechanism that the esophagus inflates in the inhalation method of air intake. The patient experiences a thoracic enlargement during pulmonary inhalation, which reduces the compression on all thoracic structures, including the esophagus. If the cricopharyngeus opening into the esophagus is slightly open at the time of the slight increase in the size of the esophagus, air from the hypopharynx will flow into the esophagus. During the exhalation phase of pulmonary respiration, when there is a general compression of thoracic structures, the esophagus also experiences some compression, which aids in the expulsion of the entrapped air. As this air passes through the approximated structures of the lower pharynx–upper esophagus (the pharyngo-esophageal junction), a vibration is set up, producing esophageal phonation. The advantage of the inhalation method of esophageal air intake is that it follows the patient's natural inclination of pulmonary inhalation followed by exhalation-phonation. Simply to take a breath and then talk is the most natural way of speaking, and for this reason the inhalation method offers the patient learning esophageal speech some early advantages. Froeschels (*61*), in commenting on the distinct advantages of learning esophageal speech by the inhalation method, stated: "The closer one approaches the natural physiologic state, the happier one can be."

In proceeding to the following steps for teaching the inhalation method, the reader should remember that the approach is best used in combination with the injection method.

1. Explain and demonstrate to the patient some aspects of normal respiration. Many normal speakers, for example, have never thought much about normal respiration, and many do not know that their voicing has always been an exhalation event. Explain to the patient that when the chest is enlarged by muscle action, the air flows into the lungs, and that in the laryngectomee's case, the air comes through the stoma opening in the trachea and down into the lungs. The clinician might point out that the chest enlarges by muscle action, not by air inflation; thus, the air comes in as the chest enlarges. When the laryngectomee's chest enlarges, there is usually a concomitant enlargement of the esophagus, and when the esophagus is enlarged, there is a greater chance for air to come into it. When the chest becomes smaller, the pulmonary air is forced out, and the air within the esophagus is much more likely to be forced out. If possible, the clinician should demonstrate esophageal voice by using this method.

2. Before making any attempt to produce voice, the patient should practice conscious relaxation and correct breathing methods (Greene, 67). He should become aware of thoracic expansion and abdominal distention on inhalation, and of thoracic contraction on exhalation. Respiration practice should only be long enough to permit him to develop this kind of breathing awareness, since patients do not seem to benefit much from extended breathing exercises per se.

3. Now the patient should attempt to add air into his esophagus during his pulmonary inhalation. Diedrich and Youngstrom recommend that "the patient [be] told to close his mouth, imagine that he is sniffing through his nose, and to do so in a fairly rapid manner" (49, p. 112). While the sniff is basically a constricted inhalation, it is frequently accompanied by esophageal dilation (the normal person often swallows what he sniffs). As an extension of the sniff, the patient should be asked to take a fairly large pulmonary breath (through the stoma, of course). When his lungs appear to be about half inflated, he should say "ah" on exhalation. This procedure can be repeated until he experiences some phonatory success.

4. For the patient who does not experience success on step 3, the following variation of the inhalation method sometimes produces good esophageal air: ask the patient to take a deep breath and, as he begins his inhalation, to cover his stoma. While the muscular enlargement of his thorax continues (despite his lack of continuing inhalation), there will be a corresponding enlargement of the esophagus, perhaps permitting air to flow into the esophagus. For the patient who can get air into the esophagus but cannot produce the air escape to produce phonation, the same mechanism applies in reverse. Here, the patient takes a deep inhalation and, as he begins to exhale, occludes his stoma; as the thorax begins to decrease in size, there will be increased pressure on the esophagus, which might well result in expulsion (and phonation) of esophageal air.

5. If esophageal phonation is achieved by either of the last two steps, the patient should proceed from his "ah" response to single monosyllabic words beginning with /p/, /b/, /t/, /d/, /k/, and /g/. He should spend considerable time practicing at this single-word level, until he masters the technique in terms of loudness, quality of sound, and articulation. This writer's greatest fault in teaching esophageal speech has been in letting too many patients move too fast; the patient who masters the basic techniques of air intake and phonation at the single-word level may well become the best esophageal speaker.

## THE INJECTION METHOD OF ESOPHAGEAL SPEECH

It is commonly observed among new laryngectomees learning esophageal speech that certain consonants appear to have a facilitating effect in producing good esophageal voice. While individual patients may have their own favorite facilitating sound, it is more often than not a plosive consonant (/p/, /b/, /t/, /d/, /k/, and /g/ or a fricative containing a plosive (/tʃ/ or /dʒ/). Stetson (154) reported many years ago that /p/, /t/, and /k/ were the easiest sounds for the new laryngectomee to use and Moolenaar-Bijl (112) found that the same phonemes produced esophageal speech faster in most patients than the traditional swallow method of teaching. Diedrich and Youngstrom (49) recommend the voiceless /p/, /t/, /k/, /s/, /ʃ/, and /tʃ/ phonemes as good sounds to employ in the injection method of air intake.

Air intake by the injection method is achieved by compressing air within the oral cavity and pharynx, which initiates the flow of air into adjacent cavities, in this case the esophagus. When the air within the oral cavity is compressed, it will flow into a less dense area; the tongue tip–alveolar process contact, for example, prevents the anterior flow of air out of the mouth, and since the velopharyngeal port is usually closed, the nasal flow of air is also prevented (Diedrich, 48). There appear to be two pressing mechanisms in the injection method of air intake, the glossal press and the glosso-pharyngeal press, as clearly demonstrated in the Diedrich and Youngstrom cinefluorographic study (49, pp. 37, 39, 40). In the glossal press, the tip of the tongue touches the anterior alveolar process, with the middle of the tongue contacting the hard and soft palate; the cinefluoro-grams also found the posterior part of the tongue moving toward the pharyngeal wall, but not touching it. In the glosso-pharyngeal press, Diedrich and Youngstrom found the same tongue-tip and middle-tongue contacts on the anterior alveolar process and hard and soft palates; how-ever, the posterior part of the tongue was found to make a backward movement toward the posterior pharyngeal wall, with some subjects showing some anterior movement of the pharyngeal wall. Diedrich and Youngstrom reported that many of their twenty-seven subjects used a combination of the inhalation and injection methods of air intake.

The injection method appears to work more often than the other two methods. Specific steps that might be employed in using this method are:

1. Discuss with the patient the dynamics of air flow, explaining that com-pressed, dense air will always flow in the direction of less dense, rarified air. Explain also how the movements of the tongue in the injection method increase the density of the air within the mouth, enabling the air to move into the esophagus. Then demonstrate how the whispered articulation of a phoneme, such as a /t/ or a /k/, is the kind of tongue movement that produces the injec-tion of air into the esophagus. After producing the whispered /t/, demonstrate for the patient an esophageal voice for the word "taw."

2. Now ask the patient to produce the phoneme /p/ by intraoral whisper. Care must be taken that the sound is made by good firm compression of the lips, with no need for stoma noise. Make sure that the patient avoids pushing out the pulmonary exhalation or using tongue and palatal-pharyngeal contact as the noise source. The intraoral whisper can be effectively taught by having the patient hold his breath and then attempt to "bite-off" a /p/ by compressing the air caught between his abruptly closed lips. He should continue practicing this until he clearly grasps the idea of true intraoral articulation, which will be

demonstrated when he is able consistently to produce a precise-sounding /p/. Once he can do this, he should move to the next voiceless plosive, /t/. Here, the tongue tip against the upper central alveolar process is the site of contact, and practice should be continued until the patient is able to produce a precise, clear /t/. The same procedure should be repeated for /k/, again first demonstrating for the patient the different site of contact.

3. When good intraoral voiceless plosives have been produced, the patient is ready to add the vowel /a/ to each plosive. With /p/, for instance, he makes the plosive, and then immediately attempts to produce an esophageal phonation of /a/, producing in effect the word "pa." If this is successful, he may combine the /p/ with a few other vowel combinations before going on to the /t/ and /k/. If the patient fails to produce the esophageal voice at this point, he should go back and work for even crisper articulation of the plosive sounds. If he is still unsuccessful after increased practice in articulation, he should attempt to adopt the inhalation method as his primary means of air intake. (The swallow method is generally used only if the other two approaches have proved non-productive.)

4. The average laryngectomee experiences some success with the injection method when using the /p/, /t/, and /k/ phonemes. Therefore, he might be provided with about five monosyllabic words for each of the phonemes—for example, for /p/, the words pa, pie, pay, paw, and pop. His task is now to say each word, one at a time, renewing his esophageal air supply *as he speaks,* which is an obvious advantage in using the injection method. It is through the mere process of articulation that the patient takes in air. After the patient has demonstrated success with these phonemes, the clinician should introduce their voiced cognates, /b/, /d/, and /g/. The same procedure should be repeated, ending with about five practice words for each new phoneme.

5. Additional phonemes, such as /s/, /z/, /ʃ/, /tʃ/, /ʒ/, and /dʒ/, may be introduced for practice. It is most important as the patient gains phonatory skill with each new consonant that he spend extra time learning to improve both the quickness and the quality of production. Too many patients err in trying to develop functional conversation too early. Considerable practice should be spent at the monosyllabic word level, practicing one word at a time and making constant efforts to produce sharp articulation and a good-sounding voice.

6. At this point, if the patient has been successful, the inhalation method can be introduced as a means of further improving air intake and esophageal phonation. The patient should carry out a normal inhalation and, at the initial moment of exhalation, produce the consonant and say his word. Selected teaching steps outlined under the inhalation method should be employed to help the patient achieve a workable combination of the two methods.

7. Once the patient is able to achieve good voice at the monosyllabic word level employing the inhalation-injection method, he will need continuous practice with materials that gradually increase in difficulty. These materials can be found in such useful booklets as *Esophageal Speech* (Doehler, *50*), *How to Speak Again* (Hyman and Keller, *84*), and *Your New Voice* (Waldrop and Gould, *163*).

Some esophageal speakers develop speaking habits which diminish the overall effectiveness of their speech. Most of these faulty kinds of behavior can be eliminated almost as they occur, if the speech clinician is alert to them. A few of the more obvious are:

1. *Unnecessary stoma noise.* It is not necessary for any laryngectomee to have to force out air from his tracheal stoma when he attempts to speak. Some laryngectomees do this, particularly those who use the inhalation method of air intake. A few make the stoma noise on inhalation, but it is observed primarily when done on exhalation, usually as part of the normal pulmonary exhalation. Since it is often produced by the patient's attempting to use too much effort to speak the patient should be reminded to take a normal pulmonary breath. Often, the identification of the problem is enough to make the patient eliminate it. However, an occasional patient will have to practice holding his breath when he attempts to speak, or practice fixing his thorax, which slows down the rapidity of exhalation. Either breath-holding or thorax-fixing will eliminate the problem, particularly when it has been identified early and not yet become a habitual response.

2. *Excessive swallowing of air.* Some laryngectomees, and many who use the swallow method of air intake, swallow too much air in their attempt to inflate the esophagus. Many patients thus become bloated, experiencing a great deal of stomach and intestinal gas with the typical discomforts of abdominal-chest fullness and pain, heartburn, etc. One way of eliminating the problem is to change the patient's method of air intake from the swallow to either the inhalation or the injection method. Another is to work with the patient to help him become less tense as he attempts to speak, putting less effort into his voice production.

3. *Distracting noises.* Gurgling esophageal noises are generally related to poor sphincteral action at the distal (bottom) end of the esophagus and are difficult to control, if they occur. Patients with low gurgling noises should avoid the swallow method. A few will profit from using antacids as a method of reducing the esophageal gurgle. A more common noise is the klunking sound that characterizes too rapid an air intake. This pharyngeal noise must be extinguished immediately by the clinician, as it can quickly become habitual. The best method of eliminating it is to have the patient practice taking in air in an easier manner, producing single words free of the "klunk." The patient then must be asked what it feels like to speak with the klunk as opposed to speaking without it; the typical patient can feel the difference, and from that point on can monitor himself so that he will not produce the klunk. But once the klunk has been established for several months, it is most difficult to eliminate.

4. *Facial grimacing.* Some laryngectomees early in their training program begin to do some unnecessary things in the attempt to take air into the esophagus. For instance, they may purse their lips, make exaggerated facial movements, blink, clench their teeth, etc. Such extraneous behavior must be quickly pointed out and eliminated. Many laryngectomees get started with some facial posture,

thinking that this helps them speak, and from that point on they assume the posture as a habit whenever they proceed to speak. A frank, frontal assault should be made by the clinician to eliminate this undesirable facial behavior. Like any other undesirable behavior, it is much easier to eliminate during its formative stages than after it has become a habit.

## PSYCHOSOCIAL ADJUSTMENT

A prominent surgeon once said to a group of people planning a laryngectomee club that he saw no reason why laryngectomees had to have a special club to assist them in their rehabilitation. To support his opinion, he cited the fact that leg amputees or patients who have survived other kinds of cancer operations do not have such clubs. What this surgeon lacked was an appreciation for the effect that losing one's voice has on the psychosocial functioning of a human being. Most veteran laryngectomees are much more sympathetic to the new laryngectomee, having themselves experienced the "despair and fear" (Whitler, *166*) and the "bewilderment" (Crowley, *39*) of emerging from an operation not being able to speak. The emotional trauma of losing one's voice is particularly poignant in the early postoperative period, when the patient is still in the hospital. It is at this time that the visit by a lay laryngectomee is so important. Whitler describes the typical patient's reaction to this visit:

One of the first persons to come to see me when I had regained a little strength was a man who had a similar operation some years ago. He walked into the room and with a cheery, broad grin said, "Hello, Mr. Whitler, you have now joined a rather exclusive group!" I was astounded. Here was a man who obviously lived by breathing through a tube in his neck, exactly like myself, did not have a larynx as I did not have one, and yet here he was talking to me. . . . I knew then that if he could so could I. [*166*, p. 3]

The great value of the laryngectomee club, usually a chapter of the International Association of Laryngectomees, appears to be the early encouragement it gives the new laryngectomee. Eventually, if his total rehabilitation is successful, the laryngectomee no longer *takes* from the organization, but belongs to it for what he is able to contribute to new laryngectomees in their first few postoperative months.

The Horn study (*82*) of 3,366 laryngectomees offers some interesting data on the psychosocial adjustment of laryngectomees: one of the primary problems the patient faces is financial loss. For example, the average laryngectomee who was employed at the time of his operation lost 153 work days (five months), which at the time of study (1961–1962), represented an average wage or income loss of over $2,000. The patient's major resources during this recovery period were found to exist in this order of frequency: personal savings, own full salary continuing, spouse's salary, company sick benefits, medical insurance. One out of five laryngectomees who answered Horn's question about borrowing stated that they had to borrow money to cover some of their medical costs. Horn reported that two out of three respondents reported a drop in income following the operation, with sixty percent of those reporting a drop attributing it to their laryngectomy and their impaired facility for communication. The percentage of those who retired doubled from 12 percent before the operation to 24 percent soon after, and the percentage of those unemployed rose from 2 percent before to 8 percent after. The greatest job and economic changes, usually to lower income levels, occurred in managerial, sales, clerical, skilled-labor and semi-skilled occupants (professional and unskilled-labor occupations reported little change in status).

Many new laryngectomees are embarrassed about using various forms of alaryngeal speech, particularly with strangers. In the study by Diedrich and Youngstrom (49), fifty percent of the seventy-two patients who responded to the question of embarrassment replied that there were continuing situations in which they experienced acute embarrassment over the way they spoke. Some situations probably become tense because of awkward, insensitive listeners whose inept responses embarrass the speaker. There is little the laryngectomee can do to reconstruct his listening world, but after continued success he learns to adjust and take in his stride the occasional bad situation. The speech pathologist may sometimes have to counsel the laryngectomee to focus on his good speech and his effective communication rather than on the occasional breakdown which may come when speaking with inadequate loudness in a noisy situation or to a person with less than adequate hearing. The laryngectomee's sensitivity to how well he will be received by others is a highly individual thing, perhaps a matter of long-established personality. Diedrich and Youngstrom reported that the most frequently listed factors in overcoming self-consciousness were the patient's "determination to talk," his feeling that "there was no other choice," and his conviction that "one had to make the best of it" (ibid., p. 75).

Some counseling of both patient and family before the operation, as well as after, seems to promote optimum long range rehabilitation. The patient should be clearly told by his surgeon what to expect after the operation with regard to such things as breathing through the stoma, feeding by tube, inability to voice, postoperative communication aids (writing pad, artificial larynx, gestures), etc. The family, also, must be given a clear picture of what the patient's postoperative problems will be. While the family should be understanding and concerned, it will be helpful for the patient if they avoid becoming overly protective (such as by cleaning the stoma for the patient); they should allow the patient to become thoroughly independent, taking care of his own nursing needs and making his own rehabilitational and vocational plans. The more that can be done to approximate the living patterns experienced by the patient before his surgery, the greater the likelihood of successful rehabilitation.

The speech pathologist must work closely with the surgeon, the family, and the local IAL club, if the patient is to use his voice functionally in the real world. Otherwise, while the patient may develop a beautiful alaryngeal voice, he may become so socially isolated that there will be no one to hear him. There is more to successful laryngectomee rehabilitation than successful surgery and effective voice therapy—the patient needs some active counseling and direction to regain his previous position in his family, his job, and in the social environment around him.

## SUMMARY

In the rehabilitation of the laryngectomee, the speech pathologist works as a member of a team with the surgeon, the nurse, and veteran laryngectomees. Special consideration is given to the pre- and postoperative visits with the new patient, with particular awareness directed to the special physical and emotional problems he may be experiencing. Speech instruction, when requested by the surgeon, may sometimes include the artificial larynx as the patient learns to entrap air esophageally by one or a combination of methods: swallow, inhalation, and injection.

# Bibliography

1. AKIN, J., *And So We Speak: Voice and Articulation* (Englewood Cliffs, N. J.: Prentice-Hall, Inc., 1958).

2. ANGELOCCI, A. A., G. A. KOPP, AND A. HOLBROOK, "The Vowel Formants of Deaf and Normal-Hearing Eleven to Fourteen-Year-Old Boys," *Journal of Speech and Hearing Disorders*, XXIX (1964), 156–70.

3. ARNDT, W. B., R. L. SHELTON, and L. J. BRADFORD, "Articulation, Voice, and Obturation in Persons with Acquired and Congenital Palate Defects," *Cleft Palate Journal*, II (1965), 377–83.

4. ARNOLD, G. E., "Vocal Nodules and Polyps: Laryngeal Tissue Reaction to Habitual Hyperkinetic Dysphonia," *Journal of Speech and Hearing Disorders*, XXVII (1962), 205–17.

5. ———, "Vocal Rehabilitation of Paralytic Dysphonia," *Archives of Oto-laryngology*, LXXVI (1962), 76–83.

6. ———, and S. PINTO, "Ventricular Dysphonia: New Interpretation of an Old Observation," *Laryngoscope*, LXX (1960), 1608–27.

7. ARONSON, A. E., J. R. BROWN, E. M. LITIN, and J. S. PEARSON, "Spastic Dysphonia: I. Voice, Neurologic, and Psychiatric Aspects," *Journal of Speech and Hearing Disorders*, XXXIII (1968), 203–18.

8. ———, H. W. PETERSON, and E. M. LITIN, "Psychiatric Symptomatology in Functional Dysphonia and Aphonia," *Journal of Speech and Hearing Disorders*, XXXI (1966), 155–27.

9. ———, "Voice Symptomatology in Functional Dysphonia and Aphonia," *Journal of Speech and Hearing Disorders*, XXIX (1964), 367–80.

10. ARTIK (Arion Products, 1022 Nicollet Avenue, Minneapolis, Minnesota 55403).

11. B. AND K. INSTRUMENTS, INC. (5111 W. 164th Street, Cleveland, Ohio 44142).

12. BAKER, D. C., "Contact Ulcers of the Larynx," *Laryngoscope*, LXIV (1954), 73–78.

13. BALLENGER, W. L., H. C. BALLENGER, AND J. J. BALLENGER, *Diseases of the Nose, Throat, and Ear* (Philadelphia: Lea and Febiger, 1947).

14. BANGS, J. L., AND A. FREIDINGER, "Diagnosis and Treatment of a Case of Hysterical Aphonia in a Thirteen Year Old Girl," *Journal of Speech and Hearing Disorders*, XIV (1949), 312–17.

15. BARTON, R. T., "The Whispering Syndrome of Hysterical Dysphonia," *Annals of Otology, Rhinology, and Laryngology*, LXIV (1960), 156–64.

16. BELL, A. M., "The 'Nasal Twang'," *Modern Language Notes*, V (1890), 75–76.

17. BISHOP, B., "Neural Regulation of Abdominal Muscle Contractions," *Sound Production in Man*, M. Krauss, ed. (New York: New York Academy of Sciences, 1968), 191–200.

18. BOHME, G., "The Efficacy of Electrotherapy in Laryngeal Diseases as Shown in the Stroboscopic Picture," *Journal of Laryngology, Rhinology, and Otology*, XLIV (1965), 481–88.

19. BOONE, D. R., "Modification of the Voices of Deaf Children," *Volta Review*, LXVIII (1966), 686–92.

20. ———, "Treatment of Functional Aphonia in a Child and an Adult," *Journal of Speech and Hearing Disorders*, XXXI (1966), 69–74.

21. BOSMA, J. F., ed., *Symposium on Oral Sensation and Perception* (Springfield, Ill.: Charles C. Thomas, 1967).

22. BOUHUYS, A., D. F. PROCTOR, AND J. MEAD, "Kinetic Aspects of Singing," *Journal of Applied Physiology*, XXI (1966), 483–96.

23. BRADFORD, L. J., A. R. BROOKS, AND R. L. SHELTON, "Clinical Judgment of Hypernasality in Cleft Palate Children," *Cleft Palate Journal, I* (1964), 329–35

24. BRODNITZ, F. S., *Vocal Rehabilitation* (Rochester, Minnesota: Whiting Press, 1967).

25. ———, "Vocal Rehabilitation in Benign Lesions of the Vocal Cords," *Journal of Speech and Hearing Disorders*, XXIII (1958), 112–17.

26. ———, AND E. FROESCHELS, "Treatment of Nodules of Vocal Cords by the Chewing Method," *Archives of Otolaryngology*, LIX (1954), 560–66.

27. BULLER, A., "Nasality: Cause and Remedy of Our American Blight," *Quarterly Journal of Speech*, XXVIII (1942), 83–84.

28. Bzoch, K. R., "The Effects of a Specific Pharyngeal Flap Operation upon the Speech of Forty Cleft-palate Persons," *Journal of Speech and Hearing Disorders*, XXIX (1964), 111–20.

29. Campbell, E. J. M., "The Respiratory Muscles," *Sound Production in Man*, M. Krauss, ed. (New York: New York Academy of Sciences, 1968), 135–40.

30. ———, *The Respiratory Muscles and the Mechanics of Breathing* (Chicago: Year Book Press, 1958).

31. Cavagna, G. A., and R. Margaria, "Airflow Rates and Efficiency Changes during Phonation," *Sound Production in Man*, M. Krauss, ed. New York: New York Academy of Sciences, 1968), 152–64.

32. Cleeland, C. E., "Definitions of Voice Quality Called X" (Ph.D. dissertation, University of Denver, 1948).

33. Clerf, L. H., "Bilateral Abductor Paralysis of the Larynx: Results of Treatment by Modified King Operation," *Annals of Otology, Rhinology, and Laryngology*, LXIV (1955), 38–46.

34. ———, "The Surgical Treatment of Bilateral Paralysis of the Larynx," *Laryngoscope*, LX (1950), 142–51.

35. *Cleveland Lost Chord Club* (Cleveland, Ohio: Cleveland Hearing and Speech Center, 1962).

36. *Cleveland Lost Chord Club, Instructions for Visitants* (Cleveland, Ohio: Cleveland Hearing and Speech Center, 1962).

37. Comroe, J. H., *The Lung* (Chicago: The Year Book Publishers, 1956).

38. Crouter, L. A., "A Cinefluorographic Comparison of Selected Vowels Spoken by Deaf and Hearing Subjects" (Master's thesis, University of Kansas, 1962).

39. Crowley, J. F., "Laughing Without Sound," *Cancer News*, (Spring, 1964), 21–22.

40. Cunning, D. S., "Unilateral Vocal Cord Paralysis," *Annals of Otology, Rhinology, and Laryngology*, LXIV (1955). 487–93.

41. Curry, E. T., "Hoarseness and Voice Change in Male Adolescents," *Journal of Speech and Hearing Disorders*, XVI (1949), 23–24.

42. Curry, R., *The Mechanism of the Human Voice* (New York: Longmans Green and Co., Inc., 1940).

43. Damste, P. H., "Voice Change in Adult Women Caused by Virilizing Agents," *Journal of Speech and Hearing Disorders*, XXXII (1967), 126–32.

44. Darley, F. L., *Diagnosis and Appraisal of Communication Disorders* (Englewood Cliffs, N. J.: Prentice-Hall, Inc., 1965).

45. Davis, D. S., and D. R. Boone, "Pitch Discrimination and Tonal Memory Abilities in Adult Voice Patients," *Journal of Speech and Hearing Research*, X (1967), 811–15.

46. Dempsey, M. E., C. L. Draegert, R. P. Siskind, and M. D. Steer, "The Purdue Pitch Meter—A Direct Reading Fundamental Frequency Analyzer," *Journal of Speech and Hearing Disorders*, XV (1950), 135–41.

47. Dickson, D. R., "An Acoustic Study of Nasality," *Journal of Speech and Hearing Research*, V (1962), 103–11.

48. DIEDRICH, W. M., "The Mechanism of Esophageal Speech," *Sound Production in Man*, M. Krauss, ed. (New York: New York Academy of Sciences, 1968), 303–17.

49. ———, and K. A. YOUNGSTROM, *Alaryngeal Speech* (Springfield, Ill.: Charles C. Thomas, 1966).

50. DOEHLER, M. A., *Esophageal Speech, A Manual for Teachers* (Boston: American Cancer Society, Massachusetts Division, 1953).

51. EBLEN, R. E., "Limitations on Use of Surface Electromyography in Studies of Speech Breathing," *Journal of Speech and Hearing Research*, VI (1963), 3–18.

52. *Echorder and Echordette* (RIL Electronics Incorporated, Street Road and Second Street Pike, Southampton, Pa. 18966).

53. EISENSON, J., *The Improvement of Voice and Diction* (New York: The Macmillan Company, 1958).

54. ERMOVICK, D. A., "A Spectrographic Analysis for Comparison of Connected Speech of Deaf Subjects and Hearing Subjects" (Master's thesis, University of Kansas, 1965).

55. FAIRBANKS, G., *Voice and Articulation Drillbook* (New York: Harper and Brothers, 1960).

56. *First Aid for Laryngectomees* (New York: American Cancer Society, Inc., 1962).

57. FISHER, H. B., *Improving Voice and Articulation* (Boston: Houghton Mifflin Company, 1966).

58. FITZHUGH, G. S., D. E. SMITH, and A. T. CHIONG, "Pathology of Three Hundred Clinically Benign Lesions of the Vocal Cords," *Laryngoscope*, LXVIII (1958), 855–61.

59. FROESCHELS, E., "Chewing Method as Therapy," *Archives of Otolaryngology*, LVI (1952), 427–34.

60. ———, "Hygiene of the Voice," *Archives of Otolaryngology*, XXXVII (1943), 122–30.

61. ———, "Remarks on Section on Surgery in Laryngectomy," *Proceedings, First Institute on Voice Pathology* (Cleveland: Cleveland Hearing and Speech Center, 1952).

62. ———, S. KASTEIN, and D. A. WEISS, "A Method of Therapy for Paralytic Conditions of the Mechanisms of Phonation, Respiration, and Glutination," *Journal of Speech and Hearing Disorders*, XX (1955), 365–70.

63. GARDNER, W. H., "Problems of Laryngectomees," *Rehabilitation Record* (1961), 15–18.

64. ———, and H. E. HARRIS, "Aids and Devices for Laryngectomees," *Archives of Otolaryngology*, LXXIII (1961), 145–52.

65. GRAY, B. B., G. ENGLAND, and J. L. MAHONEY, "Treatment of Benign Vocal Nodules by Reciprocal Inhibition," *Journal of Behavioral Research and Therapy*, III (1965), 187–93.

66. GRAY, G. W., and C. M. WISE, *The Bases of Speech* (New York: Harper and Brothers, 1959).

228     *Bibliography*

67. GREENE, M. C. L., *The Voice and Its Disorders* (New York: The Macmillan Company, 1957).
68. GRUENEWALD, B., "A Comparison Between Vocal Characteristics of Deaf and Normal Hearing Individuals" (Master's thesis, University of Kansas, 1966).
69. HAHN, E., C. W. LOMAS, D. E. HARGIS, AND D. VANDRAEGEN, *Basic Voice Training for Speech* (New York: McGraw-Hill Book Company, Inc., 1957).
70. HANLEY, C. N., AND C. C. MANNING, "Voice Quality After Adenotonsillectomy," *Journal of Speech and Hearing Disorders*, XXIII (1958), 257–62.
71. HANSON, M. L., "A Study of Velopharyngeal Competence in Children with Repaired Cleft Palates," *Cleft Palate Journal*, I (1964), 217–31.
72. HEAVER, L., "Spastic Dysphonia: II," *Logos*, II (1959), 15–24.
73. ———, AND G. E. ARNOLD, "Rehabilitation of Alaryngeal Aphonia," *Postgraduate Medicine*, XXXII (1962), 11–17.
74. HOLINGER, P. H., and K. C. JOHNSTON, "Benign Tumors of the Larynx," *Annals of Otology, Rhinology, and Laryngology*, LX (1951), 496–509.
75. ———, K. C. JOHNSTON, AND M. D. MANSUETO, "Cancer of the Larynx, Surgical Treatment," *American Journal of Nursing*, LVII (1957), 738–41.
76. HOLLIEN, H., "Vocal Fold Thickness and Fundamental Frequency of Phonation," *Journal of Speech and Hearing Research*, V (1962), 237–43.
77. ———, "Vocal Pitch Variation Related to Changes in Vocal Fold Length," *Journal of Speech and Hearing Research*, III (1960), 150–56.
78. ———, R. COLEMAN, AND P. MOORE, "Stroboscopic Laminagraphy of the Larynx During Phonation," *Acta Oto-laryngologica*, LXV (1968), 209–15.
79. ———, AND J. F. CURTIS, "A Laminagraphic Study of Vocal Pitch," *Journal of Speech and Hearing Research*, III (1960), 361–71.
80. ———, AND E. MALCIK, "Evaluation of Cross-sectional Studies of Adolescent Voice Change in Males," *Speech Monographs*, XXXIV (1967), 80–84.
81. ———, AND G. P. MOORE, "Measurements of the Vocal Folds during Changes in Pitch," *Journal of Speech and Hearing Research*, III (1960), 157–65.
82. HORN, D., "Laryngectomees: Survey Report," *International Association of Laryngectomees News*, VII (November 1962), 1.
83. HOSHIKO, M. S., "Electromyographic Investigation of the Intercostal Muscles during Speech," *Archives of Physical Medicine and Rehabilitation*, XLIII (1962), 115–19.
84. HYMAN, M., AND M. S. KELLER, *How to Speak Again* (The Ohio Division of the American Cancer Society, 1960).
85. ISSHIKI, N., "Regulatory Mechanism of Voice Intensity Variation," *Journal of Speech and Hearing Research*, VII (1964), 17–30.
86. JACKSON, C. J., AND C. L. JACKSON, *Diseases of the Nose, Throat and Ear*, II (Philadelphia: W. B. Saunders, 1959).
87. JACOBSON, E., *You Must Relax* (New York: McGraw-Hill Book Company, 1957).
88. JIMISON, C., "Nursing the Patient after Laryngectomy," *American Journal of Nursing*, LVII (June 1957), 741–43.
89. JOHNSON, W., F. L. DARLEY, AND D. C. SPRIESTERSBACH, *Diagnostic Methods in Speech Pathology* (New York: Harper and Row, 1963).

90. JUDSON, L. S., AND A. T. WEAVER, *Voice Science* (New York: Appleton-Century-Crofts, 1965).

91. KALLEN, L. A., "Vicarious Vocal Mechanisms," *Archives of Otolaryngology,* XX (1934), 360–503.

92. KANTNER, C. E., "The Rationale of Blowing Exercises for Patients with Repaired Cleft Palates," *Journal of Speech Disorders,* XII (1947), 281–86.

93. KIRCHNER, F., AND P. TOLEDO, "Vocal Cord Injection," *Journal of the Kansas Medical Society,* LXVII (1966), 125–29.

94. KRASNER, L., "Studies of the Conditioning of Verbal Behavior," *Psycholinguistics, a Book of Readings,* S. Soporta, ed. (New York: Holt, Rinehart, and Winston, 1961).

95. KRAUS, H., *Principles and Practice of Therapeutic Exercises* (Springfield, Ill.: Charles C. Thomas, 1959).

96. KUNZE, L. H., "Evaluation of Methods of Estimating Sub-glottal Air Pressure," *Journal of Speech and Hearing Research,* VII (1964), 151–64.

97. LADEFOGED, P., "Comment on Evaluation of Methods of Estimating Subglottal Air Pressure," *Journal of Speech and Hearing Research,* VII (1964), 291–92.

98. *Language Master* (Bell and Howell Co., 7100 N. McCormick Rd., Chicago, Illinois).

99. LEHMANN, Q. H., "Reverse Phonation: A New Maneuver for Examining the Larynx," *Radiology,* LXXXIV (1965), 215–22.

100. LOWENTHAL, G., "Treatment of Polypoid Laryngitis," *Laryngoscope,* LXVIII (1958), 1095–1104.

101. LUCHSINGER, R., AND G. E. ARNOLD, *Voice–Speech–Language Clinical Communicology: Its Physiology and Pathology* (Belmont, California: Wadsworth Publishing Co., Inc., 1965).

102. MARTENSSON, A., "The Functional Organization of the Intrinsic Laryngeal Muscles," *Sound Production in Man,* M. Krauss, ed. (New York: New York Academy of Sciences, 1968), 91–97.

103. MARTIN, H., "Rehabilitation of the Laryngectomee," *Cancer,* XVI (1963), 823–41.

104. McDONALD, E. T., *Articulation Testing and Treatment: A Sensory-Motor Approach* (Pittsburgh: Stanwix House, Inc., 1964).

105. MEAD, J., A. BOUHUYS, AND D. F. PROCTOR, "Mechanisms Generating Subglottic Pressure," *Sound Production in Man,* M. Krauss, ed. (New York: New York Academy of Sciences, 1968), 177–81.

106. MECKFESSEL, A. L., "A Comparison between Vocal Characteristics of Deaf and Normal Hearing Individuals" (Master's thesis, University of Kansas, 1964).

107. MILISEN, R., "Methods of Evaluation and Diagnosis of Speech Disorders," *Handbook of Speech Pathology,* L. E. Travis, ed. (New York: Appleton-Century-Crofts, Inc., 1957).

108. ———, "The Incidence of Speech Disorders," *Handbook of Speech Pathology,* L. E. Travis, ed. (New York: Appleton-Century-Crofts, Inc., 1957).

*109.* MILLARD, N., AND B. KING, *Human Anatomy and Physiology* (Philadelphia: W. B. Saunders Co., 1951).

*110.* MILLER, M. H., "The Responsibility of the Speech Therapist to the Laryngectomized Patient," *Archives of Otolaryngology,* LXX (1959), 211–16.

*111.* MOLL, K. L., "Speech Characteristics of Individuals with Cleft Lip and Palate," *Cleft Palate and Communication,* D. C. Spriestersbach and D. Sherman, eds. (New York: Academic Press, 1968).

*112.* MOOLENAAR-BIJL, A., "The Importance of Certain Consonants in Esophageal Voice after Laryngectomy," *Annals of Otology, Rhinology, and Laryngology,* LXII (1953), 979–89.

*113.* MOORE, G. P., "Voice Disorders Associated with Organic Abnormalities," *Handbook of Speech Pathology,* L. E. Travis, ed. (New York: Appleton-Century-Crofts, Inc., 1957).

*114.* ———, AND H. VON LEDEN, "Dynamic Variations of the Vibratory Pattern in the Normal Larynx," *Folia Phoniatrica,* X (1958), 205–38.

*115.* MORRIS, H. L., AND J. K. SMITH, "A Multiple Approach for Evaluating Velopharyngeal Competency," *Journal of Speech and Hearing Disorders,* XXVII (1962), 218–26.

*116.* MORRISON, W. W., "The Production of Voice and Speech following Total Laryngectomy," *Archives of Otolaryngology,* XIV (1931), 413–31.

*117.* MOSES, P. J., "The Psychology of the Castrato Voice," *Folia Phoniatrica,* XII (1960), 204–15.

*118.* ———, *The Voice of Neurosis* (New York: Grune and Stratton, 1954).

*119.* MURPHY, A. T., *Functional Voice Disorders* (Englewood Cliffs, N. J.: Prentice-Hall, Inc., 1964).

*120.* MURRAY, E., *The Speech Personality* (New York: J. B. Lippincott Co., 1944).

*121.* MURRAY, J., AND W. LEWIS, *Cardinal Aspects of Speech* (New York: Prentice-Hall, Inc., 1938).

*122.* NEGUS, V. E., *The Comparative Anatomy and Physiology of the Larynx* (New York: Grune and Stratton, 1949).

*123.* ———, "The Mechanism of the Larynx," *Laryngoscope,* LXVII (1957), 961–86.

*124.* OTIS, A. B., AND R. G. CLARK, "Ventilatory Implications of Phonation and Phonatory Implications of Ventilation," *Sound Production in Man,* M. Krauss, ed. (New York: New York Academy of Sciences, 1968), 122–28.

*125.* *Pad Pitchmeter* (Pad Laboratories, Cleveland, Ohio, 1962).

*126.* PALMER, M. T., "A New Technique in the Correction of Persistent Falsetto Voice in the Male," *Journal of Speech Disorders,* V (1940), 364–66.

*127.* PEACHER, G. M., "Vocal Therapy for Contact Ulcer of the Larynx. A Follow-up of Seventy Patients," *Laryngoscope,* LXXI (1961), 37–47.

*128.* PEACHER, G., "Contact Ulcer of the Larynx, Part IV, A Clinical Study of Vocal Re-education," *Journal of Speech Disorders,* XII (1947), 179–90.

*129.* ———, AND P. H. HOLINGER, "Contact Ulcer of the Larynx: Role of Vocal Re-education," *Archives of Otolaryngology,* XLVI (1947), 617–23.

*130.* PERKINS, W. H., "The Challenge of Functional Disorders of Voice," *Handbook of Speech Pathology,* L. E. Travis, ed. (New York: Appleton-Century-Crofts, 1957).

*131.* PETERSON, G. E., AND H. L. BARNEY, "Control Methods Used in a Study of the Vowels," *Journal of the Acoustical Society,* XXIV (1952), 175–84.

*132. Phonic Mirror* (H. C. Electronics, Inc., Belvedere-Tiburon, California 94920).

*133. A Plan for Rehabilitating the Laryngectomee: A Suggested Plan for Surgeons* (Cleveland, Ohio: Cleveland Hearing and Speech Center, 1962).

*134.* Cleveland Hearing and Speech Center, *Proceedings of First Institute on Voice Pathology* (Cleveland, Ohio, 1952).

*135.* PROCTOR, D. F., "The Physiologic Basis of Voice Training," *Sound Production in Man,* M. Krauss, ed. (New York: New York Academy of Sciences, 1968), 208–28.

*136.* RACHMAN, S., "Systematic Desensitization," *Psychological Bulletin,* LXVII (1967), 93–103.

*137.* ROBE, E., J. BRUMLIK, AND P. MOORE, "A Study of Spastic Dysphonia," *Laryngoscope,* LXX (1960), 219–45.

*138.* ROSEN, M. S., "Prosthetics for the Cleft Palate Patient," *Journal of the American Dental Association,* LX (1960), 715–21.

*139.* ROSENSTEIN, S. W., "Orthodontic Treatment for the Cleft Palate Patient," *Journal of the American Dental Association,* LX (1960), 711–14.

*140.* RUBIN, H. J., AND C. C. HIRT, "The Falsetto, a High Speed Cinematographic Study," *Laryngoscope,* LXX (1960), 1305–24.

*141.* SAUNDERS, W. H., "The Larynx," *Ciba Clinical Symposia,* XVI (1964), 67–99.

*142.* SEASHORE, C. E., E. LEWIS, AND J. G. SAETVIET, *Manual of Instructions and Interpretations for the Seashore Measures of Musical Talent* (New York: The Psychological Corporation, 1960).

*143.* SENTURIA, B. H., AND F. B. WILSON, "Otorhinolaryngic Findings in Children with Voice Deviations," *Annals of Otolology, Rhinology and Laryngology, LXXII* (1968), 1027–42.

*144.* SHELTON, R. L., A. R. BROOKS, AND K. A. YOUNGSTROM, "Clinical Assessment of Palatopharyngeal Closure," *Journal of Speech and Hearing Disorders,* XXX (1965), 37–43.

*145.* ———, E. HAHN, AND H. L. MORRIS, "Diagnosis and Therapy," *Cleft Palate and Communication,* D. C. Spriestersbach and D. Sherman, eds. (New York: Academic Press, 1968).

*146.* SHERMAN, D., "The Merits of Backward Playing of Connected Speech in the Scaling of Voice Quality Disorders," *Journal of Speech and Hearing Disorders,* XIX (1954), 312–21.

*147.* SJOSTROM, L., "Operative Treatment of Complete Adductor Paralysis," *Acta Otolaryngologica,* Supplement 109 (1953), 140–42.

*148.* SLOANE, H. N., AND B. D. MACAULAY, *Operant Procedures in Remedial Speech and Language Training* (Boston: Houghton Mifflin Co., 1968).

*149.* SNIDECOR, J. C., AND N. ISSHIKI, "Air Volume and Air Flow Relationships of Six Male Esophageal Speakers," *Journal of Speech and Hearing Disorders,* XXX (1965), 205–16.

*150.* SOMMERS, R. K., AND D. C. BRADY, *A Manual of Speech and Language Training Methods Using the Echorder* (Southampton, Pa.: RIL Electronics Co., 1964).

*151.* SONNINEN, A., "The External Frame Function in the Control of Pitch in the Human Voice," *Sound Production in Man,* M. Krauss, ed. (New York: New York Academy of Sciences, 1968), 68–90.

*152.* SPRIESTERSBACH, D. C., "Assessing Nasal Quality in Cleft Palate Speech of Children," *Journal of Speech and Hearing Disorders,* XX (1955), 266–70.

*153.* STEER, M. D., AND T. D. HANLEY, "Instruments of Diagnosis, Therapy, and Research," *Handbook of Speech Pathology,* L. E. Travis, ed. (New York: Appleton-Century-Crofts, Inc., 1957).

*154.* STETSON, R. H., "Can All Laryngectomized Patients be Taught Esophageal Speech?" *Transactions of American Laryngological Association,* LIX (1937), 59–71.

*155.* STEVENS, H., "Conversion Hysteria: A Neurologic Emergency," *Mayo Clinic Proceedings,* XLIII (1968), 54–64.

*156.* TABOR, C., *Tabor's Cyclopedic Medical Dictionary* (Philadelphia: F. A. Davis Co., 1963).

*157.* TARNEAUD, J., "The Fundamental Principles of Vocal Culturation and Therapeutics of the Voice," *Logos,* I (1958), 7–10.

*158.* THORNTON, A., "A Spectrographic Comparison of Connected Speech of Deaf Subjects and Hearing Subjects" (Master's thesis, University of Kansas, 1964).

*159.* THURMAN, W. L., "An Experimental Investigation of Certain Vocal Frequency-Intensity Relationships concerning Natural Pitch Level" (Master's thesis, University of Iowa, 1949).

*160.* ———, "Intensity Relationships and Optimum Pitch Level," *Journal of Speech and Hearing Research,* I (1958), 117–23.

*161.* VAN DEN BERG, J. W., "Register Problems," *Sound Production in Man,* M. Krauss, ed. (New York: New York Academy of Sciences, 1968), 129–34.

*162.* VAN RIPER, C., AND J. V. IRWIN, *Voice and Articulation* (Englewood Cliffs, N. J.: Prentice-Hall, Inc., 1958).

*163.* WALDROP, W. F., and M. A. GOULD, *Your New Voice* (Chicago: American Cancer Society, Illinois Division, 1956).

*164.* WALSH, T. E., AND P. R. BEAMER, "Epidermoid Carcinoma of the Larynx Occurring in Two Children with Papilloma of the Larynx," *Laryngoscope,* LX (1950), 1110–24.

*165.* WEISS, D. A., "The Pubertal Change of the Human Voice," *Folia Phoniatrica,* II (1950), 127–58.

*166.* WHITLER, L. E., "One of a Million," *Brotherhood of Locomotive Firemen and Enginemen's Magazine,* (April 1961), 1–6.

*167.* WILLIAMSON, A. B., "Diagnosis and Treatment of Seventy-Two Cases of Hoarse Voice," *Quarterly Journal of Speech,* XXXI (1945), 189–202.

168. WILSON, D. K., "Children with Vocal Nodules," *Journal of Speech and Hearing Disorders*, XXVI (1961), 19–26.

169. ———, "Voice Re-education of Adolescents with Vocal Nodules," *Archives of Otolaryngology*, LXXVI (1962), 68–73.

170. WISE, C. M., J. H. MCBURNEY, AND L. A. MALLORY, *Foundations of Speech* (Englewood Cliffs, N. J.: Prentice-Hall, Inc., 1941).

171. WOLPE, J., *Psychotherapy by Reciprocal Inhibition* (Stanford: Stanford University Press, 1958).

172. WOLKSI, W., AND J. WILEY, "Functional Aphonia in a Fourteen Year Old Boy," *Journal of Speech and Hearing Disorders*, XXX (1965), 71–75.

173. WOODMAN, D., "Bilateral Abductor Paralysis," *Archives of Otolaryngology*, LVIII (1953), 150–53.

174. WYATT, G. L., "Voice Disorders and Personality Conflicts," *Mental Hygiene*, XXV (1941), 237–50.

175. *You Can Talk Again* (a film distributed by The American Cancer Society, 219 East Forty-second Street, New York, N.Y. 10017).

176. ZALIOUK, A., "Falsetto Voice in Deaf Children," *Current Problems in Phoniatrics and Logopedics*, I (1960), 217–26.

177. ZEMLIN, W. R., *Speech and Hearing Science Anatomy and Physiology* (Englewood Cliffs, N. J.: Prentice-Hall, Inc., 1968).

178. ZOETHOUT, W. D., AND W. W. TUTTLE, *Textbook of Physiology* (St. Louis, Mo.: C. V. Mosby Co., 1955).

# Index

Abuse of voice
  description, 38, 80, 105
  elimination of, 124–26
  graphing abuses, 125
Air flow, 22, 28, 31, 36, 37
Air volumes, normal male, 19
AKIN, J., 113, 139, 140, 194
Alaryngeal speech, *defined,* 210–11
Altering tongue position, 111–12, 159,
  160, 173, 179, 181, 192
American Cancer Society, 199, 200, 203,
  208
ANGELOCCI, A. A., 156, 159
Aphonia
  functional, 64–65
  therapy for, 160–64
Approximation voice disorders, 60
  cordectomy, 69
  functional aphonia, 64–65, 160–64
  functional dysphonia, 61–62
  laryngofissure, 69
  spastic dysphonia, 62–64, 166–67
  ventricular dysphonia, 68–69, 164–66
  vocal cord paralysis, 65–68, 167–70

ARNDT, W. B., 191
ARNOLD, G. E., 2, 5, 36, *quote* 51, 52, 53,
  56, *quote* 57–58, 59–61, 63, 66,
  67, 84, *quote* 98, *quote* 154, 164,
  *quote* 166, 168, 170, *quote* 171,
  172, 212
ARONSON, A. E., 64, 65, 166
Articulation
  injection in esophageal speech, 217–19
  sharpening with artificial larynx,
    212–14
  testing in resonance evaluation, 185
Artificial larynx
  descriptions of, 200, 203, 206
  placement of instrument, 213
  teaching steps, 211–14
*Artik* recorder, 132
Assimilative nasality
  descriptions of, 101, 183
  treatment of, 194–95

*B and K* instruments, 92
BAKER, D. C., 104
BANGS, J. L., 161

*235*

BARTON, R. T., 161
Baseline measurements, 106, 125–26
BELL, A. M., 181
Bernoulli effect, 28, 30
BISHOP, B., 20, 21
BOHME, G., 66
BOONE, D. R., 64, 100, 111, 122, 153, 157,
    quote 159–60, 161, quote 162–
    63
BOSMA, J. F., 42
BRADFORD, L. J., 184, 191
BRADY, D. C., quote 124
Breathiness, 37, 62, 95
BRODNITZ, F. S., quote 2, quote 5, 53,
    quote 55, 57, 61, 62, 64, 66, 84,
    quote 96, 104, quote 117, quote
    119, 142, 143, 149
BROOKS, A. R., 184
BRUMLICK, J., 63, 166
BULLER, A., 181
BZOCH, K. R., 191

CAMPBELL, E. J. M., quote 19, 20–21
Cancer of larynx
    description of, 197
    problems after surgery, 208–10
    surgical treatment of, 198–203
    symptoms of, 198
CAVAGNA, G. A., 22
Chewing approach, 8, 104, 116–19, 137,
    139, 159, 160, 163, 173, 178,
    180
CHIONG, A. T., 53
Cinefluorography, 86, 157, 177, 187
CLARK, R. G., 19, 36
CLEELAND, C. E., 97
Cleveland Hearing and Speech Center,
    199
Cleveland Lost Chord Club, 199
Complemental air, 18
COMROE, J. H., 18
Contact ulcers, 5
    causes of, 57
    treatment of, 58
Cooper-Rand Artificial Larynx, 206
Cord thickening, 51–53
Cordectomy, 69
CROWLEY, J. F., 221
CUNNING, D. S., 167
CURRY, E. T., 19, 98
CURTIS, J. F., 59

DAMSTE, P. H., 49, 60
DARLEY, F. L., 76, quote 81, 93, quote 96,
    97, 99
DAVIS, D. S., 122

Deaf
    pitch changes observed in, 157–59
    resonance changes in, 159–60
    voice therapy for, 156–60
Deep testing, McDonald, 151
Denasality
    descriptions of, 100, 183
    treatment of, 193–94
Desensitization therapy, 79, 108
DICKSON, D. R., 188
DIEDRICH, W. M., 69, quote 199, 200,
    quote 203, 204, 206, 207, quote
    209, quote 210, 212, 214, quote
    217, 218, 222
Digital manipulation, 119–21, 159, 171–
    72
Diplophonia, 68, 173–74
DOEHLER, M. A., 207, 215, 219
Dysphagia, 198
Dysphonia
    diplophonia, 68, 173–74
    functional, 61–62
    functional-organic dichotomy in, 102
    harshness, 62
    hoarseness, 96–97
    name confusion in, 47
    spastic, 62–64, 166–67
    ventricular, 68–69, 164–66
Dyspnea, 198

Ear training, 121–24, 150, 172, 173, 178,
    181, 192, 193, 195
EBLEN, R. E., 86
Echorder recorder, 103, 117, 128, 132
EISENSON, J., 113, 115, 139, 140, 194
Elimination of abuses, 106, 124–26, 131
ENGLAND, G., 108, 135
ERMOVICK, D. A., 159
Esophageal speech
    avoiding problems in, 220–21
    inhalation method of, 207, 215–17
    injection method of, 207, 217–19
    swallow method of, 207, 214–15
Evaluation of voice problems
    case history, 76–83
    daily use–misuse, 80
    description of problem, 76–78
    laryngologist reports, 73–75
    medical information needed, 72–75
    observation of patient, 80–82, 83
    onset of problem, 78
    physical mechanisms, 82
    respiration testing, 84–89
    testing of patient, 83–101
    variability, 78–79
    voice evaluation forms, 77, 82, 83

Explanation of problem, 130–32, 161, 178, 192, 193, 195

Facilitating techniques, 109–10
  Altering Tongue Position (I), 111–12
  Change of Loudness (II), 113–16
  Chewing Approach (III), 116–19
  Digital Manipulation (IV), 119–21
  Ear Training (V), 121–24
  Elimination of Abuses (VI), 124–26
  Elimination of Hard Glottal Attack (VII), 126–27
  Establishing New Pitch (VIII), 127–30
  Explanation of Problem (IX), 130–32
  Feedback (X), 132–34
  Hierarchy Analysis (XI), 134–37
  Negative Practice (XII), 137–38
  Open Mouth Approach (XIII), 138–40
  Pitch Inflections (XIV), 140–41
  Pushing Approach (XV), 141–43
  Relaxation (XVI), 143–46
  Respiration Training (XVII), 146–49
  Target Voice Models (XVIII), 149–52
  Voice Rest (XIX), 152–53
  Yawn-sigh Approach (XX), 153–54
FAIRBANKS, G., 90, 93, 95, *quote* 97, 113, 115, 139, *quote* 140, 163, 194
Falsetto
  explanation of, 34–35
  treatment of, 171–72
Feedback, 132–34, 192, 193, 195
*First Aid for Laryngectomees,* 208
FISHER, H. B., 111, 113, 139, 140, 144, *quote* 178, 194
FITZHUGH, G. S., 53
FREIDINGER, A., 161
FROESCHELS, E., 2, 8, 104, 119, 141, 142, 169, 207, 216
Functional aphonia
  description of, 64–65
  therapy for, 160–64
Fundamental frequency
  habitual pitch, 90–91, 128
  normal pitch values, 33–34
  optimum pitch, 93–94, 128
  range of pitches, 91–92
Fundamental Frequency Indicator (FFI), 91

GARDNER, W. H., 198, 200, 204, 207, 208, 209
Glottal fry, 35, 97
GOULD, M. A., 219
Granulomas, 58
Graphic plotting of abuses, 106–7
GRAY, B. B., 108, 135

GRAY, G. W., 19, *quote* 40, 42
GREENE, M. C. L., 19, 61, *quote* 87, *quote* 161, *quote* 211–12
GRUENEWALD, B., 159

HAHN, E., 93, 177, 181, 182, *quote* 185, 187
HANLEY, T. D., 84, 86, 189
HANSON, M. L., 177, 188
Hard glottal attack, 38, 126–27, 173
HARGIS, D. E., 93
HARRIS, H. E., 200
Harshness, 62, 95, 96
HEAVER, L., 63, 166, 212
Hemangiomas, 58
Hierarchy analysis, 108, 112, 134–37, 145, 154, 163, 167, 178–81
HIRT, C. C., 35
Hoarseness, 96–97
HOLBROOK, A., 156, 159
HOLLINGER, P. H., 5, 56, 104, 198, 201, 203
HOLLIEN, H., 32, 33, 48, 91
HORN, D., 201, 204, 208, 209, 210, 221, 222
HOSHIKO, M. S., 86
*Hunter Oral Manometer,* 188
HYMAN, M., 215, 219
Hyperfunction of voice
  description of, 2
  over-articulation, 8, 9
  sites of
    phonation, 5–7, 37–39
    respiration, 3–5, 22–24
    vocal tract, 7–9, 43–44
  therapy for, 102–55
Hyperkeratosis, 58
Hypernasality
  descriptions of, 100, 182–83
  evaluation of, 183–88
  treatment for, 188–93
Hyperrhinolalia, 189
Hypofunctional voice problems, 11, 96, 141–42
Hypopharynx and hyperfunction, 7
Hysterical aphonia, 64–65, 160

Inhalation method of esophageal speech
  description of, 207
  steps in teaching, 215–17
Injection method of esophageal speech
  description of, 207
  steps in teaching, 217–19
Intensity of phonation
  air flow rate in, 28, 31, 36–37
  change of, 113–16

Intensity of phonation (*cont.*)
  glottal tension in, 30, 36, 37
  subglottal pressure in, 21, 26, 31, 34
International Association of Laryngec-
    tomees, 198, 200, 201, 203, 208,
    221, 223
Intrapulmonary pressure, 17
IRWIN, J. V., 42, *quote* 53, *quote* 115,
    *quote* 133, 148, *quote* 165, 173
ISSHIKI, N., 114, 214

JACKSON, C. J., 5, 6, *quote* 7, 11, 51
JACKSON, C. L., 5, 6, *quote* 7, 11, 51
JIMISON, C., 208
JOHNSON, W., 76, 93, 99
JOHNSTON, K. C., 104, 198, 201, 203
JUDSON, L. S., 35

KALLEN, L. A., 210
KANTNER, C. E., 181
KASTEIN, S., 142, 169
KELLER, M. S., 219
KING, B. T., 19, 170
KIRCHNER, F., 66, 168
KOPP, G. A., 156, 159
KRASNER, L., 10
KRAUS, H., 148
KUNZE, L. H., 21

LADEFOGED, P., 21
*Language Master*, 92, 132, 150
Laryngeal structures, 25–31
  extrinsic muscles, 25
  intrinsic muscles, 25
  ligaments, 25
Laryngectomy
  artificial larynx in, 200, 203, 211–14
  *definition*, 197
  economic problems after, 221–22
  esophageal speech after, 207, 210–21
  first aid after, 208
  physical problems after, 208–10
  post-operative medical care after,
    201–3
  post-operative visit after, 203–7
  pre-operative visitation before, 198–201
  psychological adjustment after, 221–23
  psychosocial adjustments after, 221–23
  structures (anatomical) after, 202
  surgery, 198, 201
  visitation after, 198–201
  voice training after, 210–21
Laryngitis, 7, 50–51, 152–53
Laryngofissure, 69
Laryngoscopy, 72, 75
LEHMANN, Q. H., 165

Leukoplakia, 58
LEWIS, W., 19
LITIN, E. M., 64
LOMAS, C. W., 93
Loudness
  change of, 113–16, 179, 192
  discussion of, 36–37
  insufficient, 23
LOWENTHAL, G., 51
LUCHSINGER, R., 36, *quote* 51, 56, *quote*
    57, 59, 60, 61, 63, 66, 84, *quote*
    98, *quote* 154, *quote* 166, 168,
    170, *quote* 171, 172
Lungs, 15

MACAULAY, B. D., 12, 65
MCBURNEY, J. H., 19
MCDONALD, E. T., 151
MAHONEY, J. L., 108, 135
MALCIK, E., 59
MALLORY, L. A., 19
Mandibular restriction, 8, 99, 104,
    116–19
MANNING, C. C., 189
Manometer, 187–88
MANSUETO, M. D., 198, 201, 203
MARGARIA, R., 22
MARTENSSON, A., 26
MARTIN, H., 204, 212
MEAD, J., 21
MECKFESSEL, A. L., 159
MILISEN, R., 47, 184
MILLARD, N., 19
MILLER, M. H., 204
MOLL, K. L., *quote* 177, 182, *quote* 187
Monotone, 38, 116, 140–41, 151
MOOLENAAR-BIJL, A., 217
MOORE, G. P., 32, 33, 35, 63, 76, 97, 166
MORRIS, H. L., 177, 181, 182, 184, *quote*
    185, 187
MORRISON, W. W., 214
MOSES, P. J., 12, 57, 60, 63, 129
MURPHY, A. T., 2, *quote* 48, 61, *quote* 94,
    *quote* 145, 149
MURRAY, E., 137
MURRAY, J., 19
Mysathenia laryngitis, 11

Nasal emission, 101, 183, 195
Nasal resonance
  description of, 100, 101
  evaluation of
    analysis of speech, 183–84
    articulation testing, 185
    cinefluorography, 157, 187
    manometric measurement, 187–88

Nasal resonance, evaluation of (*cont.*)
    peripheral oral exam, 186–87
    spectrographic analysis, 188
    stimulability testing, 184–85
    treatment by dentistry, 191
    treatment of hypernasality, 188–93
    treatment by surgeons, 191
    voice therapy for denasality, 193–94
    voice therapy for hypernasality, 192–93
Negative practice, 137–38, 160, 179, 181
NEGUS, V. E., 24

Open mouth approach, 138–40, 159, 160,
        173, 179, 180, 192
Oral-pharyngeal resonance, 176–79
Orthodontist, 191–92
OTIS, A. B., 19, 36

*PAD Pitch Meter,* 91, 157
PALMER, M. T., 172
Papilloma, 57
Paralyses of vocal folds
    abductor, bilateral, 170
    abductor, unilateral, 169–70
    adductor, bilateral, 168
    adductor, unilateral, 168
    description of, 65–68
    teflon treatment of, 168
    voice therapy for, 167–70
PEACHER, G., 104
PEACHER, G. M., 5, 57, 104, 121
Peripheral oral examination, 82, 186
PERKINS, W. H., 61
PETERSON, H. W., 64
Pharyngeal flap, 190–91, 193
Phonation
    approximation variations of, 95–97
    Bernoulli effect in, 28, 30
    description of, 24–39
    falsetto in, 34–35
    glottal fry in, 35
    hyperfunction of, 37–39
    loudness of, 36, 38, 94
    measurement of, 89–100
    normal fundamental frequencies of, 34
    phonation breaks, 98–99
    pitch breaks in, 98, 172–73
    pitch level (habitual) in, 90–91
    pitch (optimum) in, 93–94
    pitch range in, 91–92
    pitch variations in, 33, 94
    structures of, 25
Phonation breaks, 98–99
*Phonic Mirror recorder,* 103, 117,128, 132
Physical problems of laryngectomee
    air intake, 208–9

Physical problems of larynectomee (*cont.*)
    digestive, 209
    diminished taste and smell, 209
    smoking habit changes, 209–10
    weight lifting, 210
PINTO, S., 164
Pitch
    breaks in, 98, 172–73
    change effects loudness, 114
    deaf voice variations in, 157–59
    discrimination training in, 123
    establishing new level of, 127–30, 141,
            157, 178, 180, 191
    falsetto in high, 34–35, 171–72
    habitual, 90–91, 128
    inflections of, 116, 140–41, 151
    measurement of, 89–94
    optimum, 93–94, 128
    *PAD Pitch Meter* for use in, 92
    physiology of, 33
    *Purdue Pitch Meter* for use in, 92
    range of, 91–92
Pitch breaks, 98, 172–73
Pitch pipe, 90, 91, 123
Plastic surgeon, 191
Polyps
    description and causes of, 51, 55–56
    treatment of, 56
Problems in esophageal speech
    air swallowing, 220
    facial grimacing, 220–21
    noise as, 220
    stoma noise, 220
PROCTOR, D. F., *quote* 21
Prosthodontist, 191–92
Pubertal voice changes, 59
Pushing approach, 141–43, 163, 168–69

Quality judgments, 83, 110

RACHMAN, S., *quote* 12, 65, 79
Register, 35, 36, 48, 98
Relaxation, 143–46, 159–60, 163, 173,
        179–81
Residual air, 18, 23
Resonance
    assimilative nasality, 101, 183
    baby voice, 179–80
    cul de sac, 8, 159, 179, 180
    deaf voice, 159–60
    denasality, 100, 183
    hyperfunction of, 43–44
    hypernasality, 100, 182–83
    improving oral, 179–81
    mechanisms of, 40–43
    nasal emission and, 101

Resonance (cont.)
  open cavity effects on, 40
  oral-pharyngeal problems of, 176–77
  sounding board effects on, 40
  structures of, 39
  supraglottal changes of, 41
  therapy for disorders of, 175–96
Respiration
  anatomy and physiology of, 14–24
  capacity measurements of, 84–85
  complemental air in, 18
  diaphragmatic-abdominal, 87–88,
    147–48
  function measurement in, 87–89
  hyperfunction in, 22–24
  inspiration/expiration ratio in, 19
  muscles of expiration in, 15
  muscles of inspiration in, 15, 21
  prolongation of sounds in, 88–89, 147
  pulmonary laboratory report, 85
  residual air in, 18, 88
  respiratory movement and timing in, 86
  structures of, 15
  supplemental air in, 18
  tidal capacity in, 18
  vital capacity in, 18
  vitalator test, 20
  therapy in, 146–49, 159, 160, 163, 169,
    173, 180, 192
ROBE, E. J., 63, 166
ROSEN, M. S., 191
ROSENSTEIN, S. W., 191
RUBIN, H. J., 35

SAUNDERS, W. H., 69
Seashore Tests of Musical Aptitude, 122
Semon's Law, 66
SENTURIA, B. H., 47
SHELTON, R. L., 177, 181, 182, 184, quote
    185, 187, 191
SHERMAN, D., 177, 184
SJOSTROM, L., 169
SLOANE, H. N., 12, 65
SMITH, D. E., 53
SMITH, J. K., 184
SNIDECOR, J. C., 214
SOMMERS, R. K., quote 124
SONNINEN, A., 33
Spastic dysphonia
  explanation of, 5, 62
  onset of, 63
  therapy and treatment for, 63–64,
    166–67
Spectrographic analysis, 157, 159, 177,
    188
SPRIESTERSBACH, D. C., 76, 93, 99, 184

STEER, M. D., 84, 86
STEVENS, H., 13, 65, 161
Stimulability testing, 184, 194
Stridency, 178
Subglottal air pressure, 21, 26, 31, 34,
    36–37
Supplemental air, 18
Swallow method of esophageal speech,
    207, 214–15
Symptom transfer, 12
Symptomatic therapy, 9, 13, 108–9
Systematic desensitization. See Wolpe.

TABOR, C., 19
Target voice models, 133, 149–52, 193–94
TARNEUD, J., 84, 121
THORNTON, A., 159
THURMAN, W. L., 93
Thyroid cartilage, 28
Tidal capacity, 18
TOLEDO, P., 66, 168
Tracheotomy, 201–3, 208, 220
TRAVIS, L. E., 76
TUTTLE, W. W., 18

VAN DEN BERG, J. W., 34, 35
VAN RIPER, C., 2, 42, quote 53, quote 115,
    quote 133, 148, quote 165, 173
VANDRAEGEN, D., 93
Velum
  fistula of, 186
  inadequacy of movement of, 189–92,
    195
  movement of, 186
  structural adequacy of, 186, 192
Ventricular dysphonia, 68–69, 164–66
Virilizing drugs, 49, 60
Visitation of laryngectomees
  post-operative, 203–7
  pre-operative, 198–201
  visitant criteria for, 199
Vital capacity, 18, 22
Vitalator test, 20
Vocal cord paralysis, 65–68
  abductor, 66, 67
  adductor, 66–68
  causes of, 66
  Semon's Law in, 66
  voice therapy for, 167–70
Vocal folds
  adductor speed of, 26
  approximation for phonation of, 30
  Bernoulli effect of, 28, 30
  edema of, 7
  expiration, 32
  glottal configuration of, 32

Vocal folds (*cont.*)
  paralysis of, 65–68
  vibratory cycle of, 30
Vocal nodules, 6, 53, 54, 55, 105
Vocal projection, 9
Voice disorders
  approximation, 49, 60–69
  causes of, 10–11
  contact ulcers and, 57–58
  cord thickening and, 51–53, 61
  cordectomy and, 69
  endocrine changes and, 59
  functional aphonia and, 64–65
  functional dysphonia and, 61–62
  functional versus organic, 48
  granulomas and, 58
  hemangiomas and, 58
  hyperkeratosis and, 58
  incidence of, 47
  laryngitis and, 50–51
  laryngofissure and, 69
  leukoplakia and, 58
  mass-size, 49–60
  papilloma and, 56–57, 61
  spastic dysphonia and, 62–64
  ventricular dysphonia and, 68–69
  vocal cord paralysis and, 65–68
  vocal nodules and, 53–55, 61
  vocal polyps and, 55–56, 61
Voice evaluation forms, 77, 82, 83
Voice rest, 152–53
Voice therapy for vocal hyperfunction
  adolescent and adult, 107–9
  individual therapy need in, 107
  search for best production in, 103
  techniques in. *See* Facilitating techniques.
  typical approach in, 103
  young child, 105–7

Voice training for the laryngectomee,
    210–21
  avoiding problems in, 220–21
  inhalation method in, 215–17
  injection method in, 217–19
  swallow method in, 214–15
  using artificial larynx in, 211–14
VON LEDEN, H., 35, 97

WALDROP, W. F., 219
WEAVER, A. T., 35
WEISS, D. A., 59, 142, 169
*Western Electric Artificial Larynx*, 205,
    206
WHITLER, L. E., *quote* 221
WILEY, J., 161
WILLIAMSON, A. B., 181
WILSON, D. K., 2, 105, 121
WILSON, F. B., 47
WISE, G. W., 19, *quote* 40, 42
WOLPE, J., 12, 65, 79, 108, 134, 136, 144
WOLSKI, W., 161
WOODMAN, D., 170
WYATT, G. L., 10

Yawn-sigh approach, 110, 144, 153–54,
    159, 160, 173, 179, 180
*You Can Talk Again* (film), 204
YOUNGSTROM, K. A., 69, *quote* 199, 200,
    *quote* 203, 204, 206, 207, *quote*
    209, *quote* 210, 212, 214, *quote*
    217, 218, 222

ZALIOUK, A., 156
ZEMLIN, W. R., *quote* 17, 19, 26, 33, 35
ZOETHOUT, W. D., 18